Southern Living®

OUR BEST

RECIPES MADE LIGHTER

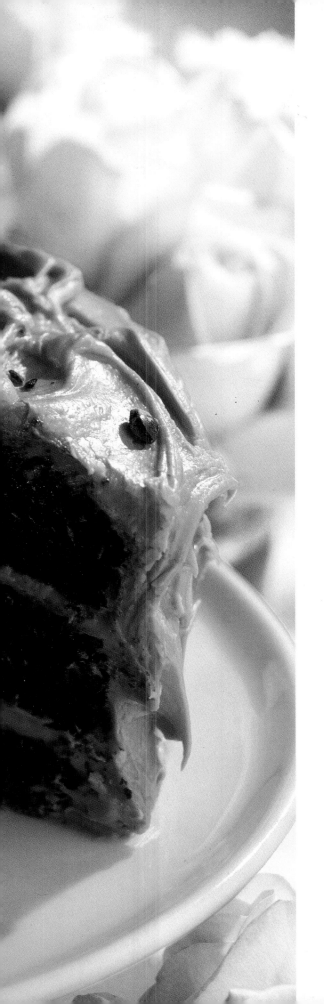

Southern Living®

OUR BEST

RECIPES MADE LIGHTER

Oxmoor House®

Library of Congress Catalog Card Number: 98-66268
ISBN: 0-8487-1850-X
Manufactured in the United States of America
First Printing 1998

We're Here for You!

We at Oxmoor House are dedicated to serving you with reliable information that expands your imagination and enriches your life. We welcome your comments and suggestions. Please write us at:
Oxmoor House, Inc.
Editor, *Southern Living*® *Our Best Recipes Made Lighter*
2100 Lakeshore Drive
Birmingham, AL 35209
To order additional publications, call 1-205-877-6560.

Oxmoor House, Inc.
    Editor-in-Chief: Nancy Fitzpatrick Wyatt
    Senior Foods Editor: Susan Payne Stabler
    Senior Editor, Editorial Services: Olivia Kindig Wells
    Art Director: James Boone

Southern Living® *Our Best Recipes Made Lighter*
    Editor: Janice Krahn Hanby
    Assistant Editor: Kathryn M. Wheeler, R.D.
    Copy Editors: Keri Bradford Anderson, Donna Baldone
    Editorial Assistants: Julie A. Cole, Valorie J. Cooper, Catherine S. Ritter
    Director, Test Kitchens: Kathleen Royal Phillips
    Assistant Director, Test Kitchens: Gayle Hays Sadler
    Test Kitchens Staff: Susan Hall Bellows, Julie Christopher, Michele Brown Fuller,
        Natalie E. King, Elizabeth Tyler Luckett, Jan Jacks Moon,
        Iris Crawley O'Brien, Jan A. Smith
    Photographer: Ralph Anderson
    Photo Stylist: Virginia R. Cravens
    Designer: Rita A. Yerby
    Publishing Systems Administrator: Rick Tucker
    Director, Production and Distribution: Phillip Lee
    Associate Production Manager: Theresa L. Beste
    Production Assistant: Valerie L. Heard
    Intern: Leslie Monk

Cover: Lemon-Herb Grilled Chicken and Marinated Tomato
    and Brie Salad (page 12)
Back cover: Orange-Strawberry Shortcake (page 144)
Page 2: Chocolate Chiffon Cake with Coffee Buttercream (page 146)

We Want Your FAVORITE RECIPES!

Southern Living cooks are simply the best cooks, and we want your secrets! Please send your favorite original recipes and a sentence about why you like each one. We can't guarantee we'll print them in a cookbook, but if we do, we'll send you $10 and a free copy of the cookbook. Send each recipe on a separate page with your name, address, and daytime phone number to:

Cookbook Recipes
Oxmoor House
2100 Lakeshore Drive
Birmingham, AL 35209

Contents

Healthy Inspiration 6

Quick Menus 9

Appetizers &
Beverages 25

Breads 41

Entrées 55

Salads 85

Side Dishes 99

Soups, Sandwiches
& Sauces 119

Desserts 133

Index 156

Healthy Inspiration

If food doesn't taste good, it doesn't matter how low in fat it is. So now with *Southern Living® Our Best Recipes Made Lighter*, you can have the best of both worlds—great-tasting, high-quality *Southern Living* recipes—made lighter.

We've made it easy to eat healthier by doing the work for you. We handpicked our favorite reader-recipes and lightened them, using creative ingredient substitutions and techniques. Then we thoroughly tested each recipe to make sure it meets our standard of excellence. Now you *can* have your cake, and eat it, too.

Our goal was to reduce the fat and calorie content of the original recipe as much as possible without sacrificing the flavor and integrity of the recipe. We also kept a close eye on cholesterol and sodium levels. We've provided a complete nutritional analysis for each recipe, plus to help you select recipes that best fit your lifestyle, we've highlighted those lower in calories, cholesterol, fat, and sodium.

In addition, we've included a menu section to help you get great-tasting dinners on the table in record time. Our five *Quick Menus* help you prepare a meal in an hour or less. And five *Super Quick Menus* let you serve dinner in 45 minutes or less.

If you want to eat healthfully, but refuse to compromise on flavor, this book is for you.

Meet Our Inspiration

These three *Southern Living* readers enjoy modifying favorite recipes and sharing their ideas with others. High-cholesterol levels, heart disease, and weight control motivated them to change the way they eat, and inspired us as we compiled this book.

Charlotte Towers

Charlotte's husband, Ben, constantly battles high cholesterol. Before they married, Charlotte watched her weight, but now she's adapted her cooking to lower cholesterol, too. Read on to learn her tips.
• When you make a casserole, replace half of the meat with rice, pasta, or vegetables. You get just as much flavor, and you cut fat, cholesterol, and calories.
• "Ben used to think that the only way to eat chicken was fried," Charlotte says. Now she marinates skinless breasts in citrus juice, wine, and a little oil, and bakes or grills them. "He's learned to love it."

Will Deller

Heart disease runs in Will's family, so he learned the importance of healthful eating and exercise at an early age. Try his tips for a healthy lifestyle.
• If you didn't like fat-free sour cream and cream cheese when they first came out, try them again. Manufacturers have improved flavor and texture, and they're slowly lowering prices.
• Use fresh fruit or vegetable purees to thicken sauces or sweeten baked goods.

Celeste Powers

Celeste controls her weight by tightening the reins whenever she's more than 10 pounds over her ideal weight. Take her advice for keeping the pounds off.
• "My husband and I grill everything—from fresh tuna to fresh vegetables."
• Grow herbs during the summer months. "You won't miss the butter on your vegetables if you mix them with fresh herbs."

Top **10** Secrets
to Lighten Your Own Recipes

Inspired by the tips from our readers, here are the Top 10 Secrets
we gleaned to lighten recipes for this book. They'll work just as well
for you when you lighten your favorite recipes.

1. Talk Turkey: If you crave sausage and bacon, try turkey sausage and turkey bacon instead. You'll get a rich, smoky flavor with less fat. (See Broccoli Salad, page 88.)

2. Broth Knows Best: Chicken broth successfully replaces part or all of the oil in many salad dressings. (See Greens and Grapefruit Salad, page 91.)

3. So Nutty: If you chop nuts a little finer than normal, they'll spread further, and you won't need as many. (See Nutty Orange Coffee Cake, page 44.)

4. Dream Cream: Either reduced-fat sour cream or evaporated skimmed milk makes a thick and creamy replacement for whipping cream in many sauce recipes. (See Dijon-Rosemary Lamb Chops, page 60, and My Favorite Pasta, page 73.)

5. Here's the Beef: If a recipe calls for ground beef, substitute leaner meats like ground round or ground skinless turkey. Brown the meat in a nonstick skillet, and then drain it in a paper towel-lined colander. Wipe the skillet dry with paper towels to eliminate even more fat before returning the meat to the skillet. (See Individual Barbecued Beef Loaves, page 56.)

6. Dressing Up: Fat-free Italian salad dressing makes a quick and easy substitution for part or all of the oil in marinades, adding flavor without fat. (See Marinated Cheese, page 33.)

7. Spray Away: Flavored vegetable cooking spray is a quick and healthy alternative to butter and oil when sautéing, moistening crumb toppings, and browning breads and pastries. (See Swiss Chicken, page 14.)

8. Sauce Savvy: Applesauce can replace part or all of the fat in many baked goods and keep them moist and tender. When lightening recipes on your own, you'll need to experiment, because this substitution makes some baked goods gummy. (See Big Batch Moist Bran Muffins, page 46.)

9. Say "Cheese," Please: Many times using a smaller amount of a highly flavored, full-bodied cheese will have more flavor impact than using a larger amount of reduced-fat or nonfat cheese. (See Cheese Wafers, page 34.)

10. Eggstra! Eggstra!: Egg substitute or egg whites can often replace all or some of the whole eggs in many recipes without an appreciable flavor difference. It works best for bread, cake, and cookie recipes or in quiches and frittatas. (See Buttercrust Corn Pie with Fresh Tomato Salsa, page 82.)

Makeover Magic

Who knew eating lighter could be so delectably doable? Here's a striking example of how we lightened our best recipes.

Baked Artichoke Dip

2 ~~1~~ (14-ounce) can**s** quartered artichoke hearts, drained and chopped

1 ~~¾~~ cup mayonnaise *(use nonfat)*

~~¾~~ ½ cup grated Parmesan cheese

1 clove garlic, minced

¼ teaspoon Worcestershire sauce *(use reduced sodium)*

~~⅛~~ ~~2 or 3 drops~~ of hot sauce **teaspoon**

- Combine all ingredients; spoon into a ~~lightly greased~~ 1-quart casserole. *(use cooking spray)*
- Bake, uncovered, at 350° for ~~20~~ **25** minutes or until thoroughly heated. Serve with melba toast rounds. **Yield:** ~~2~~ **3½** cups.

We lightened this popular high-fat dip by making a few creative substitutions. Here's what we did.

- Doubled the artichokes to increase artichoke flavor and reduce the percent of calories from fat
- Replaced regular mayonnaise with nonfat and used a bit more since we increased the artichokes
- Used less Parmesan cheese, but used the real thing for maximum flavor. (We first tried nonfat Parmesan in the original amount, but the dip lost flavor.)
- Replaced Worcestershire sauce with its reduced-sodium counterpart
- Increased the hot sauce for maximum flavor
- Used cooking spray to coat the casserole instead of greasing it
- Increased cooking time to accommodate greater volume

Before	*After*
Calories: (per 1 tablespoon) 52	Calories: (per 1 tablespoon) 14
Fat: 4.9g	Fat: 0.5g
% Calories from Fat: 85%	% Calories from Fat: 32%

Healthier Choices

Use this handy fat gram comparison to help you make healthy ingredient substitutions.

Item	Serving Size	Fat	Calories (% from Fat)
Whole Milk	8 ounces	7.3g	138 (48%)
2% Low-Fat Milk	8 ounces	4.3g	113 (34%)
Skim Milk	8 ounces	0.4g	79 (5%)
Whipping Cream	2 tbls	11.0g	103 (96%)
Half-and-Half	2 tbls	3.7g	43 (77%)
Evaporated Skimmed Milk	2 tbls	0.1g	25 (4%)
Egg-Whole	1 large	5.2g	77 (61%)
Egg Whites	2 large	0.0g	32 (0%)
Egg Substitute	¼ cup	0.0g	30 (0%)
Butter	1 tbls	11.5g	102 (100%)
Margarine	1 tbls	11.4g	101 (100%)
Light Butter	1 tbls	6.0g	50 (100%)
Reduced-Calorie Margarine	1 tbls	5.6g	50 (100%)
Cream Cheese	1 ounce	9.9g	99 (90%)
Neufchâtel Cheese	1 ounce	6.6g	74 (80%)
Nonfat Cream Cheese	1 ounce	0.0g	25 (0%)
Cheddar Cheese	1 ounce	9.4g	114 (74%)
Reduced-Fat Cheddar Cheese	1 ounce	4.5g	80 (51%)
Nonfat Cheddar Cheese	1 ounce	0.0g	40 (0%)
Sour Cream	1 tbls	3.0g	31 (87%)
Reduced-Fat Sour Cream	1 tbls	1.0g	18 (50%)
Nonfat Sour Cream	1 tbls	0.0g	8 (0%)
Mayonnaise	1 tbls	10.9g	99 (99%)
Reduced-Fat Mayonnaise	1 tbls	4.6g	44 (94%)
Nonfat Mayonnaise	1 tbls	0.0g	12 (0%)
Pork Sausage	1 ounce	11.4g	118 (87%)
Turkey Breakfast Sausage	1 ounce	3.5g	52 (61%)
Bacon	1 slice, cooked	5.7g	64 (80%)
Turkey Bacon	1 slice, cooked	2.5g	34 (66%)
Canadian Bacon	1 slice, cooked	2.0g	43 (42%)

Quick Menus

Fast-and-Fancy Beef Dinner

Blue Cheese-Walnut Stuffed Fillets
Garlic Roasted Potatoes
Green Beans with Caramelized Onions
French Bread
Serves 4
Calories per serving: 658 (31% from fat)

Beef is better than ever in this tenderloin steak stuffed with blue cheese and toasted walnuts. Accompany each serving with a 2-ounce slice of crusty French bread.

Blue Cheese-Walnut Stuffed Fillets

LOW: • Calorie • Cholesterol • Sodium

This entrée is sure to please the heartiest of appetites. We lowered fat by paring down the amount of walnuts and replacing the half-and-half with nonfat sour cream.

¼ cup crumbled blue cheese
1 tablespoon finely chopped walnuts, toasted
1 tablespoon nonfat sour cream
4 (1-inch-thick) beef tenderloin steaks
    (4 ounces each)
2 tablespoons reduced-fat margarine
2 cloves garlic, minced
4 green onions, finely chopped
½ cup Madeira wine

• **Combine** first 3 ingredients. Cut a pocket into side of each steak. Spoon blue cheese mixture evenly into steak pockets. Set aside.
• **Melt** margarine in a large nonstick skillet over medium-high heat; add garlic and green onions, and cook, stirring constantly, until tender. Remove garlic mixture; set aside.
• **Cook** steaks in skillet over medium heat 7 minutes on each side or to desired degree of doneness. Remove steaks, reserving drippings in skillet. Add wine to drippings, and cook 1 to 2 minutes or until reduced by half. Stir in garlic mixture; spoon over steaks. **Yield:** 4 servings.

Per serving: Calories 252 (52% from fat)
Fat 14.6g (4.9g saturated)   Protein 26.3g   Carbohydrate 3.0g
Fiber 0.4g   Cholesterol 76mg   Sodium 222mg

Garlic Roasted Potatoes

LOW: • Fat • Cholesterol • Sodium

1½ pounds small round red potatoes,
    quartered
Olive oil-flavored vegetable cooking spray
1 tablespoon olive oil
3 cloves garlic, minced
1 tablespoon dried rosemary, crushed
¼ teaspoon salt
¼ teaspoon pepper

• **Place** potato in a 13- x 9- x 2-inch baking dish coated with cooking spray; coat potato with cooking spray. Add olive oil; toss gently. Sprinkle with garlic and remaining ingredients; toss.
• **Bake**, uncovered, at 400° for 40 minutes or until tender, stirring once. **Yield:** 4 servings.

Per serving: Calories 155 (27% from fat)
Fat 4.7g (0.7g saturated)   Protein 3.5g   Carbohydrate 25.8g
Fiber 2.8g   Cholesterol 0mg   Sodium 158mg

Green Beans with Caramelized Onions

LOW: • Fat • Calorie • Cholesterol • Sodium

Here's a low-fat, high-flavor alternative to the familiar green bean and French fried onion casserole.

1 pound fresh green beans
1½ cups frozen pearl onions, thawed
1 tablespoon reduced-calorie margarine
2 tablespoons brown sugar

• **Arrange** beans in a steamer basket over boiling water. Cover and steam 15 minutes; set aside.
• **Place** onions in boiling water 3 minutes; drain and set aside.
• **Melt** margarine in a large heavy skillet over medium heat; add sugar, and cook, stirring constantly, until bubbly. Add onions; cook 3 minutes, stirring constantly. Add beans; cook, stirring constantly, until heated. **Yield:** 4 servings.

Per serving: Calories 87 (20% from fat)
Fat 2.0g (0.5g saturated)   Protein 2.6g   Carbohydrate 17.5g
Fiber 2.7g   Cholesterol 0mg   Sodium 41mg

Easy-Does-It Chicken Grill

Lemon-Herb Grilled Chicken
Marinated Tomato and Brie Salad
Corn on the Cob
Dinner Roll
Serves 8
Calories per serving: 459 (34% from fat)

The calories in this warm-weather menu include an ear of fresh sweet corn sprinkled with cracked pepper and a dinner roll for each person.

Lemon-Herb Grilled Chicken

LOW: • Fat • Calorie • Cholesterol • Sodium

To keep this chicken healthful, low-sodium chicken broth and lemon juice stand in for much of the original recipe's vegetable oil.

²/₃ cup lemon juice
¹/₄ cup canned low-sodium chicken broth
¹/₄ cup honey
2 tablespoons dried oregano
1 tablespoon dried rosemary
¹/₂ teaspoon salt
¹/₂ teaspoon pepper
3 tablespoons vegetable oil
4 cloves garlic
8 (4-ounce) skinned and boned chicken breast halves
Garnish: lemon slices

• **Combine** first 9 ingredients in container of an electric blender, and process until smooth, stopping occasionally to scrape down sides.
• **Place** chicken in a heavy-duty, zip-top plastic bag; pour lemon juice mixture over chicken. Seal bag, and marinate chicken in refrigerator 30 minutes.
• **Drain** and discard marinade.
• **Cook** chicken, covered with grill lid, over medium-hot coals (350° to 400°) about 5 minutes on each side or until done, turning occasionally. Garnish, if desired. **Yield:** 8 servings.

Per serving: Calories 152 (23% from fat)
Fat 3.8g (1.0g saturated)   Protein 25.8g   Carbohydrate 2.0g
Fiber 0.0g   Cholesterol 70mg   Sodium 92mg

Marinated Tomato and Brie Salad

LOW: • Sodium

Garlic plus fresh tomatoes and basil offers so much flavor that we halved the olive oil and Brie in this salad. It's still pretty high in fat, but the rest of the menu is low fat. Indulge!

¹/₂ (15-ounce) mini Brie
4 large tomatoes, seeded and cut into ¹/₂-inch cubes
1 cup fresh basil, cut into ¹/₈-inch-wide strips
4 cloves garlic, crushed
2 tablespoons olive oil
¹/₄ teaspoon salt
¹/₂ teaspoon freshly ground pepper
Garnish: fresh basil sprigs

• **Remove** and discard rind from Brie; cut Brie into ³/₄-inch cubes.
• **Combine** Brie, tomato, and next 5 ingredients; cover and let stand at room temperature 30 minutes. Garnish, if desired. **Yield:** 8 servings.

Note: Use a vegetable peeler to remove the rind from the Brie quickly and easily.

Per serving: Calories 143 (70% from fat)
Fat 11.1g (5.1g saturated)   Protein 6.6g   Carbohydrate 5.5g
Fiber 1.2g   Cholesterol 27mg   Sodium 249mg

Carefree Chicken Supper

Swiss Chicken
Baked Mushroom Rice
Asparagus Stir-Fry
Dinner Roll
Serves 6
Calories per serving: 605 (21% from fat)

Canned soups help you get this family-style meal on the table in record time. Round out the menu with a crusty dinner roll for each person.

Swiss Chicken

LOW: • Fat • Calorie • Cholesterol

We kept this easy chicken dish healthy by using reduced-fat and reduced-sodium convenience products in the recipe.

6 (4-ounce) skinned and boned chicken breast
    halves
Vegetable cooking spray
1/8 teaspoon garlic powder
1/8 teaspoon pepper
1 cup (4 ounces) shredded reduced-fat Swiss
    cheese
1 (10¾-ounce) can reduced-fat cream of
    chicken soup, undiluted
1/4 cup skim milk
3/4 cup reduced-sodium stuffing mix for
    chicken

• **Place** chicken in a 13- x 9- x 2-inch baking dish coated with cooking spray; sprinkle with garlic powder and pepper. Top each chicken breast evenly with cheese; set aside.
• **Combine** soup and milk, stirring until smooth; pour over chicken. Sprinkle with stuffing mix, and lightly coat with cooking spray.
• **Cover** and bake at 350° for 50 minutes or until chicken is done. **Yield:** 6 servings.

Per serving: Calories 243 (25% from fat)
Fat 6.7g (2.9g saturated)   Protein 35.0g   Carbohydrate 9.1g
Fiber 0.4g   Cholesterol 84mg   Sodium 561mg

Baked Mushroom Rice

LOW: • Fat • Cholesterol

2 tablespoons reduced-calorie margarine, melted
1½ cups long-grain rice, uncooked
2¾ cups canned no-salt-added chicken broth
1 (10½-ounce) can condensed French onion
    soup, undiluted
1 (2½-ounce) jar sliced mushrooms, drained

• **Combine** all ingredients in an ungreased 2-quart baking dish.
• **Cover** and bake at 350° for 1 hour. **Yield:** 6 servings.

Per serving: Calories 230 (15% from fat)
Fat 3.8g (0.4g saturated)   Protein 4.5g   Carbohydrate 42.5g
Fiber 0.9g   Cholesterol 0mg   Sodium 487mg

Asparagus Stir-Fry

LOW: • Calorie • Cholesterol • Sodium

1½ pounds fresh asparagus
Vegetable cooking spray
1 teaspoon peanut oil
½ cup canned no-salt-added chicken broth,
    divided
1 tablespoon cornstarch
1 teaspoon sugar
2 tablespoons low-sodium soy sauce
1 tablespoon sesame seeds, toasted

• **Snap** off tough ends of asparagus; remove scales from stalks with a vegetable peeler, if desired. Diagonally cut into 2-inch pieces.
• **Coat** a nonstick skillet with cooking spray; add oil, and place over medium-high heat until hot. Add asparagus; cook 2 minutes, stirring constantly. Add ¼ cup broth; cover and cook 4 minutes or until asparagus is crisp-tender.
• **Combine** remaining ¼ cup broth, cornstarch, sugar, and soy sauce; stir until smooth. Add to asparagus mixture, stirring constantly.
• **Bring** to a boil; boil 1 minute, stirring constantly. Sprinkle with seeds. **Yield:** 6 servings.

Per serving: Calories 49 (33% from fat)
Fat 1.8g (0.3g saturated)   Protein 2.4g   Carbohydrate 6.6g
Fiber 2.0g   Cholesterol 0mg   Sodium 132mg

Seafood Celebration

Tossed Salad
Crab Imperial
Herbed Cherry Tomatoes over Pasta
Dilly Garlic Bread
Serves 6
Calories per serving: 424 (27% from fat)

Toss a simple salad for this menu, using 6 cups torn mixed lettuces, 1½ cups chopped tomato, 1½ cups chopped cucumber, and ¾ cup commercial fat-free Ranch salad dressing for 6 servings.

Crab Imperial

LOW: • Calorie • Cholesterol

This classic dish contains two traditional flavor enhancers—Old Bay seasoning and dry sherry.

1 tablespoon reduced-calorie margarine
2 tablespoons chopped onion
2 tablespoons chopped green bell pepper
2 tablespoons all-purpose flour
½ cup skim milk
1 pound fresh lump crabmeat, drained
½ teaspoon Old Bay seasoning
¼ teaspoon ground black pepper
¼ cup reduced-fat mayonnaise
1 tablespoon dry sherry
¼ teaspoon low-sodium Worcestershire sauce
Vegetable cooking spray
Paprika

• **Melt** margarine in a large nonstick skillet over medium-high heat. Add onion and bell pepper; cook, stirring constantly, until tender.
• **Combine** flour and milk, stirring well. Add to vegetable mixture, and cook 2 minutes or until thickened, stirring often.
• **Add** crabmeat and next 5 ingredients. Spoon into baking shells or ramekins coated with cooking spray; sprinkle with paprika.
• **Bake** at 350° for 20 to 25 minutes or until bubbly. **Yield:** 6 servings.

Per serving: Calories 138 (36% from fat)
Fat 5.5g (0.8g saturated)   Protein 16.4g   Carbohydrate 4.2g
Fiber 0.2g   Cholesterol 79mg   Sodium 510mg

Herbed Cherry Tomatoes over Pasta

LOW: • Cholesterol • Sodium

Replacing most of the olive oil with chicken broth and balsamic vinegar makes this pasta moist and lively.

¼ cup chopped fresh basil
⅓ cup balsamic vinegar
¼ cup canned reduced-sodium chicken broth
2 tablespoons olive oil
12 ounces bow tie pasta, cooked without salt or fat
4 cups cherry tomatoes, cut in half

• **Combine** first 4 ingredients. Pour over pasta and tomatoes; toss gently. **Yield:** 6 servings.

Per serving: Calories 144 (33% from fat)
Fat 5.3g (0.7g saturated)   Protein 4.0g   Carbohydrate 21.6g
Fiber 2.4g   Cholesterol 0mg   Sodium 51mg

Dilly Garlic Bread

LOW: • Fat • Calorie • Cholesterol

Nonfat Parmesan cheese, reduced-calorie margarine, and snippets of fresh dill keep this rich-tasting bread low in fat yet high in flavor. The calories within this menu reflect 1 slice per person.

¼ cup reduced-calorie margarine
3 cloves garlic, pressed
¼ cup finely chopped fresh dill
1 (16-ounce) loaf French bread, cut in half horizontally
¼ cup grated nonfat Parmesan cheese

• **Combine** first 3 ingredients; spread mixture evenly on cut sides of bread. Sprinkle with Parmesan cheese. Place on a baking sheet.
• **Broil** 5½ inches from heat (with electric oven door partially opened) 2 to 4 minutes or until golden. Slice bread crosswise into 1-inch slices, and serve immediately. **Yield:** 1 loaf.

Per 1-inch slice: Calories 70 (21% from fat)
Fat 1.6g (0.3g saturated)   Protein 1.8g   Carbohydrate 12g
Fiber 0.5g   Cholesterol 1mg   Sodium 147mg

Short-Order Scampi

Shrimp Scampi
Eggplant Parmesan
Garlic Breadsticks
Serves 4
Calories per serving: 621 (32% from fat)

Serve this hearty, healthy Italian meal with 2 garlic breadsticks per person.

Shrimp Scampi

LOW: • Fat

For this sensational pasta dish, we cooked the shrimp in margarine, dry white wine, and a generous measure of garlic.

1 pound unpeeled medium-size fresh shrimp
8 ounces angel hair pasta, uncooked
¼ cup reduced-calorie margarine
4 cloves garlic, minced
½ cup dry white wine
¼ teaspoon salt
¼ teaspoon freshly ground pepper
½ cup grated Romano cheese
1 tablespoon chopped fresh parsley
Garnish: fresh flat-leaf parsley sprigs

• **Peel** shrimp, and devein, if desired; set shrimp aside.
• **Cook** pasta according to package directions, omitting salt and fat; drain pasta, and keep warm.
• **Melt** margarine in a large nonstick skillet over medium heat. Add garlic and shrimp, and cook, stirring constantly, 3 to 5 minutes or until shrimp turn pink; add wine, salt, and pepper. Bring to a boil, and cook 30 seconds, stirring constantly.
• **Place** pasta on a large serving platter. Pour shrimp mixture over pasta; sprinkle with cheese and parsley, and toss gently. Garnish, if desired. Serve immediately. **Yield:** 4 servings.

Per serving: Calories 440 (30% from fat)
Fat 14.6g (2.7g saturated) Protein 30.0g Carbohydrate 42.6g
Fiber 0.1g Cholesterol 144mg Sodium 595mg

Eggplant Parmesan

Eggplant Parmesan usually has breaded and fried eggplant slices. We broiled the eggplant slices instead, and slathered them with low-fat spaghetti sauce and mozzarella.

1 (1-pound) eggplant, peeled and sliced ¼ inch thick
Vegetable cooking spray
1½ teaspoons lemon juice
¼ cup grated Parmesan cheese, divided
1 cup (4 ounces) shredded part-skim mozzarella cheese, divided
1½ cups low-fat spaghetti sauce, divided

• **Place** eggplant slices on a rack of a broiler pan coated with cooking spray; brush eggplant slices with lemon juice. Broil 5½ inches from heat (with electric oven door partially opened) 6 minutes on each side or until eggplant is tender.
• **Layer** half of eggplant, 2 tablespoons Parmesan cheese, ¼ cup mozzarella cheese, and ¾ cup spaghetti sauce in an 11- x 7- x 1½-inch baking dish coated with cooking spray. Repeat layers.
• **Cover** and bake at 350° for 30 minutes; sprinkle with remaining ½ cup mozzarella cheese, and bake, uncovered, 5 additional minutes. **Yield:** 4 servings.

Per serving: Calories 153 (37% from fat)
Fat 6.3g (3.8g saturated) Protein 11.4g Carbohydrate 13.3g
Fiber 2.0g Cholesterol 20mg Sodium 521mg

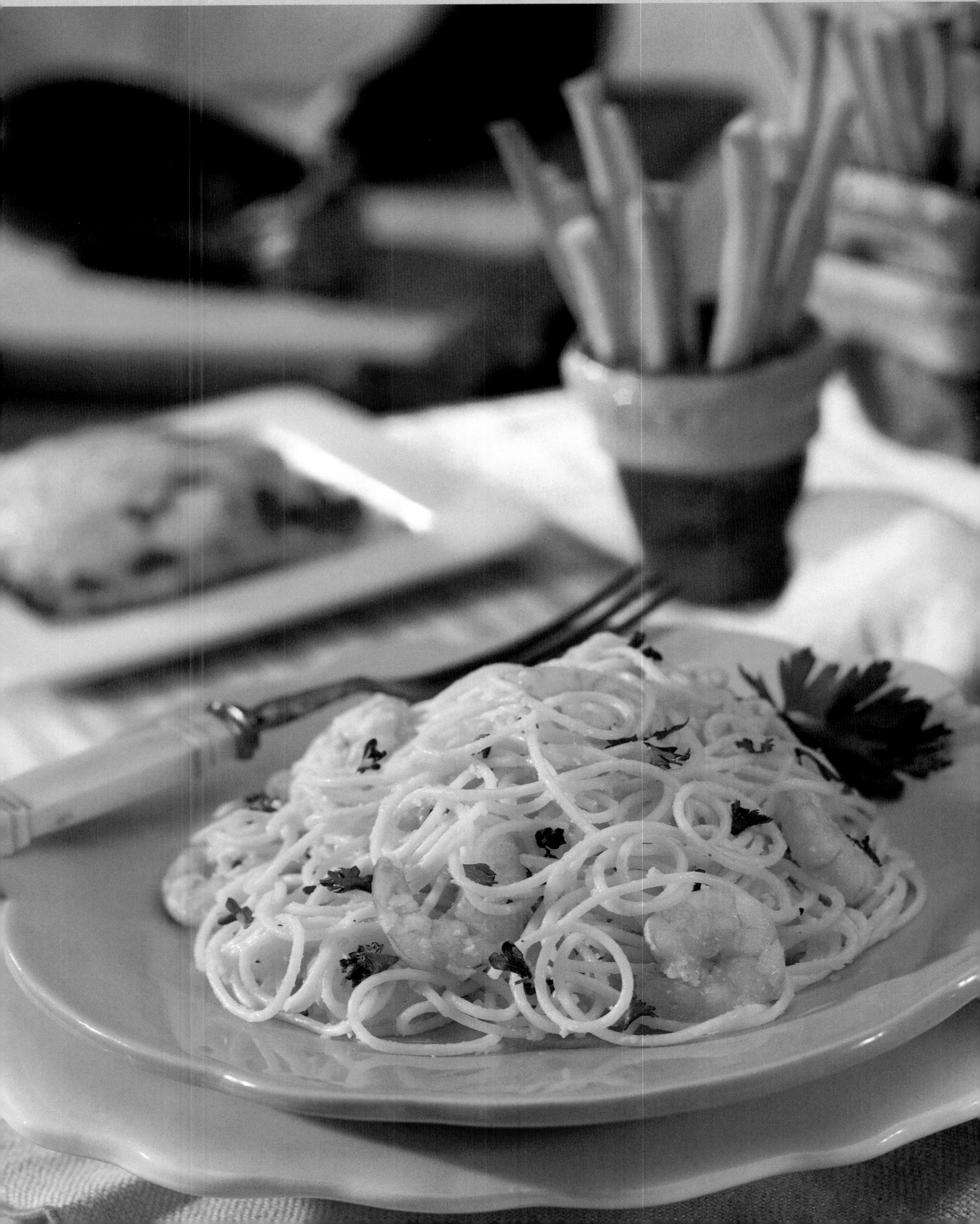

Easy Grecian Sampler

Greek Chicken Breasts
Orzo
Steamed Green Beans
Dinner Roll
Serves 4
Calories per serving: 509 (16% from fat)

Oregano, olives, capers, and feta cheese pump up the flavor of this Greek chicken. Accompany the entrée with ¾ cup cooked orzo, ¾ cup steamed green beans, and a commercial dinner roll for each person.

Greek Chicken Breasts

LOW: • Fat • Calorie • Cholesterol • Sodium

We kept the flavor in this classic Grecian chicken dish by using olive oil-flavored vegetable cooking spray in place of a good bit of olive oil. Topping the chicken mixture with a sprinkling of reduced-fat feta cheese helps cut the fat and calories.

¼ cup all-purpose flour
1 tablespoon dried oregano
4 (4-ounce) skinned and boned chicken breast halves
Olive oil-flavored vegetable cooking spray
1 tablespoon olive oil
⅓ cup dry white wine
⅓ cup canned reduced-sodium chicken broth
2 medium-size ripe tomatoes, peeled and chopped
2 tablespoons sliced ripe olives
1 teaspoon capers
2 tablespoons crumbled reduced-fat feta cheese

• **Combine** flour and oregano in a shallow dish, stirring well. Dredge chicken breasts in flour mixture.
• **Coat** a large nonstick skillet with cooking spray; add olive oil, and place over medium heat until hot. Add chicken breasts, and cook 10 minutes, turning once.
• **Add** wine and chicken broth, and simmer, uncovered, 10 to 15 minutes.
• **Add** chopped tomato, sliced olives, and capers, and cook until tomato mixture is thoroughly heated.

• **Spoon** into a serving dish; sprinkle with feta cheese. **Yield:** 4 servings.

Per serving: Calories 242 (26% from fat)
Fat 7g (1.6g saturated)   Protein 28.2g   Carbohydrate 11.4g
Fiber 1.7g   Cholesterol 68mg   Sodium 380mg

Dinner Italiano

Chicken Parmesan
Caesar Salad
Italian Breadsticks
Serves 6
Calories per serving: 650 (23% from fat)

Along with each serving of quick and easy Chicken Parmesan, serve one Italian breadstick and a simple Caesar salad made from 1 cup torn romaine lettuce, ¼ cup fat-free croutons, and 2 tablespoons commercial lite pesto-Parmesan salad dressing.

Chicken Parmesan

LOW: • Fat • Cholesterol

Low-fat cheeses and spaghetti sauce
cut the calories, but not the characteristic
flavor of this chicken classic.

6 (4-ounce) skinned and boned chicken breast
    halves
1 egg white, lightly beaten
2 tablespoons water
½ cup fine, dry breadcrumbs
¼ cup grated nonfat Parmesan cheese
1 teaspoon dried Italian seasoning
2 tablespoons vegetable oil
1 (27½-ounce) jar low-fat spaghetti sauce
1 (12-ounce) package spaghetti
1 cup (4 ounces) shredded part-skim
    mozzarella cheese
2 teaspoons grated nonfat Parmesan
    cheese
Garnish: fresh basil sprigs

• **Place** each chicken breast half between two sheets of heavy-duty plastic wrap; flatten to ¼-inch thickness, using a meat mallet or rolling pin.
• **Combine** egg white and water in a bowl. Combine breadcrumbs, ¼ cup Parmesan cheese, and Italian seasoning in a separate bowl. Dip chicken in egg white mixture; dredge in breadcrumb mixture.
• **Brown** chicken in oil in a large nonstick skillet over medium heat.
• **Add** spaghetti sauce. Cover and simmer 10 minutes.

• **Cook** spaghetti according to package directions, omitting salt and fat. Place spaghetti on a serving platter. Spoon chicken and sauce over spaghetti; sprinkle with mozzarella cheese and 2 teaspoons Parmesan cheese. Cover and let stand until cheese melts. Garnish, if desired. **Yield:** 6 servings.

Per serving: Calories 530 (19% from fat)
Fat 10.9g (3.4g saturated)   Protein 41.8g   Carbohydrate 63.2g
Fiber 3.8g   Cholesterol 77mg   Sodium 730mg

Pasta Pronto!

Artichoke and Shrimp Linguine
Broiled Tomato Halves
Spinach Salad
Serves 4
Calories per serving: 506 (25% from fat)

Artichokes, linguine, and dry white wine offer simple elegance to this shrimp dish. A broiled tomato half and a spinach salad made with 1 cup torn fresh spinach leaves and 2 tablespoons commercial fat-free Catalina salad dressing for each person keep the menu quick and easy.

Artichoke and Shrimp Linguine

LOW: • Fat • Cholesterol

We used white wine to replace most of the olive oil in this fresh shrimp recipe. It cuts the fat in half, while adding a distinctive flavor. (Most of the alcohol will evaporate during cooking.) Use freshly grated Parmesan cheese to intensify flavor.

1 **pound unpeeled medium-size fresh shrimp**
8 **ounces linguine, uncooked**
2 **tablespoons olive oil**
3 **cloves garlic, minced**
½ **teaspoon dried crushed red pepper**
1 **(14-ounce) can quartered artichoke hearts, drained**
¼ **cup dry white wine**
¼ **cup sliced ripe olives**
2 **tablespoons fresh lemon juice**
⅛ **teaspoon salt**
⅛ **teaspoon pepper**
½ **cup freshly grated Parmesan cheese**

• **Peel** shrimp, leaving tails intact, and devein, if desired. Set aside.
• **Cook** linguine according to package directions, omitting salt and fat; drain pasta, and keep warm.
• **Heat** oil in a nonstick skillet over medium-high heat; add shrimp, garlic, and red pepper, and cook, stirring constantly, 5 minutes or until shrimp turn pink.

• **Stir** in artichoke hearts and next 5 ingredients; cook 1 to 2 minutes or until thoroughly heated. Add to pasta, and sprinkle with cheese. **Yield:** 4 servings.

Per serving: Calories 436 (28% from fat)
Fat 13.6g (3.8g saturated) Protein 26.3g Carbohydrate 52.6g
Fiber 2.2g Cholesterol 96mg Sodium 545mg

Zippy Ziti Supper

Ziti with Sausage and Broccoli
Dinner Roll
Serves 4
Calories per serving: 597 (21% from fat)

Seven ingredients and a few minutes are all it takes to create a satisfying pasta supper. Serve this simple meal with commercial dinner rolls (1 per person).

Ziti with Sausage and Broccoli

LOW: • Fat • Calorie • Cholesterol

We replaced Italian sausage with turkey sausage in this robust one-dish meal. Turkey sausage keeps the bold flavor and significantly cuts the fat.

¾ pound turkey breakfast sausage links
Vegetable cooking spray
2 cloves garlic, crushed
½ teaspoon dried crushed red pepper
2 (14.5-ounce) cans diced tomatoes, undrained
8 ounces ziti pasta, uncooked
2 cups broccoli flowerets
3 tablespoons freshly grated Parmesan cheese

• **Cut** sausage diagonally into ½-inch-thick slices. Cook sausage in a large nonstick skillet over medium-high heat until browned; remove sausage, and set aside. Wipe skillet with paper towels.

• **Coat** skillet with cooking spray; place over medium heat until hot. Add garlic and pepper; cook, stirring constantly, until lightly browned. Add sausage and tomatoes; cook until thoroughly heated. Set aside, and keep warm.

• **Cook** pasta according to package directions, omitting salt and fat, and adding broccoli during last 5 minutes of cooking time. Drain and toss gently with sausage mixture and cheese. Serve immediately. **Yield:** 4 servings.

Per serving: Calories 420 (26% from fat)
Fat 12.3g (1.0g saturated)   Protein 27.0g   Carbohydrate 50.3g
Fiber 2.6g   Cholesterol 62mg   Sodium 776mg

Last-Minute Lasagna

Vegetable Lasagna
Tossed Salad
Garlic Bread
Serves 8
Calories per serving: 517 (21% from fat)

Accompany the lasagna with a salad made of 8 cups torn greens, 2 cups each of sliced carrot and chopped tomato, and 1 cup each of sliced yellow squash and radishes. Top each salad with 2 tablespoons commercial fat-free vinaigrette, and serve one slice of garlic bread.

Vegetable Lasagna

LOW: • Fat • Calorie • Cholesterol

Chock-full of vegetables and a spicy sauce, this lasagna is a meatless delight.

9 lasagna noodles, uncooked
Olive oil-flavored vegetable cooking spray
1 (10-ounce) package frozen chopped
    spinach, thawed and well drained
2 cups sliced fresh mushrooms
1 cup grated carrot (about 1 large)
½ cup chopped onion
2 tablespoons water
1 (15-ounce) can tomato sauce
1 (12-ounce) can tomato paste
1 (4.5-ounce) can chopped green chiles,
    undrained
1½ teaspoons dried oregano
2 cups nonfat cottage cheese
2 cups (8 ounces) shredded reduced-fat
    Monterey Jack cheese
¼ cup freshly grated Parmesan cheese

• **Cook** noodles according to package directions, omitting salt and fat. Drain and set aside.
• **Coat** a large nonstick skillet with cooking spray; place over medium-high heat until hot. Add spinach and next 4 ingredients; cook, stirring constantly, until tender. Stir in tomato sauce and next 3 ingredients.
• **Place** 5 noodles in a 13- x 9- x 2-inch baking dish coated with cooking spray. Layer with half each of cottage cheese, tomato sauce mixture,

Monterey Jack cheese, and Parmesan cheese. Repeat layers with remaining ingredients.
• **Bake**, uncovered, at 375° for 30 minutes or until bubbly. Let stand 10 minutes before serving.
Yield: 8 servings.

Per serving: Calories 336 (20% from fat)
Fat 7.6g (3.9g saturated)   Protein 26.3g   Carbohydrate 44.0g
Fiber 5.7g   Cholesterol 24mg   Sodium 904mg

Marinated Cheese (page 33)

Appetizers & Beverages

Cheesy Garlic-Stuffed Bread

Within a hollow loaf of earthy pumpernickel bread is a warm and mellow Swiss cheese dip.

2 cloves garlic
1 (8-ounce) package light process cream cheese, softened
1 cup loosely packed fresh parsley
½ cup (2 ounces) shredded reduced-fat Swiss cheese
2 tablespoons skim milk
1 (16-ounce) round loaf pumpernickel bread

• **Position** knife blade in food processor bowl. Drop garlic through food chute with processor running; process 3 seconds or until garlic is minced. Add cream cheese and next 3 ingredients. Process until smooth, stopping once to scrape down sides; set aside.
• **Slice** off top third of bread loaf; set top aside. Hollow out bottom half of bread loaf, leaving a 2-inch-deep bowl and a 1-inch shell. Set bread shell aside.
• **Cut** inside bread pieces into 1½-inch cubes; set aside.
• **Spoon** cheese mixture into bread shell, and replace bread top. Wrap filled bread in heavy-duty aluminum foil, and place on a baking sheet.
• **Bake** at 350° for 45 minutes or until bread is thoroughly heated.
• **Remove** bread top and cut into 1½-inch cubes. Serve cheese mixture with bread cubes. **Yield:** 5 appetizer servings.

Per serving: Calories 208 (43% from fat)
Fat 10.0g (5.8g saturated)   Protein 11.5g   Carbohydrate 19.0g
Fiber 1.8g   Cholesterol 34mg   Sodium 440mg

Tennessee Sin

LOW: • Fat

You'll feel like you're breaking all the rules each time you dip a giant crouton into this pool of melted Cheddar and cream cheese.

2 (16-ounce) loaves French bread
1 (8-ounce) package light process cream cheese, softened
1 (8-ounce) carton nonfat sour cream
2 cups (8 ounces) shredded reduced-fat Cheddar cheese
½ cup chopped cooked lean ham
⅓ cup chopped green onions
⅓ cup finely chopped green bell pepper
¼ teaspoon low-sodium Worcestershire sauce
Paprika

• **Slice** off top fourth of 1 bread loaf. Hollow out bottom section, leaving a 1-inch shell. Reserve bread top for another use. Set shell aside.
• **Cut** remaining bread loaf into 1½-inch cubes; place bread shell and cubes on two large baking sheets.
• **Bake** at 350° for 12 minutes or until lightly browned.
• **Beat** cream cheese at medium speed with an electric mixer until smooth; add sour cream, beating until creamy.
• **Stir** in Cheddar cheese and next 4 ingredients. Spoon cheese mixture into bread shell, wrap in heavy-duty aluminum foil, and place on a baking sheet.
• **Bake** at 350° for 30 minutes; unwrap and place on a serving platter. Sprinkle with paprika, and serve with toasted bread cubes. **Yield:** 13 appetizer servings.

Per serving: Calories 238 (28% from fat)
Fat 7.4g (4.1g saturated)   Protein 13.4g   Carbohydrate 27.3g
Fiber 1.1g   Cholesterol 26mg   Sodium 579mg

Baked Artichoke Dip

LOW: • Calorie • Cholesterol • Sodium

*Here's a lighter look at a popular party dip.
Nonfat mayonnaise works well in this recipe, but
stick with the real thing when it comes to the Parmesan
cheese—its sharp taste can't be imitated.*

2 (14-ounce) cans quartered artichoke hearts,
   drained and chopped
1 cup nonfat mayonnaise
¾ cup grated Parmesan cheese
1 clove garlic, minced
¼ teaspoon reduced-sodium Worcestershire
   sauce
⅛ teaspoon hot sauce
Vegetable cooking spray

• **Combine** first 6 ingredients; spoon evenly
into a 1-quart casserole coated with cooking spray.
• **Bake,** uncovered, at 350° for 25 minutes or
until thoroughly heated. Serve with melba toast
rounds. **Yield:** 3½ cups.

Per 1-tablespoon serving: Calories 14 (32% from fat)
Fat 0.5g (0.3g saturated) Protein 0.9g Carbohydrate 1.8g
Fiber 0.1g Cholesterol 1mg Sodium 89mg

Hot Crabmeat Dip

LOW: • Calorie • Cholesterol • Sodium

*This delectable dip gets its personality from pungent
additions of white wine, mustard, and horseradish.
Serve it with slices of French bread, low-fat
crackers, or fresh vegetables.*

2 (8-ounce) packages light process cream
   cheese
½ cup nonfat mayonnaise
¼ cup grated onion
½ teaspoon garlic powder
¼ teaspoon salt
½ teaspoon pepper
3 tablespoons dry white wine or dry vermouth
2 teaspoons prepared mustard
2 teaspoons prepared horseradish
½ pound fresh lump crabmeat, drained
2 tablespoons chopped fresh chives
2 tablespoons chopped fresh parsley

• **Combine** first 9 ingredients in a medium
saucepan; stir well. Cook over low heat, stirring
constantly, until cream cheese melts and mixture
is smooth.
• **Stir** in crabmeat and remaining ingredients.
Transfer to a chafing dish, and keep warm. **Yield:**
3½ cups.

Per 1-tablespoon serving: Calories 25 (54% from fat)
Fat 1.5g (0.8g saturated) Protein 1.7g Carbohydrate 1.2g
Fiber 0.1g Cholesterol 9mg Sodium 97mg

Swiss-Onion Dip

LOW: • Calorie • Cholesterol • Sodium

*If you have a penchant for cheesy concoctions,
this near-instant dip's for you. A blending
of Swiss cheese, onion, and coarse-grained mustard
is baked until soft and yielding.*

1 (10-ounce) package frozen chopped onion,
   thawed
2 cups (8 ounces) shredded reduced-fat Swiss
   cheese
1 cup nonfat mayonnaise
1 tablespoon coarse-grained Dijon mustard
⅛ teaspoon pepper

• **Drain** onion on paper towels.
• **Combine** onion and remaining ingredients.
Spoon mixture into a 1-quart baking dish.
• **Bake** at 325° for 25 minutes or until bubbly
and lightly browned. Serve dip with melba toast
rounds. **Yield:** 2¼ cups.

Per 1-tablespoon serving: Calories 28 (35% from fat)
Fat 1.1g (0.6g saturated) Protein 2.3g Carbohydrate 2.1g
Fiber 0.0g Cholesterol 4mg Sodium 103mg

Black Bean Dip

LOW: • Fat • Calorie • Cholesterol • Sodium

This gutsy southwestern bean dip is short on ingredients, but packs a powerful punch.

1 (15-ounce) can black beans, drained
1 (8-ounce) can no-salt-added tomato sauce
½ cup (2 ounces) shredded reduced-fat sharp
   Cheddar cheese
1 teaspoon chili powder

• **Combine** beans and tomato sauce in a small saucepan; bring to a boil over medium heat, stirring occasionally. Remove from heat.
• **Mash** beans with a potato masher or back of a spoon.
• **Add** cheese and chili powder; cook, stirring constantly, until cheese melts. Serve dip warm with toasted pita triangles and fresh vegetables. **Yield: 2 cups.**

Per 1-tablespoon serving: Calories 19 (19% from fat)
Fat 0.4g (0.2g saturated) Protein 1.3g Carbohydrate 2.6g
Fiber 0.5g Cholesterol 1mg Sodium 37mg

Roasted Tomatillo Salsa

LOW: • Fat • Calorie • Cholesterol • Sodium

Roasting tomatillos intensifies their fruitiness and provides a soothing backdrop to the fiery jalapeños in this Mexican sauce.

2½ pounds fresh tomatillos
6 cloves garlic, unpeeled
4 large fresh jalapeño peppers
2 large onions, quartered
½ cup nonfat sour cream
½ cup chopped fresh cilantro
½ teaspoon salt
½ teaspoon freshly ground pepper

• **Remove** and discard tomatillo husks; rinse tomatillos.
• **Place** tomatillos and next 3 ingredients in a single layer in a 15- x 10- x 1-inch jellyroll pan.
• **Bake** at 500° for 15 to 20 minutes or until vegetables are charred; cool completely. Remove and discard stems (but not seeds) from peppers. Peel garlic, discarding skins. Drain tomatillos, discarding any liquid.

• **Position** knife blade in food processor bowl; add half of roasted vegetables. Pulse 10 to 12 times or until vegetables are coarsely chopped. Repeat procedure with remaining roasted vegetables.
• **Pour** mixture into a bowl; stir in sour cream and remaining ingredients. Serve with baked tortilla chips or grilled chicken. **Yield: 6 cups.**

Per 1-tablespoon serving: Calories 7 (13% from fat)
Fat 0.1g (0.0g saturated) Protein 0.3g Carbohydrate 1.3g
Fiber 0.1g Cholesterol 0mg Sodium 14mg

Gazpacho Dip

LOW: • Calorie • Cholesterol • Sodium

Buttery chunks of avocado accented with green chiles, green onions, and ripe olives make up this feisty dip.

8 green onions, thinly sliced
2 large tomatoes, chopped
1 firm avocado, chopped
½ cup diced green bell pepper
1 (4.5-ounce) can chopped green chiles,
   undrained
½ (4.5-ounce) can chopped ripe olives,
   drained
2 cloves garlic, minced
3 tablespoons apple cider vinegar
¼ teaspoon pepper
Garnish: lime slices

• **Combine** all ingredients except the garnish, tossing gently.
• **Cover** and chill up to 4 hours. Garnish, if desired. Serve dip with baked tortilla chips. **Yield: 5 cups.**

Note: To serve this dip as a salad, spoon the mixture over shredded lettuce, and top with shredded reduced-fat Cheddar cheese and nonfat sour cream.

Per 1-tablespoon serving: Calories 7 (51% from fat)
Fat 0.4g (0.1g saturated) Protein 0.1g Carbohydrate 0.7g
Fiber 0.2g Cholesterol 0mg Sodium 8mg

Gazpacho Dip

One-Minute Salsa

LOW: • Fat • Calorie • Cholesterol • Sodium

*Got a minute? Then you have time to
make this spunky salsa. Four ingredients
and a blender are all it takes.*

1 (10-ounce) can diced tomatoes and green
   chiles, undrained
1 (14½-ounce) can no-salt-added stewed
   tomatoes, undrained
1 teaspoon pepper
1 clove garlic, minced

• **Combine** all ingredients in container of an
electric blender; process 30 seconds, stopping
once to scrape down sides. Serve with baked tortilla chips. **Yield:** 3 cups.

Per 1-tablespoon serving: Calories 3 (0% from fat)
Fat 0.0g (0.0g saturated)   Protein 0.1g   Carbohydrate 0.8g
Fiber 0.1g   Cholesterol 0mg   Sodium 21mg

Curried Chicken Mousse

LOW: • Fat • Calorie • Cholesterol • Sodium

*Curry powder blends 20 spices, herbs, and seeds
into a potent seasoning secret. Teamed with tender
chunks of chicken, this make-ahead mousse
is nothing short of marvelous.*

1 envelope unflavored gelatin
1 cup cold water, divided
2 teaspoons chicken-flavored bouillon
   granules
¼ teaspoon ground red pepper
1 teaspoon curry powder
2 teaspoons minced onion
1¼ cups finely chopped cooked chicken breast
   (skinned before cooking and cooked without salt)
¼ cup finely chopped celery
1 (2-ounce) jar diced pimiento, drained
1 tablespoon chopped fresh parsley
1 (8-ounce) carton nonfat sour cream
Vegetable cooking spray

• **Sprinkle** gelatin over ½ cup cold water in a
small saucepan; let stand 1 minute. Cook over
low heat, stirring until gelatin dissolves (about 2
minutes).

• **Add** bouillon granules, red pepper, and curry
powder, stirring until bouillon granules dissolve;
remove from heat. Add remaining ½ cup cold
water and minced onion, stirring well; chill until
consistency of unbeaten egg white.
• **Stir** in chicken and next 4 ingredients; spoon
mixture into a 4-cup mold coated with cooking
spray. Cover and chill at least 8 hours. Unmold
and serve with low-fat crackers. **Yield:** 2¾ cups.

Per 1-tablespoon serving: Calories 11 (16% from fat)
Fat 0.2g (0.1g saturated)   Protein 1.7g   Carbohydrate 0.5g
Fiber 0.0g   Cholesterol 3mg   Sodium 45mg

Crab Mousse

LOW: • Calorie • Cholesterol • Sodium

*Go ahead and pinch yourself—this creamy mousse
is decidedly luscious and low calorie. A splash
of your favorite hot sauce makes waves.*

2 teaspoons unflavored gelatin
¼ cup cold water
1 cup skim milk
3 tablespoons lemon juice
1 tablespoon grated onion
1 teaspoon dry mustard
½ teaspoon salt
¼ teaspoon paprika
¼ teaspoon hot sauce
1 (8-ounce) package Neufchâtel cheese,
   softened
8 ounces fresh crabmeat, drained
Vegetable cooking spray

• **Sprinkle** gelatin over cold water in a 1-cup
liquid measuring cup; let stand 1 minute.
• **Combine** gelatin mixture, milk, and next 6
ingredients in a heavy saucepan; cook over low
heat, stirring constantly, until gelatin dissolves
(mixture may appear curdled). Add cheese, stirring until blended. Chill until consistency of
unbeaten egg white.
• **Flake** crabmeat, removing any bits of shell;
gently fold crabmeat into gelatin mixture, and
spoon into a 4-cup mold coated with cooking
spray. Cover and chill at least 8 hours. Unmold
and serve with low-fat crackers. **Yield:** 3½ cups.

Per 1-tablespoon serving: Calories 17 (58% from fat)
Fat 1.1g (0.6g saturated)   Protein 1.4g   Carbohydrate 0.4g
Fiber 0.0g   Cholesterol 7mg   Sodium 51mg

White Bean Spread

LOW: • Fat • Calorie • Cholesterol • Sodium

Mild cannellini beans are the perfect foil for assertive fresh rosemary and anchovies in this appetizer spread.

1 (2-ounce) can anchovies, drained and
    chopped
9 cloves garlic, minced
3 tablespoons chopped fresh rosemary
2 teaspoons olive oil
4 (15-ounce) cans cannellini beans, drained
¼ cup lemon juice
½ teaspoon ground white pepper

• **Cook** anchovies, garlic, and rosemary in olive oil in a small skillet over medium heat 2 to 3 minutes, stirring constantly. Remove from heat; set aside.
• **Position** knife blade in food processor bowl; add cannellini beans. Process until beans are smooth, stopping once to scrape down sides. Add anchovy mixture, lemon juice, and pepper; process until smooth, stopping once to scrape down sides.
• **Spoon** bean mixture into a serving bowl. Serve with fresh vegetables or low-fat crackers. **Yield: 5 cups.**

Per 1-tablespoon serving: Calories 16 (11% from fat)
Fat 0.2g (0.0g saturated)   Protein 0.9g   Carbohydrate 2.5g
Fiber 0.5g   Cholesterol 0mg   Sodium 41mg

Blue Cheese Spread

LOW: • Calorie • Cholesterol

Crunchy toasted pecans meet lusty blue cheese head-on to create a medley of textures and tastes to spread on sliced apples.

1 (8-ounce) package nonfat cream cheese,
    softened
½ cup crumbled blue cheese
¼ cup chopped pecans, toasted

• **Position** knife blade in food processor bowl; add cheeses. Process 20 seconds or until blended.
• **Line** a 1-cup bowl with plastic wrap, and press cheese mixture into bowl. Cover and chill at least 8 hours.

• **Unmold** cheese spread, and remove plastic wrap. Roll outside edge of cheese mold in chopped pecans. Serve cheese spread with apple slices. **Yield: 1 cup.**

Per 1-tablespoon serving: Calories 37 (56% from fat)
Fat 2.3g (0.8g saturated)   Protein 2.9g   Carbohydrate 0.9g
Fiber 0.1g   Cholesterol 5mg   Sodium 134mg

Sherry Cheese Pâté

LOW: • Fat • Calorie • Cholesterol • Sodium

A spritz of sherry and a crown of chutney elevate this Cheddar pâté to royal stature.

6 ounces nonfat cream cheese, softened
½ cup (2 ounces) shredded reduced-fat sharp
    Cheddar cheese
2 tablespoons dry sherry
½ teaspoon curry powder
⅓ cup chutney
2 green onions, thinly sliced

• **Combine** first 4 ingredients; shape into a 5-inch circle on a serving plate, and chill. Just before serving, spread chutney over cheese, and sprinkle with green onions. Serve with low-fat crackers. **Yield: 1 cup.**

Per 1-tablespoon serving: Calories 36 (18% from fat)
Fat 0.7g (0.4g saturated)   Protein 2.6g   Carbohydrate 4.2g
Fiber 0.1g   Cholesterol 4mg   Sodium 101mg

Parmesan-Coated Brie

Parmesan-Coated Brie

LOW: • Calorie

There's just no substitute for the buttery ooze of melted Brie, so enjoy it. To assuage any guilt, ovenbake the breading to a crispy finish instead of frying it.

1 large egg, lightly beaten
1 tablespoon water
¼ cup fine, dry breadcrumbs
¼ cup grated nonfat Parmesan cheese
1½ teaspoons dried Italian seasoning
1 (15-ounce) mini Brie with herbs
Vegetable cooking spray
Garnish: fresh rosemary sprigs

• **Combine** egg and water in a shallow dish.
• **Combine** breadcrumbs, cheese, and seasoning in another shallow dish.
• **Dip** Brie into egg mixture, turning to coat top and sides (do not coat bottom). Place Brie in breadcrumb mixture, turning to coat top and sides. Repeat procedure. Place on a baking sheet coated with cooking spray. Chill at least 1 hour.
• **Bake** at 375° for 10 minutes. Garnish, if desired. Serve with French baguette slices or low-fat crackers. **Yield:** 15 appetizer servings.

Per serving: Calories 110 (65% from fat)
Fat 8.0g (5.0g saturated) Protein 6.4g Carbohydrate 2.9g
Fiber 0.1g Cholesterol 28mg Sodium 228mg

Marinated Cheese

LOW: • Calorie • Cholesterol

Trim this pert cheese with slices of cherry tomato or sprigs of any fresh herb to vary the look yet keep the analysis the same as if using basil leaves.

½ pound part-skim mozzarella cheese
½ pound reduced-fat Cheddar cheese
1 cup fat-free Italian salad dressing
¼ teaspoon freshly ground pepper
1 (12-ounce) French baguette
Garnish: fresh basil leaves

• **Cut** cheeses into ¼-inch-thick slices. (For variety, cut the cheese with a crinkle-edged cutter.) Alternate cheeses in a 13- x 9- x 2-inch dish, overlapping slightly.
• **Combine** dressing and pepper; pour over cheese. Cover and chill 8 hours.

• **Cut** baguette into ¼-inch slices. Place on baking sheets. Bake at 350° for 8 to 10 minutes or until lightly toasted, turning once.
• **Drain** cheeses. Place 1 cheese slice on each bread slice. Garnish, if desired. Serve immediately. **Yield:** 44 appetizers.

Note: To make these appetizers ahead, marinate the cheese overnight in the refrigerator. You can also toast the bread a day ahead, and store it at room temperature wrapped in cloth towels. Assemble the appetizers right before the party.

Per appetizer: Calories 52 (35% from fat)
Fat 2.0g (1.2g saturated) Protein 3.5g Carbohydrate 5.2g
Fiber 0.1g Cholesterol 7mg Sodium 163mg

Mexican Pinwheels

LOW: • Fat • Calorie • Cholesterol • Sodium

Bits of green chiles and ripe olives dance throughout these twirling temptations.

1 (8-ounce) package nonfat cream cheese, softened
½ cup nonfat sour cream
1 cup (4 ounces) shredded reduced-fat sharp Cheddar cheese
1 (4.5-ounce) can chopped green chiles, drained
1 (2¼-ounce) can sliced ripe olives, drained
⅓ cup chopped green onions
1 clove garlic, pressed
¼ teaspoon salt-free herb-and-spice blend
8 (8-inch) fat-free flour tortillas

• **Beat** cream cheese and sour cream at medium speed of an electric mixer until smooth. Stir in Cheddar cheese and next 5 ingredients. Spread cheese mixture evenly over each tortilla; roll up tortillas, jellyroll fashion. Wrap each separately in plastic wrap. Chill up to 8 hours.
• **Unwrap** each roll, and cut into 12 slices. Secure pinwheels with wooden picks, if desired. **Yield:** 8 dozen.

Per pinwheel: Calories 17 (16% from fat)
Fat 0.3g (0.2g saturated) Protein 1.0g Carbohydrate 2.4g
Fiber 0.1g Cholesterol 1mg Sodium 64mg

Oregano Cheese Puffs

LOW: • Fat • Calorie • Cholesterol • Sodium

A provocative pairing of oregano and Swiss excites these delicate appetizers. Egg substitute lets them puff just as high as with whole eggs.

⅔ cup skim milk
2 tablespoons reduced-calorie stick margarine
¾ cup all-purpose flour
¼ teaspoon salt
⅛ teaspoon pepper
¾ cup egg substitute
½ cup (2 ounces) shredded reduced-fat Swiss cheese, divided
2 teaspoons dried oregano
Vegetable cooking spray

• **Bring** milk and margarine to a boil in a medium saucepan. Reduce heat to low; add flour, salt, and pepper all at once, stirring vigorously, until mixture leaves sides of pan and forms a smooth ball. Remove from heat, and cool 5 to 10 minutes.
• **Add** egg substitute, ¼ cup at a time, beating with a wooden spoon after each addition. Stir in ¼ cup cheese and oregano. Drop by level tablespoonfuls onto baking sheets coated with cooking spray.
• **Bake** at 400° for 16 to 18 minutes. Sprinkle with remaining ¼ cup cheese, and bake 1 to 2 additional minutes. Serve immediately. **Yield:** 29 appetizers.

Per appetizer: Calories 27 (30% from fat)
Fat 0.9g (0.3g saturated)   Protein 1.8g   Carbohydrate 3.0g
Fiber 0.1g   Cholesterol 1mg   Sodium 43mg

Cheese Wafers

LOW: • Calorie • Cholesterol • Sodium

These salty tidbits are seriously delicious. The intense flavor of extra sharp Cheddar maximizes cheese appeal while crisp rice cereal guarantees crunch.

¼ cup margarine, softened
1 cup (4 ounces) shredded reduced-fat extra sharp Cheddar cheese
¼ cup nonfat buttermilk
1½ cups crisp rice cereal
1 cup all-purpose flour
⅛ teaspoon salt
⅛ teaspoon ground red pepper
Dash of paprika

• **Position** knife blade in food processor bowl; add margarine, cheese, and buttermilk. Process until blended, stopping once to scrape down sides.
• **Add** cereal and remaining 4 ingredients; process until mixture forms a ball, stopping often to scrape down sides.
• **Shape** dough into ½-inch balls. Place balls about 2 inches apart on ungreased baking sheets. Flatten each ball in a crisscross pattern with a fork dipped in flour.
• **Bake** at 350° for 15 minutes or until lightly browned. Remove to wire racks to cool. **Yield:** 4½ dozen.

Per wafer: Calories 26 (45% from fat)
Fat 1.3g (0.5g saturated)   Protein 0.9g   Carbohydrate 2.5g
Fiber 0.1g   Cholesterol 2mg   Sodium 40mg

Grilled Eggplant Appetizer

LOW: • Fat • Calorie • Cholesterol • Sodium

A garlicky puree of grilled eggplant is spread on crunchy baguette slices, crowned with a scarlet splice of tomato, strewn with freshly grated Parmesan, and broiled to warm satisfaction.

2 (1-pound) eggplants, peeled and cut into
  ½-inch slices
½ teaspoon salt
½ cup coarsely chopped fresh basil
¼ cup fat-free Italian salad dressing
2 cloves garlic, minced
Vegetable cooking spray
¼ teaspoon ground red pepper
1 (22-inch) French baguette, cut into ½-inch
  slices
4 Roma tomatoes, each cut into 10 slices
¼ cup freshly grated Parmesan cheese

• **Sprinkle** eggplant with salt, and let stand 30 minutes.
• **Combine** basil, Italian dressing, and garlic; set aside.
• **Rinse** eggplant slices, and pat dry.
• **Coat** food rack with cooking spray; place rack on grill over medium coals (300° to 350°). Place eggplant slices on rack in a single layer.
• **Cook**, without grill lid, 8 to 10 minutes on each side. Place half of eggplant slices in an airtight container, and sprinkle with basil mixture; top with remaining eggplant slices. Cover and chill 8 hours.
• **Position** knife blade in food processor bowl; add eggplant mixture and red pepper. Process until smooth, stopping once to scrape down sides.
• **Spread** about 1½ teaspoons eggplant mixture on each of 40 baguette slices, and top each with a tomato slice. Sprinkle evenly with cheese.
• **Broil** 5½ inches from heat (with electric oven door partially opened) 2 to 3 minutes or until cheese melts. Serve immediately. **Yield:** 40 appetizers.

Per appetizer: Calories 16 (17% from fat)
Fat 0.3g (0.1g saturated)   Protein 0.7g   Carbohydrate 3.0g
Fiber 0.4g   Cholesterol 1mg   Sodium 69mg

Oven-Baked Tomato Appetizers

LOW: • Fat • Calorie • Cholesterol

Feta cheese is fresh and tangy against crisp-edged slices of French baguette. There's no need to coat the bread with olive oil before toasting to get a rich golden hue. We lightly sprayed ours with olive oil-flavored vegetable cooking spray instead.

1 (12-ounce) French baguette
Olive oil-flavored vegetable cooking spray
12 small Roma tomatoes (1 pound)
½ teaspoon sugar
½ teaspoon salt
1 teaspoon dried thyme
⅓ cup crumbled reduced-fat feta cheese

• **Cut** 24 (½-inch) slices from baguette; place on a baking sheet. Coat lightly with cooking spray. Bake at 400° for 5 minutes; cool.
• **Cut** tomatoes in half lengthwise; scoop out seeds and pulp, and reserve for another use. Place tomato halves, cut side up, on a rack in broiler pan. Sprinkle evenly with sugar, salt, and thyme.
• **Bake** at 350° for 30 minutes. Place tomato halves, cut side up, on bread; sprinkle with cheese. Serve immediately. **Yield:** 2 dozen.

Per appetizer: Calories 52 (16% from fat)
Fat 0.9g (0.3g saturated)   Protein 1.8g   Carbohydrate 8.9g
Fiber 0.6g   Cholesterol 1mg   Sodium 156mg

Spicy Buffalo Wings

LOW: • Calorie • Cholesterol

The hot sauce in these wild wings is so rambunctious that we never missed the ¾ cup butter from the original recipe. Serve them with nonfat blue cheese salad dressing to beat the peppery heat.

3 pounds chicken wings
Vegetable cooking spray
½ cup hot sauce
¼ cup water
1 (1-ounce) envelope dry onion soup mix
1 to 3 teaspoons ground red pepper
1 (8-ounce) bottle nonfat blue cheese salad
 dressing

• **Cut** off and discard wingtips; cut wings in half at joint. Place chicken on a rack of broiler pan coated with cooking spray; set aside.
• **Combine** hot sauce, water, soup mix, and red pepper. Brush chicken with half of hot sauce mixture.
• **Bake,** uncovered, at 375° for 30 minutes. Remove from oven; turn chicken, and brush with remaining hot sauce mixture. Bake 10 to 15 additional minutes or until tender. Serve warm with salad dressing. **Yield:** 3 dozen.

Per wing: Calories 66 (34% from fat)
Fat 2.5g (0.7g saturated) Protein 7.1g Carbohydrate 2.9g
Fiber 0.2g Cholesterol 24mg Sodium 185mg

Turkey Sausage Turnovers

LOW: • Fat • Calorie • Cholesterol

Browned crumbles of turkey sausage and bits of onion are cloaked in refrigerated pizza crust dough and baked until chestnut colored.

½ pound ground turkey breakfast sausage
½ cup finely chopped onion
1 tablespoon all-purpose flour
1 tablespoon dry sherry
1 (10-ounce) can refrigerated pizza crust
 dough
Olive oil-flavored vegetable cooking spray
Paprika
1 cup fat-free spaghetti sauce

• **Cook** sausage and onion in a large skillet over high heat, stirring until sausage crumbles.

Remove from heat; drain. Return sausage and onion to skillet. Stir in flour and sherry; cool.
• **Roll** pizza crust into a 12-inch square on a lightly floured surface. Cut into 16 (3-inch) squares. Place 1 tablespoon sausage mixture on half of each square. Moisten edges of squares with water, and fold in half, pressing edges to seal; crimp with a fork. Place on baking sheets coated with cooking spray. Coat tops with cooking spray. Cut 3 small slits in top of each turnover.
• **Bake** at 375° for 16 to 18 minutes, and sprinkle with paprika. Serve warm with spaghetti sauce. **Yield:** 16 turnovers.

Per turnover: Calories 74 (23% from fat)
Fat 1.9g (0.4g saturated) Protein 3.8g Carbohydrate 10.1g
Fiber 0.3g Cholesterol 7mg Sodium 210mg

Smoked Salmon and Cucumber Tartlets

LOW: • Fat • Calorie • Cholesterol • Sodium

Fresh dill, horseradish, and vodka flatter the salmon filling in these golden layers of phyllo pastry.

1 cup 1% low-fat cottage cheese
½ cup peeled, seeded, and finely chopped
 cucumber
⅓ pound smoked salmon
1 (8-ounce) package nonfat cream cheese,
 softened
3 tablespoons pepper vodka
2 tablespoons lemon juice
1 tablespoon Dijon mustard
2 teaspoons prepared horseradish
2 tablespoons capers, rinsed and drained
⅛ teaspoon freshly ground pepper
2 tablespoons chopped fresh dill
Phyllo Tartlet Shells
Garnish: fresh dill sprigs

• **Place** cottage cheese in a wire-mesh strainer lined with two layers of cheesecloth. Place strainer over a medium bowl, and cover and chill 8 hours.
• **Drain** chopped cucumber well, patting between layers of paper towels. Set aside.
• **Position** knife blade in food processor bowl; add cottage cheese, salmon, and next 5 ingredients. Process until smooth, stopping once to scrape down sides. Stir in drained cucumber, capers, pepper, and chopped dill; cover and chill.

• **Spoon** salmon mixture evenly into cooled Phyllo Tartlet Shells; garnish, if desired. **Yield: 4 dozen.**

Phyllo Tartlet Shells

8 sheets frozen phyllo pastry, thawed
Butter-flavored vegetable cooking spray

• **Place** 1 sheet of phyllo on a flat surface (keep remaining phyllo covered with a slightly damp towel). Lightly spray phyllo with cooking spray. Repeat procedure with 3 more sheets of phyllo and cooking spray. Cut layered phyllo into 24 (3-inch) squares, using kitchen scissors or a sharp knife.
• **Coat** miniature (1³⁄₄-inch) muffin pans with cooking spray, and place 1 square of layered phyllo into each muffin cup, pressing gently in center to form a pastry shell. Repeat procedure with remaining 4 sheets of phyllo and butter-flavored cooking spray.
• **Bake** tartlet shells at 350° for 8 minutes or until lightly browned. Carefully remove shells from pans, and let cool on wire racks. **Yield: 4 dozen.**

Note: You can store unfilled baked shells in an airtight container.

Per tartlet: Calories 24 (19% from fat)
Fat 0.5g (0.1g saturated) Protein 2.1g Carbohydrate 2.2g
Fiber 0.0g Cholesterol 2mg Sodium 109mg

Pizza Bites

LOW: • Fat • Calorie • Cholesterol

Mini English muffins instead of refrigerated flaky biscuits transform these plucky little pies into unpretentious low-fat fare.

³⁄₄ cup (3 ounces) shredded part-skim
    mozzarella cheese
¹⁄₃ cup freshly grated Parmesan cheese
1 (14-ounce) package mini English muffins
¹⁄₃ cup diced Canadian bacon
¹⁄₃ cup diced green bell pepper

• **Combine** mozzarella and Parmesan cheeses, and set aside.
• **Cut** each muffin in half horizontally.
• **Sprinkle** bacon, green pepper, and cheese mixture evenly on muffin halves. Place on an ungreased baking sheet.

• **Bake** at 400° for 10 to 12 minutes or until lightly browned, and serve warm. **Yield: 2 dozen.**

Per appetizer: Calories 56 (19% from fat)
Fat 1.2g (0.7g saturated) Protein 3.5g Carbohydrate 7.8g
Fiber 0.0g Cholesterol 5mg Sodium 147mg

Ham-Pineapple Nibbles

LOW: • Calorie • Cholesterol

Rubbed sage adds an interesting nuance to these half-moon-shaped appetizers, enhancing the sweet pineapple and salty ham flavors rather than disguising them.

4¹⁄₂ ounces lean cooked ham, coarsely chopped
1 (15¹⁄₄-ounce) can crushed pineapple in juice,
    drained
¹⁄₂ cup (2 ounces) shredded part-skim
    mozzarella cheese
¹⁄₃ cup soft breadcrumbs
¹⁄₄ cup minced green bell pepper
¹⁄₄ cup egg substitute
4 green onions, chopped
¹⁄₄ teaspoon rubbed sage
¹⁄₄ cup all-purpose flour
3 (8-ounce) cans refrigerated crescent rolls

• **Position** knife blade in food processor bowl; add ham. Process until ground, stopping once to scrape down sides.
• **Combine** ham, pineapple, and next 6 ingredients in a large bowl; set aside.
• **Sprinkle** flour evenly over work surface. Separate each package of rolls into 4 rectangles, pressing perforations to seal. Roll each rectangle into an 8- x 4-inch rectangle; cut each crosswise into thirds.
• **Place** about 1 tablespoon ham mixture in center of each third of dough. Fold dough over ham mixture, pressing edges to seal; crimp with a fork. Place on ungreased baking sheets.
• **Bake** at 375° for 10 minutes or until golden. **Yield: 3 dozen.**

Per appetizer: Calories 84 (44% from fat)
Fat 4.1g (1.2g saturated) Protein 2.7g Carbohydrate 9.3g
Fiber 1.5g Cholesterol 3mg Sodium 205mg

Bacon-Jalapeño-Tomato Quesadillas

LOW: • Calorie • Cholesterol

Blanketed with shredded Monterey Jack cheese and sprinkled with morsels of smoky turkey bacon, these wedge-shaped appetizers are filling and full of flavor.

4 (9-inch) flour tortillas
Butter-flavored vegetable cooking spray
2 cups (8 ounces) shredded reduced-fat
    Monterey Jack cheese
4 slices turkey bacon, cooked and crumbled
1 small tomato, peeled, seeded, and chopped
4 pickled jalapeño peppers, finely chopped
1 teaspoon ground cumin
Garnish: fresh cilantro sprigs
½ cup no-salt-added salsa

• **Lightly** spray 1 side of each tortilla with cooking spray. Place tortillas, coated side up, on large ungreased baking sheets.
• **Bake** at 400° for 3 minutes or until lightly browned. (Tortillas may be baked up to 2 hours ahead.)
• **Combine** cheese and next 4 ingredients, stirring gently. Sprinkle cheese mixture evenly over tortillas.
• **Bake** at 400° for 5 minutes or until cheese is bubbly. Cut each tortilla into four wedges; garnish, if desired. Serve quesadillas with salsa. **Yield:** 16 appetizers.

***

Per appetizer: Calories 93 (39% from fat)
Fat 4.0g (1.7g saturated) Protein 5.8g Carbohydrate 8.2g
Fiber 0.3g Cholesterol 11mg Sodium 293mg

Piña Coladas

LOW: • Fat • Calorie • Cholesterol • Sodium

With rum and coconut extracts, our sunny concoction has a fraction of the calories and fat that you'd get from rum and cream of coconut.

1 (12-ounce) can evaporated skimmed milk
1 (8-ounce) can pineapple chunks, undrained
½ cup frozen pineapple-orange juice
    concentrate, undiluted
1 large banana, sliced
½ teaspoon rum extract
½ teaspoon coconut extract

• **Combine** all ingredients in container of an electric blender. Add enough ice to measure 5 cups. Process until smooth, stopping once to scrape down sides. **Yield:** 5 cups.

***

Per 1-cup serving: Calories 157 (2% from fat)
Fat 0.3g (0.1g saturated) Protein 5.7g Carbohydrate 32.9g
Fiber 1.2g Cholesterol 3mg Sodium 80mg

Piña Colada Slush

LOW: • Fat • Calorie • Cholesterol • Sodium

This coconut- and rum-laced drink is seductively smooth and frosty.

1 (46-ounce) can pineapple juice
2 (12-ounce) cans frozen lemonade
    concentrate, thawed and undiluted
3 cups water
2 cups light rum
1 (14-ounce) can low-fat coconut milk
1 (3-liter) bottle diet lemon-lime carbonated
    beverage, chilled

• **Combine** first 5 ingredients in a large plastic container.
• **Cover** and freeze at least 8 hours, stirring twice during freezing process. To serve, combine equal portions of frozen mixture and lemon-lime beverage, stirring well. Serve immediately. Cover and refreeze any remaining frozen mixture. **Yield:** 7 quarts.

***

Per 1-cup serving: Calories 127 (6% from fat)
Fat 0.8g (0.8g saturated) Protein 0.2g Carbohydrate 18.4g
Fiber 0.1g Cholesterol 0mg Sodium 22mg

Piña Colada Slush

Rasp-Berry Good Tea

LOW: • Fat • Calorie • Cholesterol • Sodium

Stimulate your senses with this aromatic beverage of raspberry zinger herb tea and fizzy ginger ale.

2 cups boiling water
4 raspberry zinger herb tea bags
3 tablespoons sugar
2 cups reduced-calorie ginger ale, chilled

• **Pour** boiling water over tea bags; cover and steep 5 minutes.
• **Remove** tea bags from water, squeezing gently. Stir in sugar, and let tea mixture cool.
• **Stir** in chilled ginger ale. Pour over ice. **Yield:** 4 cups.

Per 1-cup serving: Calories 37 (0% from fat)
Fat 0.0g (0.0g saturated)   Protein 0.0g   Carbohydrate 9.5g
Fiber 0.0g   Cholesterol 0mg   Sodium 18mg

Spicy Tomato Warm-Up

LOW: • Fat • Calorie • Cholesterol

We slashed the sodium in this pick-me-up by a third, and then jazzed it up with celery seeds, onion powder, and garlic powder.

1 (46-ounce) can no-salt-added tomato juice
1 (14¼-ounce) can no-salt-added beef broth
3 tablespoons lemon juice
3 tablespoons low-sodium Worcestershire sauce
½ teaspoon salt
½ teaspoon pepper
½ teaspoon celery seeds
½ teaspoon hot sauce
¼ teaspoon garlic powder
¼ teaspoon onion powder

• **Combine** all ingredients in a large saucepan; cook over medium heat until thoroughly heated. Serve warm. **Yield:** 8 cups.

Per 1-cup serving: Calories 45 (0% from fat)
Fat 0.0g (0.0g saturated)   Protein 1.8g   Carbohydrate 10.4g
Fiber 0.1g   Cholesterol 0mg   Sodium 189mg

Mocha Punch

LOW: • Fat • Calorie • Cholesterol • Sodium

Here's a punch so thick and rich it could double as dessert. Frozen yogurt and whipped topping keep the texture and taste in harmony.

1 (2-ounce) jar instant coffee granules
1 cup boiling water
¾ cup sugar
1 gallon skim milk
½ gallon chocolate nonfat frozen yogurt, softened
½ gallon vanilla nonfat frozen yogurt, softened
1 cup frozen reduced-calorie whipped topping, thawed

• **Combine** coffee granules and boiling water, stirring until coffee dissolves. Add sugar, stirring until sugar dissolves. Cover and chill.
• **Combine** coffee mixture and milk in a large punch bowl; gently stir in frozen yogurts. Spoon whipped topping on top. **Yield:** about 2½ gallons.

Per 1-cup serving: Calories 124 (3% from fat)
Fat 0.4g (0.1g saturated)   Protein 6.3g   Carbohydrate 24.7g
Fiber 0.0g   Cholesterol 2mg   Sodium 98mg

Honey Angel Biscuits (page 49)

Breads

Rosemary Biscuits

LOW: • Fat • Calorie • Cholesterol

Rosemary's heady aroma and distinctive lemon-pine flavor permeate each bite of these flaky biscuits.

4 cups reduced-fat biscuit and baking mix
1½ teaspoons dried rosemary, crushed
1⅓ cups skim milk
Butter-flavored vegetable cooking spray

• **Combine** biscuit mix and rosemary in a large bowl. Add milk, stirring with a fork until dry ingredients are moistened. Turn dough out onto a lightly floured surface, and knead lightly 3 or 4 times.
• **Roll** dough to ½-inch thickness; cut with a 2-inch round cutter, and place on a baking sheet coated with cooking spray. Coat tops of biscuits with cooking spray.
• **Bake** at 450° for 8 to 10 minutes or until lightly browned. **Yield:** 2½ dozen.

Per biscuit: Calories 86 (2% from fat)
Fat 0.2g (0.0g saturated)   Protein 2.0g   Carbohydrate 21.9g
Fiber 0.0g   Cholesterol 0mg   Sodium 278mg

Mexican Fiesta Spoon Biscuits

LOW: • Cholesterol

Check your local market for the brand of refrigerated biscuits that's lowest in fat. We found that store brands often have less.

3 (12-ounce) cans refrigerated buttermilk biscuits
1 (16-ounce) jar chunky salsa
Vegetable cooking spray
1 cup (4 ounces) shredded reduced-fat Monterey Jack cheese
1 small green bell pepper, chopped
½ cup sliced green onions

• **Cut** each biscuit into 8 pieces.
• **Combine** biscuits and salsa in a 13- x 9- x 2-inch baking dish coated with cooking spray, tossing gently to coat. Top with cheese and remaining ingredients.
• **Bake,** uncovered, at 350° for 45 minutes or until edges are golden and center is set; let stand

10 minutes. Cut into squares, and serve with soup or salad. **Yield:** 15 biscuits.

Per biscuit: Calories 234 (40% from fat)
Fat 10.5g (2.8g saturated)   Protein 6.3g   Carbohydrate 30.5g
Fiber 0.2g   Cholesterol 5mg   Sodium 974mg

Onion-and-Sesame Rolls

LOW: • Fat • Calorie • Cholesterol

Refrigerated pizza dough creates the quick and low-fat base for these rolls. Brush the dough with fat-free Italian salad dressing to keep them moist, tender, and tasty.

1½ tablespoons grated Parmesan cheese
1 tablespoon instant minced onion
½ teaspoon garlic powder
1 (10-ounce) can refrigerated pizza dough
Butter-flavored vegetable cooking spray
2 tablespoons fat-free Italian salad dressing
1 tablespoon sesame seeds

• **Combine** first 3 ingredients; set cheese mixture aside.
• **Unroll** pizza dough, and pat into a 10- x 8-inch rectangle. Coat dough with cooking spray, and brush with salad dressing. Sprinkle cheese mixture over dough, leaving a ½-inch border. Roll up, jellyroll fashion, starting with short side; pinch seams to seal.
• **Cut** into 10 (1-inch-thick) slices, and place on an ungreased baking sheet. Coat tops of rolls with cooking spray, and sprinkle with sesame seeds.
• **Bake** at 400° for 10 to 12 minutes or until rolls are lightly browned; serve immediately. **Yield:** 10 rolls.

Per roll: Calories 87 (20% from fat)
Fat 1.9g (0.4g saturated)   Protein 3.1g   Carbohydrate 14.4g
Fiber 0.5g   Cholesterol 1mg   Sodium 204mg

Quick Rolls

LOW: • Cholesterol

Ever had those ridiculously rich and easy rolls made with biscuit mix, sour cream and butter? We thought they couldn't be matched until we made them using lower fat ingredients. We gave this lighter version the same high rating as the original.

2¼ cups reduced-fat biscuit and baking mix, divided
1 (8-ounce) carton reduced-fat sour cream
½ cup reduced-calorie margarine, melted
Vegetable cooking spray

• **Combine** 2 cups biscuit mix, sour cream, and margarine, stirring well.
• **Sprinkle** remaining ¼ cup biscuit mix on a flat surface. Drop dough by level tablespoonfuls onto biscuit mix, and roll into balls. Place 3 balls into each of 12 muffin cups coated with cooking spray.
• **Bake** at 350° for 20 minutes or until rolls are golden. **Yield:** 1 dozen.

Per roll: Calories 155 (51% from fat)
Fat 8.8g (2.1g saturated)   Protein 2.3g   Carbohydrate 17.1g
Fiber 0.0g   Cholesterol 7mg   Sodium 349mg

Cheesy French Bread

LOW: • Fat • Calorie • Cholesterol

A generous measure of Monterey Jack cheese spiked with just the right amount of fresh garlic melts invitingly over crusty French bread.

1½ cups (6 ounces) shredded reduced-fat Monterey Jack cheese
½ cup reduced-fat mayonnaise
1½ teaspoons dried parsley flakes
1 clove garlic, pressed
1 (16-ounce) loaf French bread, cut in half horizontally

• **Combine** first 4 ingredients. Spread on cut sides of bread; place on a baking sheet.
• **Bake** at 350° for 15 minutes or until cheese is melted. Serve immediately. **Yield:** 1 loaf.

Per 1-inch slice: Calories 71 (30% from fat)
Fat 2.4g (0.7g saturated)   Protein 3.1g   Carbohydrate 8.7g
Fiber 0.4g   Cholesterol 6mg   Sodium 154mg

Garlic Bread

LOW: • Fat • Calorie • Cholesterol

Parmesan cheese and herbs spice up this meat-and-potatoes staple. Be sure to have plenty on hand.

¼ cup reduced-calorie margarine, softened
¼ cup grated nonfat Parmesan cheese
2 cloves garlic, pressed
¼ teaspoon dried marjoram
¼ teaspoon dried oregano
1 (16-ounce) loaf French bread, cut into 1-inch slices

• **Combine** first 5 ingredients, and spread between bread slices.
• **Reassemble** loaf, and wrap in heavy-duty aluminum foil; place on a baking sheet.
• **Bake** at 350° for 20 minutes. Open foil, and bake 5 additional minutes or until crisp and golden. Serve immediately. **Yield:** 1 loaf.

Note: The margarine mixture does double-duty as a tasty topping for baked potatoes.

Per 1-inch slice: Calories 92 (21% from fat)
Fat 2.1g (0.2g saturated)   Protein 2.3g   Carbohydrate 15.1g
Fiber 0.6g   Cholesterol 1mg   Sodium 196mg

Nutty Orange Coffee Cake

LOW: • Cholesterol

Line these biscuits up like dominos to create this citrusy breakfast bread. Little nuggets of nonfat cream cheese hide inside each biscuit.

½ cup sugar
¼ cup finely chopped pecans
2 teaspoons grated orange rind
½ (8-ounce) package nonfat cream cheese
2 (12-ounce) cans refrigerated buttermilk
    biscuits
Butter-flavored vegetable cooking spray
½ cup sifted powdered sugar
1 tablespoon fresh orange juice

• **Combine** first 3 ingredients; set aside.
• **Place** about 1 teaspoon cream cheese on half of each biscuit; fold biscuit over cheese, pressing edges to seal.
• **Coat** biscuits with cooking spray; dredge in sugar mixture. Place, curved side down, in a 12-cup Bundt pan coated with cooking spray, spacing evenly. Coat tops with cooking spray; sprinkle with remaining sugar mixture.
• **Bake** at 350° for 35 minutes or until done. Immediately invert onto a serving plate.
• **Combine** powdered sugar and orange juice, stirring well; drizzle over warm coffee cake. Serve immediately. **Yield:** 10 servings.

Per serving: Calories 296 (35% from fat)
Fat 11.4g (2.2g saturated)   Protein 5.9g   Carbohydrate 45.2g
Fiber 0.2g   Cholesterol 2mg   Sodium 788mg

Eggnog French Toast

LOW: • Fat

This dish is special enough to serve during the holiday season. Rum extract adds a calorie-conscious kick to the syrup.

1½ cups commercial refrigerated eggnog
½ teaspoon freshly grated nutmeg
8 (1-inch-thick) slices French bread
Vegetable cooking spray
Rum Syrup

• **Combine** eggnog and nutmeg in a large shallow dish. Place bread slices in dish, turning to coat evenly.

• **Coat** a large nonstick skillet or griddle with cooking spray; place over medium-high heat until hot. Remove bread slices from eggnog mixture, allowing excess to drain. Cook in skillet 3 minutes on each side or until golden. Serve immediately with Rum Syrup. **Yield:** 4 servings.

Rum Syrup
1 cup lite maple syrup
½ teaspoon rum extract

• **Combine** syrup and rum extract in a small saucepan; cook over low heat until heated, stirring often. **Yield:** 1 cup.

Per serving: Calories 313 (23% from fat)
Fat 8.1g (4.2g saturated)   Protein 8.2g   Carbohydrate 52.2g
Fiber 1.3g   Cholesterol 58mg   Sodium 404mg

Macadamia Nut French Toast

LOW: • Fat

This dish is definitely worth the calories. Three egg whites instead of two of the whole eggs in the original recipe allow us the indulgence of macadamia nuts.

3 egg whites, lightly beaten
2 large eggs, lightly beaten
¼ cup sugar
¼ teaspoon ground nutmeg
⅔ cup orange juice
⅓ cup skim milk
½ teaspoon vanilla extract
1 (16-ounce) loaf Italian bread, cut into 12
    (1-inch) slices
Vegetable cooking spray
¼ cup macadamia nuts, chopped and toasted
Garnish: ground nutmeg

• **Combine** first 7 ingredients; stir well.
• **Fit** bread slices in a single layer into a 13- x 9- x 2-inch baking dish coated with cooking spray. Pour egg mixture over bread slices; cover and chill at least 8 hours, turning bread once.
• **Place** bread in a single layer in a 15- x 10- x 1-inch jellyroll pan coated with cooking spray.
• **Bake** at 400° for 10 minutes; sprinkle with nuts. Bake 10 additional minutes. Garnish, if desired. Serve immediately. **Yield:** 6 servings.

Per serving: Calories 345 (21% from fat)
Fat 7.9g (1.4g saturated)   Protein 11.9g   Carbohydrate 56.0g
Fiber 2.2g   Cholesterol 75mg   Sodium 498mg

Macadamia Nut French Toast

Big Batch Moist Bran Muffins

We gave these lighter muffins a higher rating than the original recipe because they're extra moist and memorable. But don't use the applesauce trick we used to replace part of the fat in all bread recipes–it sometimes makes bread gummy.

5 cups all-purpose flour
1⅔ cups sugar
1 tablespoon plus 2 teaspoons baking soda
1 tablespoon plus 1 teaspoon ground
      cinnamon
1½ teaspoons salt
1 quart nonfat buttermilk
½ cup vegetable oil
½ cup unsweetened applesauce
3 large eggs
1 (16-ounce) can fruit cocktail in juice,
      undrained
1 (15-ounce) package wheat bran flakes cereal
      with raisins
Vegetable cooking spray

• **Combine** all ingredients except vegetable cooking spray in a large mixing bowl; beat at medium speed with an electric mixer 2 minutes. Spoon into muffin pans coated with cooking spray, filling two-thirds full.

• **Bake** at 400° for 16 to 18 minutes or until muffins are done. Remove muffins from pans immediately. **Yield:** 4 dozen.

Note: You can store batter, covered tightly, in refrigerator up to 1 week. Do not stir before using.

Per muffin: Calories 142 (20% from fat)
Fat 3.2g (0.6g saturated)   Protein 3.1g   Carbohydrate 26.4g
Fiber 1.6g   Cholesterol 14mg   Sodium 278mg

Coconut Muffins

Here's a morning treat that's sure to charm coconut lovers.

2 cups all-purpose flour
½ cup sugar
2 teaspoons baking powder
¼ teaspoon salt
¼ cup flaked coconut
1 large egg, lightly beaten
1 egg white, lightly beaten
1 (8-ounce) carton vanilla low-fat yogurt
¼ cup vegetable oil
¼ teaspoon coconut extract
Vegetable cooking spray

• **Combine** first 5 ingredients in a large bowl; make a well in center of mixture.

• **Combine** egg and next 4 ingredients; add to dry ingredients, stirring just until moistened. Spoon into muffin pan coated with cooking spray, filling three-fourths full.

• **Bake** at 400° for 19 to 20 minutes or until lightly browned. Remove muffins from pan immediately. **Yield:** 1 dozen.

Per muffin: Calories 184 (31% from fat)
Fat 6.3g (1.7g saturated)   Protein 4.0g   Carbohydrate 28.0g
Fiber 0.7g   Cholesterol 19mg   Sodium 77mg

Coconut Muffins

Dilly Cheese Muffins

LOW: • Fat • Calorie • Cholesterol

Feathery bits of fresh dill heighten the Swiss cheese and mustard message in these low-fat, low-calorie muffins.

3 cups reduced-fat biscuit and baking mix
1 cup (4 ounces) shredded reduced-fat Swiss cheese
1 tablespoon sugar
1¼ cups nonfat buttermilk
¼ cup egg substitute
1½ tablespoons chopped fresh dill
½ teaspoon dry mustard
1½ teaspoons vegetable oil
Vegetable cooking spray

• **Combine** first 3 ingredients in a large bowl, and make a well in center of mixture.
• **Combine** buttermilk and next 4 ingredients in a bowl, stirring well; add to dry ingredients, stirring just until moistened.
• **Place** paper baking cups in muffin pans, and coat with cooking spray; spoon batter into cups, filling two-thirds full.
• **Bake** at 350° for 25 to 28 minutes or until lightly browned. Remove muffins from pans immediately. **Yield:** 1½ dozen.

Per muffin: Calories 135 (14% from fat)
Fat 2.1g (0.7g saturated) Protein 5.1g Carbohydrate 28.4g
Fiber 0.0g Cholesterol 4mg Sodium 373mg

Sour Cream Corn Muffins

LOW: • Calorie • Cholesterol

Cream-style corn and reduced-fat sour cream make these muffins moist beyond measure. Don't be tempted to substitute nonfat sour cream— the muffins won't be as tender.

1 cup self-rising yellow cornmeal mix
1 (8.5-ounce) can cream-style corn
1 (8-ounce) carton reduced-fat sour cream
¼ cup egg substitute
2 tablespoons vegetable oil
Vegetable cooking spray

• **Combine** first 5 ingredients, stirring until smooth. Spoon into a muffin pan coated with cooking spray, filling two-thirds full.

• **Bake** at 400° for 25 minutes or until golden. Remove muffins from pan immediately. **Yield:** 1 dozen.

Per muffin: Calories 90 (52% from fat)
Fat 5.2g (1.9g saturated) Protein 2.1g Carbohydrate 11.0g
Fiber 4.3g Cholesterol 7mg Sodium 209mg

Baked Hush Puppies

LOW: • Calorie • Sodium

These cute little pups bake in miniature muffin cups for a significant fat and calorie savings compared with traditional deep-fried versions.

1 cup yellow cornmeal
1 cup all-purpose flour
1 tablespoon baking powder
1 teaspoon sugar
1 teaspoon salt
⅛ teaspoon ground red pepper
2 large eggs, lightly beaten
¾ cup skim milk
¼ cup vegetable oil
½ cup finely chopped onion
Vegetable cooking spray

• **Combine** first 6 ingredients in a large bowl; make a well in center of mixture. Set aside.
• **Combine** eggs and next 3 ingredients, stirring well; add to dry mixture, stirring just until dry ingredients are moistened.
• **Coat** miniature (1¾-inch) muffin pans with cooking spray. Spoon about 1 tablespoon batter into each muffin cup. (Cups will be about three-fourths full.)
• **Bake** at 425° for 15 minutes or until done. Remove from pans immediately. **Yield:** 3 dozen.

Per hush puppy: Calories 55 (39% from fat)
Fat 2.4g (0.2g saturated) Protein 1.3g Carbohydrate 6.9g
Fiber 0.4g Cholesterol 13mg Sodium 71mg

Spinach Cornbread

Here's a cornbread you'll cash in on–it's laced with spinach for extra flavor and nutrition. No need to worry about selecting and cleaning your greens. Our recipe uses convenient frozen chopped spinach.

1 (10-ounce) package frozen chopped spinach, thawed
1 (6-ounce) package Mexican cornbread mix
1 cup chopped onion
¾ cup nonfat cottage cheese
½ cup nonfat buttermilk
¼ cup vegetable oil
2 large eggs, lightly beaten
Vegetable cooking spray

• **Drain** spinach well, pressing between layers of paper towels to remove excess moisture. Place spinach in a bowl; add cornbread mix and next 5 ingredients, stirring until blended. Pour into an 8-inch baking dish coated with cooking spray.
• **Bake** at 400° for 30 minutes or until lightly browned. Serve immediately. **Yield:** 9 servings.

Per serving: Calories 176 (48% from fat)
Fat 9.4g (1.8g saturated)   Protein 7.2g   Carbohydrate 18.0g
Fiber 2.0g   Cholesterol 50mg   Sodium 411mg

Spoonbread

LOW: • Fat • Calorie

Whipped egg whites folded in this Southern classic keep it light as a cloud.

1½ cups boiling water
1 cup cornmeal
¾ teaspoon salt
2 tablespoons reduced-calorie margarine
1 cup skim milk
1 egg, separated
1 teaspoon baking powder
1 egg white
Vegetable cooking spray

• **Pour** boiling water over cornmeal gradually, stirring until smooth. Add salt and margarine, stirring until blended; cool 10 minutes. Gradually stir in milk and egg yolk. Add baking powder, stirring until blended.
• **Beat** egg whites at high speed with an electric mixer until stiff peaks form. Gently fold beaten egg whites into cornmeal mixture. Pour mixture into a 1½-quart baking dish coated with cooking spray.
• **Bake** at 375° for 45 minutes or until lightly browned. **Yield:** 6 servings.

Per serving: Calories 125 (30% from fat)
Fat 4.2g (0.4g saturated)   Protein 4.7g   Carbohydrate 18.0g
Fiber 2.2g   Cholesterol 38mg   Sodium 378mg

Honey Angel Biscuits

LOW: • Calorie • Cholesterol

A drizzle of golden honey sweetens these reach-for-the-sky biscuits.

1 package active dry yeast
¼ cup warm water (105°to 115°)
3 cups all-purpose flour
1 teaspoon baking powder
1 teaspoon baking soda
½ teaspoon salt
1 cup nonfat buttermilk
½ cup vegetable oil
3 tablespoons honey

• **Combine** yeast and warm water in a 1-cup liquid measuring cup; let stand 5 minutes.
• **Combine** flour and next 3 ingredients in a large bowl.
• **Combine** yeast mixture, buttermilk, oil, and honey, and add to dry ingredients, stirring just until dry ingredients are moistened.
• **Turn** dough out onto a lightly floured surface, and knead 4 or 5 times.
• **Pat** dough to ½-inch thickness. Cut with a 2-inch round cutter, and place on an ungreased baking sheet.
• **Bake** at 400° for 10 minutes or until golden. **Yield:** 1½ dozen.

Per biscuit: Calories 146 (39% from fat)
Fat 6.3g (1.2g saturated)   Protein 2.8g   Carbohydrate 19.7g
Fiber 0.7g   Cholesterol 0mg   Sodium 150mg

Butter Crescent Rolls

LOW: • Fat • Calorie • Cholesterol • Sodium

*Buttery-tasting crescent rolls without butter?
Pretty darn close. Using yogurt in the dough and
coating the rolls with butter-flavored vegetable
cooking spray keep them rich.*

1 package active dry yeast
¼ cup warm water (105° to 115°)
¼ cup sugar
½ cup plain nonfat yogurt
3 tablespoons margarine, melted
2 egg whites, lightly beaten
¾ teaspoon salt
3¼ cups all-purpose flour
Butter-flavored vegetable cooking spray

• **Combine** yeast and warm water in a 1-cup liquid measuring cup; let stand 5 minutes.
• **Combine** yeast mixture, sugar, and next 4 ingredients in a large bowl, stirring until blended. Gradually stir in enough flour to make a soft dough.
• **Turn** dough out onto a lightly floured surface, and knead 3 or 4 times. Place in a bowl coated with cooking spray, turning to coat top.
• **Cover** and let rise in a warm place (85°), free from drafts, 1 hour or until doubled in bulk.
• **Punch** dough down, and divide into thirds; shape each portion into a ball. Roll each ball into a 12-inch circle on a lightly floured surface; coat lightly with cooking spray. Cut each circle into 12 wedges. Roll up each wedge, starting with wide end; place rolls, point side down, on baking sheets coated with cooking spray.
• **Cover** and let rise in a warm place (85°), free from drafts, 30 minutes or until doubled in bulk.
• **Bake** at 375° for 12 minutes or until golden. Serve immediately. **Yield:** 3 dozen.

Per roll: Calories 59 (17% from fat)
Fat 1.1g (0.2g saturated)   Protein 1.6g   Carbohydrate 10.3g
Fiber 0.4g   Cholesterol 0mg   Sodium 65mg

Make-Ahead Yeast Rolls

LOW: • Fat • Calorie • Cholesterol • Sodium

*Here's a convenient roll recipe you'll turn to
again and again. We stripped a significant amount
of fat from this recipe and still have a dough that
would make Grandma jealous. It's so supple you
can shape it any way you want.*

2 packages active dry yeast
¼ cup warm water (105° to 115°)
4½ cups bread flour, divided
1¾ cups nonfat buttermilk
⅓ cup sugar
2 tablespoons margarine, softened
1½ teaspoons salt
Vegetable cooking spray

• **Combine** yeast and warm water in a 1-cup liquid measuring cup; let stand 5 minutes.
• **Combine** yeast mixture, 2 cups flour, and next 4 ingredients in a large bowl; beat with a wooden spoon 2 minutes. Gradually stir in enough remaining flour to make a soft dough.
• **Cover** and let rise in a warm place (85°), free from drafts, 1 hour.
• **Punch** dough down; cover and chill at least 8 hours.
• **Punch** dough down; turn dough out onto a lightly floured surface, and knead 3 or 4 times. Divide dough in half; shape each portion into 16 (2-inch) balls. Place balls in two 9-inch square pans coated with cooking spray.
• **Cover** and let rise in a warm place (85°), free from drafts, 1½ hours or until dough is doubled in bulk.
• **Bake** at 375° for 12 minutes or until golden. **Yield:** 32 rolls.

Per roll: Calories 90 (11% from fat)
Fat 1.1g (0.2g saturated)   Protein 3.0g   Carbohydrate 16.9g
Fiber 0.1g   Cholesterol 0mg   Sodium 133mg

Quick Yeast Rolls

LOW: • Fat • Calorie • Cholesterol

Enjoy these puffy pan rolls with dinner in about an hour. We removed the egg from the original recipe, but kept its rich egg flavor by using egg substitute.

2 packages active dry yeast
½ cup warm water (105° to 115°)
1 cup skim milk
¼ cup egg substitute
2 tablespoons sugar
1 tablespoon vegetable oil
1½ teaspoons salt
4 cups all-purpose flour, divided
Butter-flavored vegetable cooking spray

• **Combine** yeast and warm water in a 2-cup liquid measuring cup; let stand 5 minutes.
• **Combine** yeast mixture, milk, and next 4 ingredients in a large bowl. Gradually add 1 cup flour, stirring until smooth. Gradually stir in enough remaining flour to make a soft dough. Place in a bowl coated with cooking spray, turning to coat top.
• **Cover** and let stand in a warm place (85°), free from drafts, 15 minutes.
• **Punch** dough down; cover and let stand in a warm place (85°), free from drafts, 15 additional minutes.
• **Turn** dough out onto a lightly floured surface; knead 3 or 4 times. Divide dough into 24 pieces; shape into balls. Place in two 9-inch square pans or round pans coated with cooking spray.
• **Cover** and let stand in a warm place (85°), free from drafts, 15 minutes.
• **Bake** at 400° for 15 minutes or until golden. **Yield:** 2 dozen.

Per roll: Calories 92 (8% from fat)
Fat 0.8g (0.2g saturated) Protein 3.0g Carbohydrate 17.7g
Fiber 0.7g Cholesterol 0mg Sodium 156mg

Moravian Sugar Cake

LOW: • Fat

Mouth-watering scents of cinnamon and brown sugar will waft through your house as this sweet bread bakes.

2 packages active dry yeast
½ teaspoon sugar
½ cup warm water (105° to 115°)
½ cup margarine, melted and divided
¼ cup water
½ cup sugar
¼ cup instant potato flakes
2 tablespoons instant nonfat dry milk powder
½ teaspoon salt
1 large egg
1 egg white
3 cups all-purpose flour, divided
Vegetable cooking spray
½ cup firmly packed brown sugar
½ teaspoon ground cinnamon

• **Combine** first 3 ingredients in a large mixing bowl; let stand 5 minutes.
• **Add** ¼ cup melted margarine, ¼ cup water, and next 6 ingredients. Add 1 cup flour; beat at low speed with an electric mixer 2 minutes. Stir in remaining 2 cups flour to make a soft dough.
• **Cover** and let rise in a warm place (85°), free from drafts, 45 minutes or until doubled in bulk.
• **Punch** dough down; spread in a 15- x 10- x 1-inch jellyroll pan coated with cooking spray. Cover and let rise in a warm place (85°), free from drafts, 30 minutes.
• **Make** shallow indentations in dough at 1-inch intervals, using the handle of a wooden spoon. Drizzle with remaining ¼ cup melted margarine.
• **Combine** brown sugar and cinnamon; sprinkle over dough.
• **Bake** at 375° for 12 to 15 minutes. Cut into squares. **Yield:** 15 servings.

Per serving: Calories 215 (28% from fat)
Fat 6.7g (1.4g saturated) Protein 4.1g Carbohydrate 34.7g
Fiber 1.0g Cholesterol 15mg Sodium 167mg

Monkey Bread

Monkey Bread

LOW: • Fat • Cholesterol

A pull-apart bread recipe like this one typically dips each piece of dough into a bowl of melted butter. Egad! We simply brushed the dough with a little reduced-calorie margarine and found it hard to resist pulling extra portions.

2 packages active dry yeast
2 cups warm water (105° to 115°)
5½ cups all-purpose flour
⅓ cup sugar
1½ teaspoons salt
¼ cup reduced-calorie margarine, melted
Vegetable cooking spray

• **Combine** yeast and 1 cup warm water in a 2-cup liquid measuring cup; let stand 5 minutes. Add remaining 1 cup warm water, flour, sugar, and salt, stirring until blended. Cover and chill at least 8 hours.
• **Punch** dough down; divide in half. Turn 1 portion out onto a heavily floured surface, and knead 3 or 4 times. Roll to ¼-inch thickness; cut into 4- x 1½-inch strips.
• **Brush** strips with half of melted margarine, and layer, overlapping, in a 12-cup Bundt or 10-inch tube pan coated with cooking spray. Repeat procedure with remaining dough and melted margarine in another coated Bundt or tube pan. Cover and let rise in a warm place (85°), free from drafts, 45 minutes or until doubled in bulk.
• **Bake** at 350° for 30 to 35 minutes or until golden. **Yield:** 20 servings.

Per serving: Calories 152 (11% from fat)
Fat 1.9g (0.3g saturated)   Protein 3.8g   Carbohydrate 29.8g
Fiber 1.1g   Cholesterol 0mg   Sodium 198mg

English Muffin Bread

LOW: • Fat • Calorie • Cholesterol

This bread resembles English muffins in taste and texture. Whole wheat flour, oat bran, and cornmeal team up to impart an earthy, whole grain goodness in every slice.

3½ to 3¾ cups all-purpose flour, divided
1 cup whole wheat flour
½ cup oat bran
2 teaspoons salt
1 package rapid-rise yeast
1 cup skim milk
1 cup water
3 tablespoons reduced-calorie margarine
Vegetable cooking spray
2 tablespoons cornmeal

• **Combine** 1½ cups all-purpose flour, wheat flour, and next 3 ingredients in a large mixing bowl, and set aside.
• **Combine** skim milk, water, and margarine in a 4-cup liquid measuring cup. Microwave at HIGH 2 minutes; pour over flour mixture. Beat at medium speed with an electric mixer 2 minutes. Gradually stir in 2 cups all-purpose flour. Turn dough out onto a lightly floured surface; if dough is sticky, knead in remaining ¼ cup flour.
• **Cover** dough with a large bowl; let stand 10 minutes.
• **Coat** two 8½- x 4½- x 3-inch loafpans with cooking spray; sprinkle evenly with cornmeal. Divide dough in half; shape each portion into a loaf, and place in pan.
• **Cover** and let dough rise in a warm place (85°), free from drafts, 1 hour or until dough is doubled in bulk.
• **Bake** at 400° for 25 minutes. Remove loaves from pans, and cool on a wire rack. **Yield:** 2 loaves.

Per ½-inch slice: Calories 77 (10% from fat)
Fat 0.9g (0.1g saturated)   Protein 2.5g   Carbohydrate 14.6g
Fiber 1.0g   Cholesterol 0mg   Sodium 154mg

Roasted Red Bell Pepper Bread

LOW: • Fat • Calorie • Cholesterol

The vibrant color of roasted red peppers, sharp flavor of Parmesan, and fresh scent of rosemary make this bread a sensational sensory experience. Serve it with soup, toast it for a snack, or slice it for sandwiches.

1 (7-ounce) jar roasted red bell peppers
1 package active dry yeast
1 teaspoon sugar
1⅓ cups warm water (105° to 115°)
3½ cups bread flour
1 cup grated nonfat Parmesan cheese
2 tablespoons chopped fresh rosemary
1 teaspoon salt
1 tablespoon cracked pepper
Vegetable cooking spray

• **Drain** bell peppers on paper towels; chop and set aside.
• **Combine** yeast, sugar, and warm water in a 2-cup liquid measuring cup; let stand 5 minutes. Set aside.
• **Combine** flour, bell peppers, Parmesan cheese, and next 3 ingredients in a large bowl; gradually add yeast mixture, stirring until blended.
• **Turn** dough out onto a well-floured surface, and knead until smooth and elastic (about 10 minutes). Place dough in a bowl coated with cooking spray, turning to coat top.
• **Cover** and let rise in a warm place (85°), free from drafts, 1 hour or until doubled in bulk.
• **Punch** dough down; turn out onto a lightly floured surface, and knead 4 or 5 times. Divide dough in half. Shape each portion into a 12-inch loaf. Place loaves on a large baking sheet coated with cooking spray. Let rise in a warm place (85°), free from drafts, 45 minutes or until doubled in bulk.
• **Bake** at 450° for 25 minutes or until loaves sound hollow when tapped, covering with aluminum foil after 15 minutes to prevent excessive browning. Remove from baking sheet immediately; cool on wire racks. **Yield:** 2 loaves.

Per 1-inch slice: Calories 93 (4% from fat)
Fat 0.4g (0.1g saturated)   Protein 2.5g   Carbohydrate 18.7g
Fiber 0.2g   Cholesterol 0mg   Sodium 191mg

Mini Swiss Cheese Loaves

LOW: • Fat • Calorie

These eight little loaves of bread get a big bang of flavor from Swiss cheese and toasted sesame seeds. Share a loaf or two with a friend.

1 package active dry yeast
¼ cup warm water (105° to 115°)
2⅓ cups all-purpose flour, divided
2 tablespoons sugar
1 teaspoon salt
¼ teaspoon baking soda
1 (8-ounce) carton plain nonfat yogurt
1 large egg
1 cup (4 ounces) shredded reduced-fat Swiss cheese
Vegetable cooking spray
2 teaspoons sesame seeds, toasted

• **Combine** yeast and warm water in a 1-cup liquid measuring cup; let stand 5 minutes.
• **Combine** yeast mixture, 1 cup flour, and next 5 ingredients in a large mixing bowl.
• **Beat** at low speed with an electric mixer 30 seconds. Beat at high speed 2 minutes.
• **Stir** in remaining flour and Swiss cheese, mixing well.
• **Divide** batter evenly among eight 5- x 3- x 2-inch loafpans coated with cooking spray; sprinkle evenly with sesame seeds.
• **Cover** and let rise in a warm place (85°) free from drafts, 1 hour. (Batter may not double in bulk.)
• **Bake** at 350° for 25 minutes or until golden. Remove from pans; serve warm, or cool on a wire rack. **Yield:** 8 loaves.

Per loaf: Calories 226 (20% from fat)
Fat 4.9g (2.3g saturated)   Protein 10.7g   Carbohydrate 34.2g
Fiber 1.3g   Cholesterol 38mg   Sodium 380mg

Fruitcake-Stuffed Pork Loin (page 60)

Entrées

Marinated Flank Steak

LOW: • Calorie • Cholesterol

Two salty sauces, soy and Worcestershire, accent these sizzling slices of steak and onion.

½ cup low-sodium soy sauce
⅓ cup red wine vinegar
¼ cup lemon juice
3 tablespoons low-sodium Worcestershire
　sauce
2 tablespoons vegetable oil
2 tablespoons Dijon mustard
1 teaspoon freshly ground pepper
1 large onion, sliced
1 clove garlic, minced
2 (1-pound) flank steaks

• **Combine** all ingredients except steaks in a shallow dish or large heavy-duty, zip-top plastic bag; add steaks. Cover or seal, and chill 8 to 12 hours, turning occasionally.
• **Remove** steaks and onion slices from marinade, discarding marinade. Wrap onion in heavy-duty aluminum foil.
• **Cook** steaks and onion slices, covered with grill lid, over medium-hot coals (350° to 400°) about 15 minutes or to desired degree of doneness, turning occasionally.
• **Cut** steaks diagonally across the grain into thin strips, and serve with onion slices. **Yield:** 8 servings.

Per serving:　Calories 246 (56% from fat)
Fat 15.4g (5.6g saturated)　Protein 20.1g　Carbohydrate 4.3g
Fiber 0.4g　Cholesterol 55mg　Sodium 588mg

Individual Barbecued Beef Loaves

LOW: • Fat • Calorie • Cholesterol

A tangy blend of ketchup, cider vinegar, and brown sugar tops these little meat loaves. Serve them with Roasted Garlic Mashed Potatoes (page 109) and English peas for a comfort-food dinner on the lighter side.

½ cup reduced-calorie ketchup
⅓ cup cider vinegar
3 tablespoons brown sugar
1 teaspoon beef-flavored bouillon granules
1½ pounds ground round
1 cup fine, dry breadcrumbs
1 cup evaporated skimmed milk
2 tablespoons finely chopped onion
¼ teaspoon salt
¼ teaspoon pepper
Vegetable cooking spray

• **Combine** first 4 ingredients in a small saucepan; cook over medium heat, stirring constantly, until bouillon granules dissolve. Set barbecue sauce aside.
• **Combine** ground round and next 5 ingredients, stirring until mixture is thoroughly blended.
• **Shape** mixture into 6 loaves; place loaves on a rack of broiler pan coated with cooking spray. Brush half of barbecue sauce over loaves.
• **Bake**, uncovered, at 350° for 40 minutes. Brush remaining half of barbecue sauce over loaves, and bake 5 additional minutes. Serve immediately. **Yield:** 6 servings.

Per serving:　Calories 290 (21% from fat)
Fat 6.8g (2.3g saturated)　Protein 30.3g　Carbohydrate 24.1g
Fiber 0.8g　Cholesterol 67mg　Sodium 909mg

Individual Barbecued Beef Loaf with
English peas and Roasted Garlic Mashed
Potatoes (page 109)

Casserole Spaghetti

LOW: • Fat • Calorie • Cholesterol • Sodium

Kids will love the saucy goodness and familiar flavors of this spaghetti casserole made light and easy with reduced-fat versions of cream of mushroom soup and Cheddar cheese. The addition of pimiento-stuffed olives and chili powder will satisfy the grown-ups' palates.

1½ pounds ground round
1½ cups chopped onion
1 cup chopped green bell pepper
½ cup chopped celery
2 cloves garlic, crushed
1 (10¾-ounce) can low-fat, reduced-sodium cream of mushroom soup, undiluted
¾ cup water
1 (14.5-ounce) can no-salt-added whole tomatoes, undrained and chopped
2 tablespoons chili powder
¼ teaspoon salt
¼ teaspoon pepper
1 (8-ounce) package spaghetti
2 ounces reduced-fat sharp Cheddar cheese, cut into ½-inch cubes
2 tablespoons chopped pimiento-stuffed olives
Vegetable cooking spray
½ cup (2 ounces) shredded reduced-fat sharp Cheddar cheese

• **Cook** first 5 ingredients in a Dutch oven, stirring until meat crumbles; drain well, and return to Dutch oven.
• **Stir** in soup and next 5 ingredients.
• **Bring** mixture to a boil over medium heat. Cover, reduce heat, and simmer 1 hour, stirring occasionally.
• **Cook** spaghetti according to package directions, omitting salt and fat; drain.
• **Stir** spaghetti, cheese cubes, and olives into meat sauce. Spoon mixture into a 13- x 9- x 2-inch baking dish coated with cooking spray.
• **Cover** and bake at 325° for 20 minutes or until thoroughly heated. Sprinkle with ½ cup shredded cheese, and bake, uncovered, 10 additional minutes. **Yield:** 8 servings.

Per serving: Calories 331 (27% from fat)
Fat 9.8g (3.9g saturated)   Protein 27.5g   Carbohydrate 32.5g
Fiber 2.8g   Cholesterol 65mg   Sodium 436mg

Grilled Lamb with Mango Salsa

LOW: • Calorie • Cholesterol • Sodium

1 (4-pound) boneless leg of lamb
1 teaspoon cumin seeds
1 teaspoon coriander seeds
½ cup dry white wine
¼ cup tequila
¼ cup olive oil
2 tablespoons fresh lime juice
2 tablespoons minced fresh garlic
2 tablespoons chopped fresh cilantro
2 jalapeño peppers, seeded and finely chopped
¼ teaspoon salt
½ teaspoon freshly ground pepper
Mango Salsa

• **Cut** large half of leg of lamb to, but not through, other side. Flip cut piece over; set aside.
• **Cook** cumin and coriander seeds in a heavy skillet, stirring constantly, until browned; crush.
• **Combine** crushed seeds, wine, and next 8 ingredients in a large shallow dish. Add lamb; cover and chill 8 hours, turning occasionally.
• **Prepare** charcoal fire in one end of grill; let burn 15 to 20 minutes. Place lamb on grill opposite medium-hot coals (350° to 400°). Cook lamb, without grill lid, 1 hour or until meat thermometer inserted in thickest portion of meat registers 150° (medium-rare), turning once.
• **Cut** into thin slices; serve with Mango Salsa. **Yield:** 16 servings.

Mango Salsa

4 medium mangoes, peeled and chopped
¼ cup chopped celery
¼ cup finely chopped green onions
¼ cup chopped yellow or red bell pepper
⅓ cup chopped fresh cilantro
1 jalapeño pepper, seeded and minced
¼ cup honey
2 tablespoons olive oil
2 tablespoons fresh lime juice
¼ teaspoon salt

• **Combine** first 6 ingredients. Combine honey and remaining 3 ingredients; pour over mango mixture, and toss. Chill 30 minutes. **Yield:** 4 cups.

Per serving: Calories 230 (41% from fat)
Fat 10.6g (2.6g saturated)   Protein 20.0g   Carbohydrate 10.6g
Fiber 0.7g   Cholesterol 62mg   Sodium 125mg

Grilled Lamb with Mango Salsa

Dijon-Rosemary Lamb Chops

LOW: • Sodium

These lamb chops are awash in a creamy Dijon mustard and wine sauce. Nonfat sour cream aptly stands in for the whipping cream in the original recipe; be sure to keep the heat on low after adding the sour cream to the sauce, or it may curdle.

8 (4-ounce) lean lamb loin chops
2 tablespoons Dijon mustard
1 tablespoon dried rosemary, crushed
¼ cup all-purpose flour
Vegetable cooking spray
1 tablespoon olive oil
1 cup dry white wine, divided
½ cup nonfat sour cream
⅛ teaspoon pepper

• **Trim** fat from chops. Spread mustard over lamb chops; sprinkle evenly with rosemary. Dredge chops in flour, shaking off excess flour.
• **Coat** a large nonstick skillet with cooking spray; add oil, and place skillet over medium-high heat until hot. Add chops, and cook until browned, turning once. Reduce heat to medium; cover and cook 7 minutes.
• **Turn** chops over; add ⅓ cup wine. Cook 8 additional minutes or to desired degree of doneness. Remove chops from skillet; keep warm.
• **Add** remaining ⅔ cup wine to pan drippings, stirring to loosen browned particles that cling to bottom.
• **Cook** 10 minutes or until liquid is reduced to about ¾ cup, stirring occasionally. Gradually stir in sour cream; cook until thoroughly heated (do not boil). Stir in pepper. Serve sauce with lamb chops. **Yield:** 4 servings.

Per serving: Calories 576 (72% from fat)
Fat 45.8g (18.8g saturated)   Protein 28.4g   Carbohydrate 9.4g
Fiber 0.4g   Cholesterol 115mg   Sodium 336mg

Fruitcake-Stuffed Pork Loin

LOW: • Calorie • Cholesterol • Sodium

In a twist on tradition, this pork roast is rolled with a sweetly spiced filling of fat-free fruit bar cookies instead of calorie-laden fruitcake.

Olive oil-flavored vegetable cooking spray
⅓ cup chopped onion
1 clove garlic, minced
1½ cups crumbled fat-free fig-filled bar cookies
1½ cups crumbled fat-free apple-filled bar cookies
¼ cup chopped pecans
¼ teaspoon ground cloves
⅛ teaspoon ground cinnamon
1 (5-pound) lean rolled boneless pork loin roast
¼ teaspoon salt
¼ teaspoon pepper
2 tablespoons dried thyme, divided
1 cup unsweetened apple juice
1 cup canned no-salt-added chicken broth
3 tablespoons bourbon, divided
2 tablespoons honey
2 tablespoons all-purpose flour
¼ cup evaporated skimmed milk
1 tablespoon reduced-calorie margarine
Garnish: fresh thyme sprigs

• **Coat** a large nonstick skillet with cooking spray; place over medium-high heat until hot. Add onion and garlic; cook, stirring constantly, until tender. Remove skillet from heat; stir in cookies, pecans, cloves, and cinnamon.
• **Remove** pork loin from elastic net. (There should be 2 pieces.) Trim excess fat. Make a cut lengthwise down the center of each piece, cutting to, but not through, bottom. Starting from center cut of each piece, slice horizontally toward 1 side, stopping ½ inch from edge. Repeat on opposite side. Unfold each piece of meat so that it lies flat.
• **Flatten** to ½-inch thickness, using a meat mallet or rolling pin.
• **Sprinkle** salt, pepper, and 1 tablespoon thyme evenly over pork. Sprinkle cookie mixture over pork.
• **Roll** each loin half, jellyroll fashion, starting with long side. Secure with string, and place, seam side down, in a shallow roasting pan.
• **Pour** apple juice and chicken broth around rolled pork loins in pan.

• **Combine** 2 tablespoons bourbon and honey. Brush lightly over rolled pork loins. Sprinkle with remaining 1 tablespoon thyme.

• **Bake**, uncovered, at 350° for 1 hour and 25 minutes or until meat thermometer inserted in thickest portion registers 160°, basting occasionally with pan drippings. Remove pork loins from pan, reserving pan drippings; keep pork warm.

• **Skim** fat from pan drippings. Pour pan drippings into a saucepan; bring to a boil, and cook 5 minutes or until mixture is reduced to 1 cup. Set aside.

• **Combine** flour and milk, stirring until smooth. Melt margarine in a heavy saucepan over low heat; add flour mixture, stirring until smooth. Cook 1 minute, stirring constantly. Gradually add reduced drippings and remaining 1 tablespoon bourbon; cook over medium heat, stirring constantly, until mixture thickens and boils. Serve sauce with sliced pork. Garnish, if desired. **Yield:** 20 servings.

Per serving: Calories 242 (42% from fat)
Fat 11.3g (3.5g saturated)   Protein 20.0g   Carbohydrate 12.2g
Fiber 0.7g   Cholesterol 65mg   Sodium 116mg

Pork Medaillons with Port Wine and Dried Cranberry Sauce

LOW: • Calorie • Cholesterol • Sodium

Port wine and dried cranberries distinguish the sauce that accompanies this pork tenderloin, while balsamic vinegar and fresh ginger deliver a piquant punch.

1 large red bell pepper
1 teaspoon olive oil
1 medium-size purple onion, finely chopped
2 shallots, finely chopped
2 tablespoons minced fresh ginger
½ cup port wine
⅓ cup balsamic vinegar
2 tablespoons sugar
1 ripe pear, peeled, cored, and chopped
2 teaspoons grated orange rind
½ cup dried cranberries
1 cup reduced-sodium chicken broth
2 tablespoons fresh thyme leaves
¼ teaspoon ground red pepper
2 (1-pound) pork tenderloins, trimmed
½ teaspoon salt
½ teaspoon freshly ground pepper

• **Place** red bell pepper on an aluminum foil-lined baking sheet. Bake at 500° for 20 minutes or until skin looks blistered, turning once.

• **Place** pepper immediately into a heavy-duty, zip-top plastic bag; seal and let stand 10 minutes to loosen skin. Peel pepper; remove and discard seeds. Cut pepper into strips; set aside.

• **Pour** oil into a large skillet; place over medium heat until hot. Add onion and shallot, and cook 10 minutes, stirring often.

• **Add** minced ginger and next 3 ingredients; bring to a boil. Reduce heat, and simmer 10 minutes or until liquid is reduced by three-fourths, stirring often.

• **Add** pepper strips, pear, and next 5 ingredients; simmer 10 minutes or until pear is tender, stirring occasionally. Remove from heat, and keep warm.

• **Cut** each tenderloin into 8 slices. Place each slice between two sheets of heavy-duty plastic wrap; flatten slightly, using a meat mallet or rolling pin. Sprinkle each side of slices with salt and pepper; arrange in a single layer on a rack in broiler pan.

• **Broil** 5½ inches from heat (with electric oven door partially opened) 3 minutes on each side or to desired degree of doneness. Serve with sauce. **Yield:** 8 servings.

Per serving: Calories 254 (32% from fat)
Fat 9.0g (3.0g saturated)   Protein 25.0g   Carbohydrate 18.3g
Fiber 1.7g   Cholesterol 66mg   Sodium 204mg

Honey-Mustard Pork Tenderloin

LOW: • Fat • Calorie • Cholesterol • Sodium

A sweet kiss of honey tames the Dijon mustard and apple cider vinegar in this basting sauce. Brush the mixture on the pork before baking and then again during cooking for maximum impact.

2 (¾-pound) boneless pork tenderloins, trimmed
Vegetable cooking spray
¼ cup honey
2 tablespoons apple cider vinegar
1 tablespoon Dijon mustard
½ teaspoon paprika

• **Place** tenderloins on a rack coated with cooking spray; place rack in broiler pan. Set aside.
• **Combine** honey and next 3 ingredients. Spoon one-third of honey mixture over tenderloins; set remaining honey mixture aside.
• **Bake**, uncovered, at 350° for 30 minutes or until meat thermometer inserted in thickest portion registers 160°, basting occasionally with remaining honey mixture. Cut tenderloins into thin slices. **Yield:** 6 servings.

Per serving: Calories 183 (21% from fat)
Fat 4.3g (1.4g saturated) Protein 22.9g Carbohydrate 12.0g
Fiber 0.0g Cholesterol 64mg Sodium 121mg

Hash Brown Bake

LOW: • Calorie • Cholesterol

The shredded potato crust of this ham and cheese pie emerges from the oven crisp and browned. It's at home on the breakfast or dinner table.

3 cups frozen shredded potatoes
Vegetable cooking spray
1 tablespoon reduced-calorie margarine, melted
1 cup finely chopped lean cooked ham
1 cup (4 ounces) shredded reduced-fat sharp Cheddar cheese
¼ cup finely chopped green bell pepper
½ cup egg substitute
½ cup skim milk
¼ teaspoon pepper

• **Thaw** potato between layers of paper towels to remove excess moisture. Press potato in bottom and up sides of a 9-inch pieplate coated with cooking spray. Brush potato with margarine, and coat lightly with cooking spray.
• **Bake**, uncovered, at 425° for 20 minutes or until lightly browned; cool potato shell on a wire rack 10 minutes.
• **Combine** ham, cheese, and bell pepper; spoon into potato shell. Combine egg substitute, milk, and pepper; pour over ham mixture.
• **Bake**, uncovered, at 350° for 25 minutes or until set; let stand 10 minutes before serving. **Yield:** 6 servings.

Per serving: Calories 147 (39% from fat)
Fat 6.3g (3.0g saturated) Protein 13.9g Carbohydrate 9.0g
Fiber 0.6g Cholesterol 28mg Sodium 539mg

Ham and Cheese Pie

LOW: • Calorie • Cholesterol

The buttery flavor, flaky texture, and sheer convenience of refrigerated crescent rolls make them a winner. We found a lighter way to use the rolls by teaming them with lean ham and cheeses.

1 (8-ounce) can refrigerated crescent rolls
1½ cups finely chopped lean cooked ham
1 (8-ounce) package reduced-fat Monterey Jack cheese, cubed
2 tablespoons grated nonfat Parmesan cheese
2 tablespoons finely chopped onion
¾ cup egg substitute

• **Unroll** crescent rolls, and separate into 8 triangles. Fit 5 triangles into a 9-inch pieplate, pressing edges together to seal.
• **Combine** chopped ham and next 3 ingredients; spoon into pieplate. Pour egg substitute over ham mixture.
• **Cut** remaining 3 triangles into thin strips; arrange over mixture.
• **Bake**, uncovered, on lower rack of oven at 325° for 45 minutes. (Cover edges with aluminum foil during the last 15 minutes of baking to prevent excessive browning, if necessary.) Let stand 5 minutes before serving. **Yield:** 6 servings.

Per serving: Calories 319 (47% from fat)
Fat 16.6g (7.0g saturated) Protein 25.0g Carbohydrate 17.5g
Fiber 0.1g Cholesterol 51mg Sodium 1,207mg

Ham Stroganoff on Cheesy Onion Biscuits

LOW: • Fat • Cholesterol

If ham biscuits give you solace, you'll love this concoction. Parmesan cheese and bits of green onion infuse the biscuits with flavor; then they're split and smothered with a ham-studded sour cream sauce.

Vegetable cooking spray
1 teaspoon reduced-calorie margarine
2 cups chopped lean cooked reduced-sodium ham
¼ cup finely chopped onion
1 (10¾-ounce) can low-sodium cream of chicken soup, undiluted
½ cup skim milk
1 (8-ounce) carton nonfat sour cream
⅛ teaspoon pepper
Cheesy Onion Biscuits

• **Coat** a large nonstick skillet with cooking spray; add margarine. Place skillet over medium-high heat until margarine melts; add ham and onion, and cook, stirring constantly, until onion is tender.
• **Stir** in soup and milk; cover and cook over medium heat 3 to 4 minutes. Stir in sour cream and pepper; cook over low heat until mixture is thoroughly heated. Serve between split Cheesy Onion Biscuits. **Yield:** 4 servings.

Cheesy Onion Biscuits
2 cups all-purpose flour
3 tablespoons instant nonfat dry milk powder
4 teaspoons baking powder
½ teaspoon salt
⅓ cup reduced-calorie margarine
⅓ cup grated nonfat Parmesan cheese
2 tablespoons finely chopped green onions
¾ cup water
Vegetable cooking spray

• **Combine** first 4 ingredients in a large bowl; cut in margarine with pastry blender or fork until mixture is crumbly. Stir in Parmesan cheese and green onions. Add water, stirring with a fork until dry ingredients are moistened.
• **Turn** biscuit dough out onto a lightly floured surface, and knead lightly 5 or 6 times.
• **Pat** dough to ½-inch thickness; cut with a 3-inch round cutter. Place on a baking sheet coated with cooking spray.

• **Bake** at 400° for 15 minutes or until lightly browned. **Yield:** 8 biscuits.

Per serving (with 2 biscuits): Calories 577 (28% from fat) Fat 18.1g (3.9g saturated) Protein 28.0g Carbohydrate 73.3g Fiber 1.9g Cholesterol 58mg Sodium 1,773mg

Ham-Mushroom-Stuffed Artichokes

LOW: • Fat • Calorie • Cholesterol

A sauce thick with Swiss cheese and ham fills every nook and cranny of these artichokes.

2 medium-size fresh artichokes
Lemon wedge
1½ tablespoons fresh lemon juice
1 cup sliced fresh mushrooms
Olive oil-flavored vegetable cooking spray
3 ounces lean cooked ham, cut into strips
1 tablespoon dry vermouth or evaporated skimmed milk
¼ cup evaporated skimmed milk
2 tablespoons chopped fresh chives
½ cup (2 ounces) shredded reduced-fat Swiss cheese

• **Wash** artichokes. Cut off stem end; trim about ½ inch from top of each artichoke. Remove any loose bottom leaves. Trim one-fourth off top of each outer leaf; rub top and edges of leaves with lemon wedge.
• **Place** artichokes in a large nonaluminum Dutch oven; cover with water, and add lemon juice.
• **Bring** to a boil; cover, reduce heat, and simmer 35 minutes or until lower leaves pull out easily. Drain. Spread leaves apart gently to reach center; scrape out the fuzzy thistle center (choke) with a spoon. Place artichokes in a pan; set aside.
• **Cook** mushrooms in a large skillet coated with cooking spray over medium-high heat 3 minutes, stirring often. Add ham, and cook 3 minutes, stirring often. Add vermouth and milk; cook 3 minutes. Remove from heat; stir in chives and cheese.
• **Spoon** sauce over artichokes. Broil 5½ inches from heat (with electric oven door partially opened) 3 minutes or until golden. **Yield:** 2 servings.

Per serving: Calories 342 (22% from fat) Fat 8.5g (4.1g saturated) Protein 29.4g Carbohydrate 45.3g Fiber 16.9g Cholesterol 45mg Sodium 930mg

Oven-Fried Chicken

Oven-Fried Chicken

LOW: • Fat • Calorie • Cholesterol

Succumb to the lure of crispy fried chicken and rejoice—this oven-fried version doesn't make a greasy mess. This chicken has plenty of crunch and taste, thanks to corn flakes cereal and Creole and Italian seasonings.

1 quart water
1 teaspoon salt
6 chicken drumsticks, skinned
4 (6-ounce) bone-in chicken breast halves, skinned
½ cup nonfat buttermilk
5 cups corn flakes cereal, coarsely crushed
2 to 3 teaspoons Creole seasoning
2 teaspoons dried Italian seasoning
½ teaspoon garlic powder
⅛ teaspoon freshly ground black pepper
⅛ teaspoon ground red pepper
Vegetable cooking spray

• **Combine** water and salt in a large bowl; add chicken pieces. Cover and chill 8 hours.
• **Drain** chicken; rinse with cold water, and pat dry. Place chicken in a shallow dish; pour buttermilk over chicken, turning pieces to coat.
• **Combine** corn flake crumbs and next 5 ingredients in a large heavy-duty, zip-top plastic bag. Place 2 pieces chicken in bag; seal. Shake to coat completely. Remove chicken, and repeat procedure with remaining pieces.
• **Place** coated chicken, bone side down, in a 15- x 10- x 1-inch jellyroll pan coated with cooking spray, and spray chicken with cooking spray. Place pan on the lowest rack in oven.
• **Bake**, uncovered, at 400° for 45 minutes (do not turn). **Yield:** 7 servings.

Per serving: Calories 210 (14% from fat)
Fat 3.3g (0.9g saturated)   Protein 27.6g   Carbohydrate 15.4g
Fiber 0.3g   Cholesterol 80mg   Sodium 1,143mg

Forty-Cloves-of-Garlic Chicken

LOW: • Fat • Calorie • Cholesterol • Sodium

Roasting chicken with this much garlic floods it with flavor and fills your kitchen with an irresistible aroma. Some of the cloves are tucked inside the chicken, while the rest are roasted to use in a mellow sauce.

4 heads garlic
Olive oil-flavored cooking spray
1 (3-pound) broiler-fryer, skinned
½ cup dry white wine
½ cup plus 2 tablespoons canned reduced-sodium chicken broth, divided
½ cup evaporated skimmed milk
1 tablespoon cornstarch
⅛ teaspoon pepper

• **Peel** outer skin from garlic heads, and discard. Cut off top one-third of each garlic head. Separate garlic heads into 40 cloves. Reserve any remaining cloves for another use. Place 35 cloves in center of a piece of heavy-duty aluminum foil; coat garlic with cooking spray. Fold foil over garlic, sealing tightly. Set aside garlic packet and remaining 5 cloves.
• **Place** chicken, breast side up, on a rack in a shallow roasting pan. Place 5 reserved garlic cloves in cavity. Place garlic packet on rack in roasting pan.
• **Bake**, uncovered, at 375° for 20 minutes.
• **Pour** wine over chicken, and bake 40 minutes, basting occasionally with pan juices.
• **Remove** garlic from pan, and let cool 10 minutes. Bake chicken 30 additional minutes or until done.
• **Remove** and discard papery skin from garlic. Squeeze pulp from garlic cloves into container of a mini food processor. Add 2 tablespoons broth; process until smooth, stopping once to scrape down sides. Set aside.
• **Combine** remaining ½ cup broth, evaporated milk, and cornstarch in a small saucepan, stirring until smooth. Cook over medium-high heat 2 to 3 minutes, stirring occasionally. Stir garlic mixture and pepper into broth mixture. Serve chicken with garlic sauce immediately. **Yield:** 6 servings.

Per serving: Calories 235 (28% from fat)
Fat 7.4g (2.0g saturated)   Protein 30.3g   Carbohydrate 6.9g
Fiber 0.2g   Cholesterol 87mg   Sodium 168mg

Lemon-Roasted Chicken

LOW: • Calorie

To maximize flavor, rub a simple mix of spiky rosemary leaves, salt, and pepper under the skin of the chicken. We've roasted the chicken with the skin on to keep it moist. Be sure to remove the skin before serving.

1½ teaspoons salt
2 teaspoons freshly ground pepper
2 to 3 teaspoons dried rosemary, crushed
1 (3-pound) broiler-fryer
1 medium lemon, cut in half

• **Combine** first 3 ingredients; set aside.
• **Loosen** skin from chicken breast by running fingers between the two; rub 1 teaspoon seasoning mixture under skin. Rub remaining mixture over outside of chicken. Place chicken in a heavy-duty, zip-top plastic bag; seal and chill 8 hours.
• **Remove** chicken from bag. Insert lemon halves in cavity; tie ends of legs together with string. Lift wing tips up and over back, and tuck under bird. Place chicken, breast side down, in a lightly greased shallow pan.
• **Bake**, uncovered, at 450°, turning over every 15 minutes, for 50 minutes or until a meat thermometer inserted in thigh registers 180°. Let stand 10 minutes. Remove skin before serving. **Yield:** 4 servings.

Per serving: Calories 225 (35% from fat)
Fat 8.6g (2.3g saturated)   Protein 33.3g   Carbohydrate 3.9g
Fiber 0.5g   Cholesterol 101mg   Sodium 978mg

Gold Nugget Chicken

LOW: • Fat • Calorie • Cholesterol

Here's a company-worthy dish. Encased in each bundle of chicken is a nugget of sharp Cheddar cheese that melts to perfection.

8 (4-ounce) skinned and boned chicken breast halves
8 ounces reduced-fat sharp Cheddar cheese, cut into 8 equal pieces
½ cup egg substitute
¾ cup fine, dry breadcrumbs
¼ cup reduced-calorie margarine
Vegetable cooking spray
1 cup sliced fresh mushrooms
½ cup chopped onion
½ cup chopped green bell pepper
1 cup canned reduced-sodium chicken broth
2 tablespoons all-purpose flour
½ teaspoon salt
½ teaspoon pepper
3 cups cooked long-grain rice (cooked without salt or fat)
1 (2-ounce) jar diced pimiento, drained
Garnish: fresh oregano sprigs

• **Place** chicken between two sheets of heavy-duty plastic wrap, and flatten to ¼-inch thickness, using a meat mallet or rolling pin. Place a piece of cheese in center of each breast; fold over all sides of breast, enclosing cheese, and secure with wooden picks.
• **Dip** chicken in egg substitute, draining excess; dredge in breadcrumbs, coating all sides.
• **Melt** margarine in a large nonstick skillet coated with cooking spray. Cook chicken bundles on both sides over medium-high heat until browned; remove from skillet. Set aside, and keep warm.
• **Add** mushrooms, onion, and bell pepper to skillet, and cook, stirring constantly, until tender.
• **Gradually** add broth to flour, stirring until smooth. Add broth mixture, salt, and pepper to skillet; cook, stirring constantly, until thickened.
• **Add** rice and pimiento; pour into a 13- x 9- x 2-inch baking dish coated with cooking spray. Place chicken bundles on top.
• **Bake**, uncovered, at 400° for 20 minutes. Remove wooden picks before serving. Garnish, if desired. **Yield:** 8 servings.

Per serving: Calories 382 (27% from fat)
Fat 11.4g (4.2g saturated)   Protein 40.0g   Carbohydrate 28.6g
Fiber 1.3g   Cholesterol 85mg   Sodium 664mg

Gold Nugget Chicken

Chicken Lasagna Florentine

LOW: • Calorie • Cholesterol

A buttery-tasting topping embellishes this chicken and spinach lasagna with just the right amount of crisp texture and nutty goodness.

6 lasagna noodles, uncooked
1 (10-ounce) package frozen chopped spinach, thawed
2 cups chopped cooked chicken breast (skinned before cooking and cooked without salt)
1½ cups (6 ounces) shredded reduced-fat sharp Cheddar cheese
1 cup sliced fresh mushrooms
⅓ cup finely chopped onion
1 (10¾-ounce) can reduced-fat cream of mushroom soup, undiluted
1 (8-ounce) carton nonfat sour cream
⅓ cup nonfat mayonnaise
1 tablespoon cornstarch
1 tablespoon low-sodium soy sauce
¼ teaspoon freshly ground nutmeg
¼ teaspoon pepper
Butter-flavored vegetable cooking spray
3 tablespoons reduced-calorie margarine
¼ cup finely chopped pecans
½ cup fine, dry breadcrumbs
½ cup grated Parmesan cheese

• **Cook** noodles according to package directions, omitting salt and fat; drain and set aside.
• **Drain** spinach well, pressing between layers of paper towels to remove excess moisture.
• **Combine** spinach, chicken, and next 10 ingredients in a large bowl; stir well.
• **Arrange** 2 noodles in an 11- x 7- x 1½-inch baking dish coated with cooking spray. Spread half of chicken mixture over noodles. Repeat procedure with remaining noodles and chicken mixture. Set aside.
• **Melt** margarine in a medium-size nonstick skillet over medium heat; add pecans, and cook 1 minute. Remove from heat; stir in breadcrumbs and cheese. Sprinkle topping over casserole. Coat with cooking spray.
• **Cover** and bake at 350° for 55 to 60 minutes or until hot and bubbly. Let stand 15 minutes before serving. **Yield:** 8 servings.

Per serving: Calories 369 (32% from fat)
Fat 13.2g (4.6g saturated)   Protein 26.8g   Carbohydrate 30.8g
Fiber 2.8g   Cholesterol 50mg   Sodium 893mg

Creamy Ham and Chicken Lasagna

LOW: • Fat • Calorie • Cholesterol

In this lighter lasagna, succulent morsels of chicken and ham are nestled among noodles and bathed in a cheese sauce.

2 (4-ounce) skinned and boned chicken breast halves
2 cups chopped lean cooked ham
9 lasagna noodles, uncooked
Vegetable cooking spray
½ pound sliced fresh mushrooms
3 tablespoons all-purpose flour
4 cups evaporated skimmed milk
3 tablespoons reduced-calorie margarine
1¼ cups freshly grated Parmesan cheese, divided
¾ teaspoon dried basil
¼ teaspoon freshly ground pepper
Garnishes: chopped fresh parsley, paprika

• **Place** chicken breasts in a saucepan; add water to cover. Bring to a boil over high heat; cover, reduce heat to medium, and cook 20 minutes or until chicken is tender. Drain; cool slightly.
• **Chop** chicken into bite-size pieces, and place in a large bowl; add chopped ham.
• **Cook** lasagna noodles according to package directions, omitting salt and fat; drain. Place wax paper on a baking sheet; coat wax paper with cooking spray. Place cooked noodles in a single layer on wax paper; cover with additional wax paper coated with cooking spray. Continue layering noodles and wax paper. Set aside.
• **Coat** a large nonstick skillet with cooking spray; place over medium-high heat until hot. Add mushrooms, and cook, stirring constantly, until tender. Drain and stir into meat mixture; set aside.
• **Combine** flour and evaporated milk in a small bowl, stirring until smooth. Melt margarine in skillet over medium-high heat. Gradually stir in milk mixture; cook, stirring constantly, about 3 minutes or until bubbly. Stir in 1 cup Parmesan cheese, basil, and pepper; cook until cheese melts and mixture is thickened. Add chicken mixture to cheese mixture, stirring well.
• **Place** 3 lasagna noodles in a 2-quart shallow baking dish coated with cooking spray. Spread one-third of meat mixture over lasagna noodles. Repeat layers twice. Sprinkle with remaining ¼ cup Parmesan cheese.

• **Cover** and bake at 350° for 30 minutes. Remove from oven; let stand 10 minutes before serving. Garnish, if desired. **Yield:** 8 servings.

Per serving: Calories 402 (25% from fat)
Fat 11.0g (4.7g saturated)   Protein 33.9g   Carbohydrate 39.9g
Fiber 1.6g   Cholesterol 58mg   Sodium 1,011mg

Simply Good Chicken Casserole

LOW: • Cholesterol

Here's a simply good, simply made chicken casserole. The rich flavors of reduced-fat cream soups, sour cream, and buttery cracker crumbs belie their low-cholesterol nature.

6 (6-ounce) skinned chicken breast halves
1 quart water
1 teaspoon salt
1 teaspoon pepper
1 (10¾-ounce) can reduced-fat cream of chicken soup, undiluted
1 (10¾-ounce) can reduced-fat cream of celery soup, undiluted
1 (8-ounce) carton reduced-fat sour cream
½ teaspoon pepper
8 ounces reduced-fat oval-shaped buttery crackers, crushed
Vegetable cooking spray
2 tablespoons margarine, melted

• **Combine** first 4 ingredients in a large Dutch oven; bring to a boil. Cover, reduce heat, and simmer 1 hour or until tender. Remove chicken, and cool slightly.
• **Bone** chicken; cut chicken into bite-size pieces. Combine chicken, chicken soup, and next 3 ingredients, stirring well.
• **Place** half of crushed crackers in an 11- x 7- x 1½-inch baking dish coated with cooking spray; spoon chicken mixture evenly over crackers. Top with remaining crackers, and drizzle with margarine.
• **Bake,** uncovered, at 325° for 35 minutes or until lightly browned. **Yield:** 8 servings.

Per serving: Calories 306 (38% from fat)
Fat 12.9g (4.4g saturated)   Protein 26.3g   Carbohydrate 17.0g
Fiber 0.1g   Cholesterol 79mg   Sodium 836mg

Chicken and Dumplings with Herbed Broth

LOW: • Fat

½ cup self-rising flour
½ teaspoon pepper
6 chicken leg-thigh combinations (3 pounds), skinned
Vegetable cooking spray
2 tablespoons vegetable oil
1 medium onion, chopped
2 cloves garlic, minced
1 tablespoon self-rising flour
5 cups canned reduced-sodium chicken broth
2 tablespoons chopped fresh basil
2 tablespoons chopped fresh thyme
1 tablespoon chopped fresh rosemary
½ teaspoon grated lemon rind
2 tablespoons lemon juice
2 cups self-rising flour
1 cup nonfat buttermilk
¼ cup reduced-fat sour cream

• **Combine** ½ cup flour and pepper in a large heavy-duty, zip-top plastic bag. Add chicken, and seal bag securely. Shake gently to coat.
• **Coat** a Dutch oven with cooking spray. Add oil; place over medium heat until hot. Add chicken; cook until golden, turning once. Remove chicken from pan, reserving drippings in pan.
• **Cook** onion and garlic in drippings, stirring constantly, until tender.
• **Add** 1 tablespoon flour, and cook 1 minute, stirring constantly; gradually add broth, stirring constantly.
• **Add** basil and next 4 ingredients; bring to a boil. Return chicken to Dutch oven; cover, reduce heat, and simmer 30 minutes.
• **Remove** from Dutch oven, and keep warm. Reserve broth mixture in Dutch oven.
• **Combine** 2 cups flour and buttermilk in a large bowl, stirring with a fork.
• **Bring** reserved broth mixture to a rolling boil. Drop dough by heaping tablespoonfuls into broth. Cover, reduce heat, and simmer, without stirring, 7 to 10 minutes or until dumplings are firm in center. Remove from heat. Stir in sour cream. Serve over chicken. **Yield:** 6 servings.

Per serving: Calories 476 (25% from fat)
Fat 13.0g (3.4g saturated)   Protein 39.7g   Carbohydrate 46.9g
Fiber 0.8g   Cholesterol 123mg   Sodium 1,253mg

Chicken Dumpling Pie

LOW: • Fat • Calorie • Cholesterol

Tender dumplings atop a savory stew of chicken and vegetables fill this dish to the brim with homemade goodness.

3 cups chopped cooked chicken breast (skinned before cooking and cooked without salt)
2 cups frozen mixed vegetables, thawed and drained
2 (10¾-ounce) cans reduced-fat cream of chicken soup, undiluted
1 (10½-ounce) can low-sodium chicken broth
½ teaspoon poultry seasoning
Vegetable cooking spray
2 cups reduced-fat biscuit and baking mix
1 (8-ounce) carton reduced-fat sour cream
1 cup skim milk

• **Combine** first 5 ingredients in a large bowl, stirring well. Pour chicken mixture into a 13- x 9- x 2-inch baking dish coated with cooking spray.
• **Combine** biscuit mix, sour cream, and milk in medium bowl; spoon over chicken mixture.
• **Bake**, uncovered, at 350° for 50 to 60 minutes or until topping is golden. **Yield:** 6 servings.

Per serving: Calories 429 (25% from fat)
Fat 11.9g (4.5g saturated)   Protein 31.4g   Carbohydrate 48.8g
Fiber 1.9g   Cholesterol 86mg   Sodium 987mg

Chicken Pot Pie

LOW: • Calorie • Cholesterol

Our pie is plump with chunks of chicken, hard-cooked egg, and vegetables. We were so satisfied with the tender top crust that we skipped the bottom crust altogether.

2 tablespoons reduced-calorie margarine
⅓ cup all-purpose flour
1 (12-ounce) can evaporated skimmed milk
1 cup canned reduced-sodium chicken broth
½ teaspoon freshly ground pepper
Vegetable cooking spray
1 (8-ounce) package presliced fresh mushrooms
1 small onion, chopped
3 stalks celery, sliced
3½ cups chopped cooked chicken breast (skinned before cooking and cooked without salt)
3 hard-cooked egg whites, chopped
½ (15-ounce) package refrigerated piecrusts

• **Melt** margarine in a heavy saucepan over low heat. Combine flour and evaporated milk, stirring until smooth. Add milk mixture and chicken broth to saucepan; cook over medium heat, stirring constantly, until thickened and bubbly. Stir in pepper; set sauce aside.
• **Coat** a large nonstick skillet with cooking spray; place over medium-high heat until hot. Add mushrooms, onion, and celery; cook, stirring constantly, until tender. Stir vegetable mixture, chicken, and egg whites into sauce.
• **Coat** a 2-quart round casserole with cooking spray. Spoon filling into casserole; top with piecrust. Trim off excess pastry. Fold edges under, and flute. Cut slits in top.
• **Bake**, uncovered, at 375° for 40 to 50 minutes or until golden. **Yield:** 6 servings.

Per serving: Calories 443 (34% from fat)
Fat 16.6g (5.3g saturated)   Protein 36.9g   Carbohydrate 35.5g
Fiber 1.4g   Cholesterol 78mg   Sodium 669mg

Chicken Tostadas

LOW: • Fat • Calorie • Cholesterol

A spritz of fresh lime juice and a scattering of chopped cilantro perk up these simple tostadas.

1 pound skinned and boned chicken breast halves, cut into ¾-inch cubes
½ cup fresh lime juice
4 (8-inch) flour tortillas
¼ teaspoon pepper
Vegetable cooking spray
1 cup picante sauce
2 tablespoons finely chopped fresh cilantro
2 tablespoons reduced-fat sour cream
4 cups shredded lettuce
2 medium tomatoes, chopped
6 fresh mushrooms, sliced

• **Place** chicken in a shallow dish or heavy-duty, zip-top plastic bag; pour lime juice over chicken. Cover or seal, and chill 30 minutes.
• **Place** tortillas on a baking sheet; bake at 350° for 3 to 5 minutes or until lightly browned and crisp. Set aside.
• **Remove** chicken from lime juice, discarding juice. Sprinkle chicken with pepper.
• **Coat** a nonstick skillet with cooking spray; place over medium heat until hot. Add chicken, and cook 4 minutes or until done, stirring often.
• **Stir** in picante sauce, cilantro, and sour cream. Return to a simmer, and cook 5 minutes, stirring occasionally.
• **Place** tortillas on serving plates; spoon chicken mixture evenly onto tortillas. Top with lettuce, tomato, and mushrooms. Cut into wedges; serve immediately. **Yield:** 4 servings.

Per serving: Calories 304 (16% from fat)
Fat 5.4g (1.4g saturated)   Protein 31.9g   Carbohydrate 31.9g
Fiber 2.8g   Cholesterol 69mg   Sodium 923mg

Turkey and Peppers in Cornbread Crust

LOW: • Fat • Calorie • Cholesterol

Roasted sweet red peppers and green chiles add an intriguing kick to leftover turkey.

2 cups chopped cooked turkey breast
1 (7-ounce) jar roasted sweet red peppers, drained and sliced
1 (4.5-ounce) can chopped green chiles, undrained
1 (10¾-ounce) can reduced-fat cream of chicken soup, undiluted
½ cup nonfat sour cream
¼ cup skim milk
1 teaspoon chili powder
Vegetable cooking spray
1 (11.5-ounce) can refrigerated cornbread twists

• **Combine** first 7 ingredients. Spoon mixture into an 8-inch square baking dish coated with cooking spray.
• **Bake**, uncovered, at 375° for 35 minutes. Separate cornbread twists into 16 strips. Twist strips 2 or 3 times, and place evenly over turkey mixture.
• **Bake**, uncovered, at 375° for 20 additional minutes. Let stand 5 minutes before serving. **Yield:** 6 servings.

Per serving: Calories 313 (30% from fat)
Fat 10.4g (2.8g saturated)   Protein 21.0g   Carbohydrate 32.7g
Fiber 1.1g   Cholesterol 44mg   Sodium 958mg

The King Henry Pizza

LOW: • Calorie • Cholesterol

If Henry VIII were alive today, he no doubt would have the well-known drumstick in one hand (skinless, of course) and a slice of this sturdy pizza in the other—it's topped with a generous helping of three meats and four cheeses.

1¼ cups pizza pasta sauce
1 (12-inch) refrigerated pizza crust
½ pound freshly ground turkey breakfast sausage, cooked and drained
1 ounce sliced pepperoni, coarsely chopped
8 slices turkey bacon, cooked and crumbled
¾ cup (3 ounces) shredded part-skim mozzarella cheese
¾ cup (3 ounces) shredded reduced-fat sharp Cheddar cheese
¼ cup (1 ounce) shredded fontina cheese
¼ cup grated Parmesan cheese

• **Spread** sauce over pizza crust, and top evenly with remaining ingredients.
• **Bake** at 425° for 10 minutes or until bubbly. **Yield:** 8 servings.

Per serving: Calories 272 (42% from fat)
Fat 12.6g (4.4g saturated)   Protein 18.0g   Carbohydrate 20.8g
Fiber 1.4g   Cholesterol 46mg   Sodium 802mg

Sausage and Noodle Casserole

LOW: • Fat • Calorie • Cholesterol

It's hard to tell any difference in the flavor of ground turkey breakfast sausage versus pork sausage, but there's a substantial savings in fat, cholesterol, and calories.

1 (8-ounce) package medium egg noodles
1 pound freshly ground turkey breakfast sausage
1 (10¾-ounce) can low-fat, reduced-sodium cream of chicken soup, undiluted
1 (8-ounce) carton nonfat sour cream
⅓ cup crumbled blue cheese
1 (4½-ounce) jar sliced mushrooms, drained
1 (2-ounce) jar diced pimiento, drained
2 tablespoons finely chopped green bell pepper
Vegetable cooking spray
½ cup soft breadcrumbs
2 teaspoons reduced-calorie margarine, melted

• **Cook** noodles according to package directions, omitting salt and fat; drain and set aside.
• **Brown** sausage in a large nonstick skillet, stirring until it crumbles; drain and set aside.
• **Combine** soup, sour cream, and blue cheese in a large saucepan; cook over medium heat, stirring constantly, until cheese melts.
• **Add** noodles, sausage, mushrooms, pimiento, and bell pepper, tossing to coat. Spoon mixture into an 11- x 7- x 1½-inch baking dish coated with cooking spray.
• **Combine** breadcrumbs and margarine; sprinkle over casserole.
• **Bake**, uncovered, at 350° for 30 minutes. **Yield:** 6 servings.

Per serving: Calories 349 (30% from fat)
Fat 11.8g (3.8g saturated)   Protein 21.7g   Carbohydrate 38.3g
Fiber 1.1g   Cholesterol 88mg   Sodium 694mg

My Favorite Pasta

LOW: • Fat • Calorie • Cholesterol

A rich white sauce smothers these supple strands of spinach linguine. The sauce is made with evaporated skimmed milk and a little cornstarch to simulate the rich, creamy taste of its whipping cream version.

4 ounces spinach linguine, uncooked
½ cup evaporated skimmed milk
½ cup canned reduced-sodium chicken broth
1 tablespoon cornstarch
½ cup frozen English peas, thawed
2 slices turkey bacon, cooked and crumbled
½ cup freshly grated Parmesan cheese

• **Cook** linguine according to package directions, omitting salt and fat; drain and keep warm.
• **Combine** evaporated milk, broth, and cornstarch in a small saucepan, stirring until smooth. Cook over medium heat, stirring constantly, until mixture is thickened and bubbly.
• **Stir in** peas and bacon, and toss with linguine. Sprinkle with cheese, and serve immediately. **Yield:** 2 servings.

Per serving: Calories 406 (19% from fat)
Fat 8.5g (3.7g saturated)   Protein 24.4g   Carbohydrate 55.8g
Fiber 3.6g   Cholesterol 28mg   Sodium 794mg

Spinach and Mushrooms with Bow Tie Pasta

LOW: • Fat • Cholesterol

Fresh garlic, lemon, Parmesan cheese, and pepper energize the flavor of the fresh spinach in this pasta dish for two.

Vegetable cooking spray
½ pound sliced fresh mushrooms
3 large cloves garlic, minced
1 cup evaporated skimmed milk
2 teaspoons cornstarch
1½ tablespoons lemon juice
½ teaspoon salt
¾ teaspoon freshly ground pepper
8 ounces bow tie pasta, uncooked
4 cups loosely packed torn fresh spinach
3 tablespoons shaved Parmesan cheese

• **Coat** a large nonstick skillet with cooking spray; place over medium-high heat until hot. Add mushrooms and garlic, and cook, stirring constantly, 5 to 6 minutes or until tender.
• **Combine** evaporated milk and cornstarch in a small bowl, stirring until smooth.
• **Add** cornstarch mixture to skillet; bring to a boil, and cook 1 minute, stirring constantly. Stir in lemon juice, salt, and pepper. Remove mixture from heat.
• **Cook** pasta according to package directions, omitting salt and fat, adding spinach during last minute of cooking time. Drain and toss gently with mushroom mixture. Sprinkle evenly with shaved Parmesan cheese, and serve immediately. **Yield:** 2 servings.

Per serving: Calories 614 (7% from fat)
Fat 4.9g (1.7g saturated)   Protein 31.1g   Carbohydrate 112g
Fiber 6.8g   Cholesterol 10mg   Sodium 905mg

Oven-Fried Catfish

LOW: • Calorie • Cholesterol

Don't pass up this recipe even if you don't care for catfish—any type of whitefish fillets will do. Corn flakes cereal and a coating of cooking spray create a mighty crunch. Lemony Tartar Sauce (page 132) makes the perfect partner.

¾ cup crushed corn flakes cereal
¾ teaspoon celery salt
¼ teaspoon onion powder
¼ teaspoon paprika
Dash of pepper
4 (6-ounce) skinless farm-raised catfish fillets
Vegetable cooking spray

• **Combine** first 5 ingredients; set aside. Cut fillets in half. Spray with cooking spray; coat with corn flake mixture. Arrange in a single layer on a baking sheet coated with cooking spray. Spray tops with cooking spray.
• **Bake**, uncovered, at 350° for 30 minutes or until fish flakes easily when tested with a fork. **Yield:** 4 servings.

Per serving: Calories 247 (32% from fat)
Fat 8.7g (1.6g saturated) Protein 25.5g Carbohydrate 14.0g
Fiber 0.2g Cholesterol 77mg Sodium 673mg

Caribbean Banana Fish

LOW: • Fat • Calorie • Cholesterol • Sodium

Banana, rum, and coconut milk create a lyrical combo of flavors in this fish dish.

¼ teaspoon coriander seeds
¼ teaspoon lemon pepper
¼ teaspoon ground nutmeg
¼ teaspoon ground allspice
¼ teaspoon salt
¼ teaspoon pepper
Vegetable cooking spray
4 (4-ounce) red snapper fillets, skinned
¼ cup all-purpose flour
2 bananas, peeled and sliced
4 small green onions, chopped
¼ cup sweetened coconut milk
¼ cup rum

• **Crush** coriander seeds, using a mortar and pestle; add lemon pepper and next 4 ingredients, stirring well. Set aside.
• **Coat** a large nonstick skillet with cooking spray, and place over medium heat until hot.
• **Dredge** snapper fillets in flour, and arrange in hot skillet. Sprinkle half of spice mixture over fillets, and cook over medium-high heat until lightly browned. Turn fillets; sprinkle with remaining spice mixture, and cook until browned.
• **Place** banana slices over fillets, and sprinkle with chopped green onions. Add coconut milk, and cook until fish flakes easily when tested with a fork.
• **Add** rum to skillet; cover and let stand 5 minutes. **Yield:** 4 servings.

Per serving: Calories 286 (22% from fat)
Fat 7.1g (3.8g saturated) Protein 25.3g Carbohydrate 21.9g
Fiber 2.4g Cholesterol 42mg Sodium 224mg

Grilled Swordfish with Caper Sauce

LOW: • Calorie • Cholesterol • Sodium

These swordfish steaks have a decidedly herbal attitude. They're marinated in a mixture of white wine, rosemary, and garlic and then grilled and topped with additional rosemary. If you keep herb-flavored oils on hand, you can even substitute your favorite for the olive oil in the topping.

½ cup dry white wine
5 cloves garlic, minced
2 teaspoons chopped fresh rosemary, divided
¼ teaspoon salt
¼ teaspoon pepper
4 (4-ounce) swordfish steaks
Vegetable cooking spray
⅓ cup lemon juice
3 tablespoons fine, dry breadcrumbs
3 tablespoons extra virgin olive oil
1 tablespoon capers
Garnish: fresh rosemary sprigs

• **Combine** wine, garlic, and 1 teaspoon rosemary in an 8-inch square baking dish.
• **Sprinkle** salt and pepper over fish; place fish in baking dish, turning to coat. Cover and chill at least 1 hour. Remove fish from marinade, discarding marinade.
• **Coat** food rack with cooking spray; place rack on grill over hot coals (400° to 500°). Cook fish, covered with grill lid, 4 to 5 minutes on each side or until fish flakes easily when tested with a fork.
• **Combine** remaining 1 teaspoon rosemary, lemon juice, and next 3 ingredients. Spoon over fish. Garnish, if desired, and serve immediately. **Yield:** 4 servings.

Per serving: Calories 271 (50% from fat)
Fat 15.1g (2.7g saturated)   Protein 23.6g   Carbohydrate 7.5g
Fiber 0.4g   Cholesterol 44mg   Sodium 461mg

Grilled Trout

LOW: • Calorie • Cholesterol • Sodium

Herb lovers—you can substitute any fresh herb for the tarragon in this recipe. And you may even want to place a few sprigs on the coals for a double dose of herbiness.

2 tablespoons herb-flavored vegetable oil
¼ cup lemon juice
½ teaspoon salt
2 (2-pound) dressed trout
4 sprigs fresh tarragon
1 lemon, sliced
Vegetable cooking spray

• **Combine** oil, lemon juice, and salt in a small bowl, stirring well with a wire whisk. Brush half of mixture inside each trout. Place 2 sprigs tarragon and 2 lemon slices inside each trout.
• **Place** trout in a large baking dish. Pour remaining oil mixture over trout. Cover and chill 2 hours.
• **Place** trout in a grill basket coated with cooking spray. Cook, covered with grill lid, over hot coals (400° to 500°) 5 to 7 minutes on each side or until fish flakes easily when tested with a fork. **Yield:** 6 servings.

Per serving: Calories 206 (52% from fat)
Fat 11.8g (2.1g saturated)   Protein 22.3g   Carbohydrate 2.9g
Fiber 0.1g   Cholesterol 61mg   Sodium 251mg

Crabmeat-Topped Potatoes

LOW: • Fat • Cholesterol

Using crabmeat as a potato topper gives spuds a touch of class. Neufchâtel cheese and nonfat sour cream create a rich-tasting, creamy base for the sauce.

4 large baking potatoes (about 3 pounds)
Vegetable cooking spray
¼ cup chopped green bell pepper
¼ cup chopped green onions
1 (8-ounce) package Neufchâtel cheese, softened
1 (6-ounce) can crabmeat, drained
¼ cup skim milk
½ cup nonfat sour cream
¼ teaspoon ground white pepper
¼ teaspoon garlic powder

• **Scrub** potatoes, and prick several times with a fork.

• **Bake** potatoes at 400° for 1 hour and 20 minutes or until done.

• **Coat** a large nonstick skillet with cooking spray; place over medium-high heat until hot. Add bell pepper and green onions, and cook, stirring constantly, until tender.

• **Add** cheese, crabmeat, and milk. Cook over low heat, stirring constantly, until mixture is smooth.

• **Remove** from heat; stir in sour cream, white pepper, and garlic powder. Serve over split baked potatoes. **Yield:** 4 servings.

Per serving: Calories 492 (25% from fat)
Fat 13.9g (8.5g saturated)   Protein 23.7g   Carbohydrate 69.4g
Fiber 6.4g   Cholesterol 65mg   Sodium 513mg

Chesapeake Bay Crab Cakes

LOW: • Calorie • Cholesterol

These chunky crab cakes are topped with a layer of mayonnaise spiked with Old Bay seasoning before they're baked until golden.

1 egg white, lightly beaten
4 low-sodium saltine crackers, crushed
1½ tablespoons chopped fresh parsley
¾ teaspoon Old Bay seasoning
½ teaspoon low-sodium Worcestershire sauce
4 drops of hot sauce
⅛ teaspoon freshly ground pepper
3 tablespoons reduced-fat mayonnaise
1 pound fresh lump crabmeat, drained
Vegetable cooking spray
2 tablespoons reduced-fat mayonnaise
¼ teaspoon Old Bay seasoning
Paprika
Tartar Sauce
Garnishes: fresh oregano sprigs, lemon slices

• **Combine** first 8 ingredients in a bowl; stir in crabmeat.

• **Shape** into 6 (3-inch) patties. Place on a baking sheet coated with cooking spray.

• **Combine** 2 tablespoons mayonnaise and ¼ teaspoon Old Bay seasoning; spread evenly on crab cakes. Sprinkle with paprika.

• **Bake,** uncovered, at 350° for 20 minutes or until crab cakes are golden. (Do not overbake.) Serve with Tartar Sauce. Garnish, if desired. **Yield:** 6 servings.

Tartar Sauce
¾ cup reduced-fat mayonnaise
1 tablespoon finely chopped fresh parsley
2 teaspoons chopped fresh chives
2 teaspoons sweet pickle relish
1 teaspoon capers, chopped
¾ teaspoon Dijon mustard
1 hard-cooked egg white, finely chopped

• **Combine** all ingredients; cover and chill. **Yield:** ¾ cup.

Per serving: Calories 206 (57% from fat)
Fat 13.1g (1.9g saturated)   Protein 16.3g   Carbohydrate 5.2g
Fiber 0.1g   Cholesterol 86mg   Sodium 819mg

Chesapeake Bay Crab Cake

Crab-Stuffed Lobster Tails

Plunge each bite of these fancy stuffed tails into the Garlic-Butter Sauce. And don't think twice about soaking up every last drop, because we made it lighter with reduced-calorie margarine and lemon juice.

2 quarts water
2 (1- to 1½-pound) live lobsters
½ pound fresh crabmeat
1 clove garlic, minced
1 tablespoon chopped fresh parsley
2 tablespoons freshly grated Parmesan cheese
2 tablespoons fine, dry breadcrumbs
¼ teaspoon Old Bay seasoning
¼ teaspoon pepper
1 tablespoon reduced-calorie margarine, melted
1 teaspoon lemon juice
Garlic-Butter Sauce
Garnishes: fresh parsley sprigs, lemon halves

• **Place** water in a large Dutch oven; bring to a boil. Plunge lobsters, head first, into boiling water; return to a boil. Cover, reduce heat, and simmer 10 minutes; drain and let cool.
• **Break** off large claws and legs. Crack claw and leg shells, using a seafood cracker or nut cracker; remove meat, and set aside. Break off tail. Cut top side of tail shell lengthwise in a 1-inch strip, using kitchen scissors. Cut through center of meat and remove vein. Leave meat in shell. Rinse and set aside.
• **Drain** and flake crabmeat, removing any bits of shell. Combine crabmeat and next 8 ingredients; toss gently. Spoon into lobster tail. Place on a baking sheet.
• **Bake**, uncovered, at 400° for 12 minutes or until thoroughly heated. Serve with Garlic-Butter Sauce and claw and leg meat. Garnish, if desired. **Yield:** 2 servings.

Garlic-Butter Sauce

2 tablespoons reduced-calorie margarine
¼ cup lemon juice
1 clove garlic, minced

• **Melt** margarine in a small saucepan over low heat. Stir in lemon juice and garlic. **Yield:** about ⅓ cup.

Per serving: Calories 408 (35% from fat)
Fat 15.9g (3.2g saturated)   Protein 54.4g   Carbohydrate 11.4g
Fiber 0.5g   Cholesterol 214mg   Sodium 1,326mg

Seared Scallops with Tomato-Mango Salsa

LOW: • Calorie • Cholesterol

Wake up your taste buds with this salsa's sassy combination of fresh tomato, mango, purple onion, and basil.

1 medium tomato, finely chopped
¾ cup finely chopped mango
3 tablespoons finely chopped purple onion
2 tablespoons finely chopped fresh basil
2 tablespoons red wine vinegar
1 tablespoon capers
1 tablespoon olive oil
12 sea scallops
¼ teaspoon salt
¼ teaspoon pepper
¼ avocado, sliced
Garnish: fresh basil sprigs

• **Combine** first 6 ingredients. Cover and chill salsa at least 30 minutes.
• **Heat** olive oil in a skillet over medium-high heat until hot. Add scallops; cook 3 minutes or until scallops are opaque, turning once. Remove from skillet; sprinkle with salt and pepper.
• **Arrange** scallops, salsa, and avocado slices on plates. Garnish, if desired. **Yield:** 2 servings.

Per serving: Calories 246 (41% from fat)
Fat 11.2g (1.7g saturated)   Protein 17.0g   Carbohydrate 21.7g
Fiber 2.9g   Cholesterol 30mg   Sodium 782mg

Stuffed Shrimp with Hollandaise Sauce

LOW: • Calorie

These crawfish-stuffed jumbo shrimp are dressed lavishly in a hollandaise sauce. Our sauce is lighter because we used reduced-calorie mayonnaise and lemon juice instead of eggs and butter.

24 unpeeled jumbo fresh shrimp
Vegetable cooking spray
1 medium onion, finely chopped
½ red bell pepper, finely chopped
½ green bell pepper, finely chopped
2 cloves garlic, minced
½ cup fine, dry breadcrumbs
1 tablespoon Creole seasoning
1 egg white, lightly beaten
⅓ cup reduced-calorie mayonnaise
1 pound frozen crawfish tails, thawed and chopped
2 tablespoons lemon juice
2 tablespoons dry white wine
Hollandaise Sauce

• **Peel** shrimp, leaving tails on; devein, if desired. Butterfly by making a deep slit down the back of each from the large end to the tail, cutting to, but not through, the inside curve. Set aside.
• **Coat** a large saucepan with cooking spray; place over medium-high heat until hot. Add onion and next 3 ingredients; cook until tender, stirring often. Stir in breadcrumbs and seasoning.
• **Combine** egg white, mayonnaise, and crawfish; stir into onion mixture.
• **Stuff** slit in each shrimp with crawfish mixture; arrange on an aluminum foil-lined 15- x 10- x 1-inch jellyroll pan.
• **Combine** lemon juice and wine. Drizzle mixture over shrimp.
• **Bake,** uncovered, at 400° for 20 minutes. Serve with Hollandaise Sauce. **Yield:** 8 servings.

Hollandaise Sauce
⅔ cup reduced-calorie mayonnaise
¼ cup water
½ teaspoon grated lemon rind
1 tablespoon lemon juice
¼ teaspoon salt

• **Combine** all ingredients in a saucepan; stir with a wire whisk until mixture is smooth. Cook over low heat, stirring constantly, 3 to 4 minutes or until thoroughly heated. Serve warm. **Yield:** 1 cup.

Per serving: Calories 260 (41% from fat)
Fat 11.8g (2.1g saturated)   Protein 27.3g   Carbohydrate 11.3g
Fiber 1.0g   Cholesterol 216mg   Sodium 982mg

Mediterranean Shrimp and Pasta

LOW: • Fat

With this recipe, you can create healthy Mediterranean cuisine right in your own kitchen. The shrimp simmer in a tomato sauce flavored with artichoke hearts, white wine, and lite olive oil vinaigrette.

1 pound unpeeled medium-size fresh shrimp
8 ounces linguine, uncooked
Olive oil-flavored vegetable cooking spray
1 tablespoon olive oil
½ cup sliced green onions
3 cloves garlic, minced
1 (14-ounce) can quartered artichoke hearts, drained
6 Roma tomatoes, chopped
1 cup sliced fresh mushrooms
½ cup lite olive oil vinaigrette
¼ cup dry white wine
2 teaspoons dried Italian seasoning
¼ teaspoon dried rosemary, crushed
¼ teaspoon pepper
2 tablespoons freshly grated Parmesan cheese

• **Peel** shrimp, and devein, if desired; set aside.
• **Cook** linguine according to package directions, omitting salt and fat. Drain and keep warm.
• **Coat** a large nonstick skillet with cooking spray; add oil, and place over medium-high heat until hot. Add green onions and garlic, and cook, stirring constantly, until tender. Stir in artichoke hearts and next 7 ingredients.
• **Bring** to a boil; reduce heat, and simmer, uncovered, 5 minutes.
• **Add** shrimp; cook 3 minutes or until shrimp turn pink, stirring occasionally. Serve over pasta, and sprinkle with cheese. **Yield:** 4 servings.

Per serving: Calories 489 (25% from fat)
Fat 13.7g (1.6g saturated)   Protein 32.5g   Carbohydrate 61.4g
Fiber 3.5g   Cholesterol 152mg   Sodium 517mg

Oven Shrimp

Oven Shrimp

LOW: • Calorie • Sodium

These buttery-tasting shrimp are addictive. Be sure to serve plenty of crusty French bread to sop up the spicy sauce. The recipe serves 24 and can easily be halved if you're having a smaller gathering.

1 cup dry white wine
1 pound reduced-calorie margarine
4 lemons, thinly sliced
¾ cup low-sodium Worcestershire sauce
¼ cup freshly ground pepper
1 teaspoon salt
1 teaspoon dried rosemary
1 teaspoon hot sauce
10 pounds unpeeled medium-size fresh shrimp
Garnish: fresh rosemary sprigs

• **Combine** first 8 ingredients in a large saucepan; bring to a boil. Remove from heat.
• **Place** shrimp in two large roasting pans. Pour margarine mixture over shrimp, stirring to coat.
• **Bake,** uncovered, at 400° for 20 to 25 minutes, stirring occasionally. Garnish, if desired. **Yield:** 24 servings.

Per serving: Calories 250 (45% from fat)
Fat 12.4g (2.5g saturated) Protein 29.1g Carbohydrate 5.1g
Fiber 0.3g Cholesterol 215mg Sodium 487mg

The Best-of-the-Bayou Pizza

LOW: • Fat • Calorie • Cholesterol • Sodium

This pizza, made with a refrigerated pizza crust, is bursting with a bounty of ingredients from the Bayou region—fresh shrimp, Creole seasoning, and roasted garlic.

1 pound unpeeled large fresh shrimp
Vegetable cooking spray
½ cup chopped green bell pepper
½ cup chopped onion
½ cup chopped celery
2 teaspoons salt-free Creole seasoning
⅔ cup Roasted Garlic Sauce
1 (12-inch) refrigerated pizza crust
1 cup (4-ounces) shredded part-skim mozzarella cheese
¼ cup freshly grated Parmesan cheese

• **Peel** shrimp, and devein, if desired.
• **Coat** a large nonstick skillet with cooking spray; place over medium-high heat until hot. Add shrimp, bell pepper, and next 3 ingredients to skillet, and cook 3 to 5 minutes or until shrimp turn pink.
• **Spread** Roasted Garlic Sauce over pizza crust; top with shrimp mixture. Sprinkle with cheeses.
• **Bake,** uncovered, at 425° for 10 minutes or until bubbly, and serve immediately. **Yield:** 8 servings.

Roasted Garlic Sauce

2 heads garlic, unpeeled
2 teaspoons canned reduced-sodium chicken broth
Olive oil-flavored vegetable cooking spray
1½ tablespoons reduced-calorie margarine
1½ tablespoons all-purpose flour
⅔ cup canned reduced-sodium chicken broth

• **Place** garlic on a piece of aluminum foil, and drizzle each head with 2 teaspoons chicken broth. Coat with cooking spray. Fold edges of foil together to seal.
• **Bake** at 425° for 45 minutes; let cool.
• **Melt** margarine in a heavy saucepan over medium-high heat. Cut top off each garlic head, and squeeze cooked garlic into pan. (Garlic will be soft and sticky.)
• **Add** flour, and cook, stirring constantly with a wire whisk, 1 minute or until lightly browned.
• **Add** ⅔ cup chicken broth. Cook, stirring constantly, until mixture is thick and bubbly. **Yield:** ⅔ cup.

Per serving: Calories 223 (23% from fat)
Fat 5.6g (2.6g saturated) Protein 15.8g Carbohydrate 25.2g
Fiber 1.2g Cholesterol 59mg Sodium 396mg

Sunday Egg Casserole

LOW: • Fat • Calorie • Sodium

A splash of sherry spikes this hearty egg casserole, while crisp water chestnuts add crunch. We halved the number of eggs from the original recipe, adding fresh mushrooms instead. The mushrooms grow tender and succulent as they bake.

1 pound fresh mushrooms, sliced
¼ cup dry sherry, divided
1 (10¾-ounce) can reduced-sodium cream of chicken soup, undiluted
1 (8-ounce) carton nonfat sour cream
2 tablespoons all-purpose flour
½ teaspoon salt
½ teaspoon pepper
1 tablespoon finely chopped onion
1 (2-ounce) jar chopped pimiento, drained
1 (10-ounce) package frozen English peas, thawed and drained
7 large hard-cooked eggs, cut lengthwise into 4 wedges
1 (8-ounce) can sliced water chestnuts, drained
Butter-flavored vegetable cooking spray
1 cup soft breadcrumbs
1½ teaspoons reduced-calorie margarine, melted

• **Cook** mushrooms and 2 tablespoons sherry in a large nonstick skillet over medium heat 5 minutes or until mushrooms are tender, stirring occasionally. Drain well; set aside.

• **Combine** remaining 2 tablespoons sherry, soup, and next 6 ingredients in a medium saucepan. Cook over medium-high heat 2 minutes or until mixture is bubbly; stir in mushrooms and peas.

• **Arrange** egg wedges and water chestnuts in bottom of an 11- x 7- x 1½-inch baking dish coated with cooking spray. Pour soup mixture evenly over top.

• **Combine** breadcrumbs and melted margarine. Sprinkle over soup mixture.

• **Bake**, uncovered, at 375° for 30 minutes or until top is golden. **Yield:** 8 servings.

Per serving: Calories 184 (28% from fat)
Fat 5.8g (1.5g saturated) Protein 12.0g Carbohydrate 20.4g
Fiber 2.6g Cholesterol 191mg Sodium 447mg

Buttercrust Corn Pie with Fresh Tomato Salsa

LOW: • Calorie • Cholesterol

1 cup finely crushed low-sodium saltine crackers
3 tablespoons grated nonfat Parmesan cheese
⅓ cup reduced-calorie margarine, melted
Vegetable cooking spray
1¼ cups skim milk, divided
2 cups fresh or frozen corn
½ teaspoon onion salt
¼ teaspoon ground white pepper
2 tablespoons all-purpose flour
2 tablespoons chopped ripe olives
½ cup sliced green onions
½ cup egg substitute
Paprika
Fresh Tomato Salsa

• **Combine** first 3 ingredients; reserve 2 tablespoons. Press remaining mixture in bottom of a 9-inch pieplate coated with cooking spray.

• **Combine** 1 cup milk, corn, onion salt, and pepper in a saucepan; bring to a boil over medium heat. Reduce heat, and simmer 3 minutes.

• **Combine** remaining ¼ cup milk and flour, stirring until smooth. Gradually add flour mixture to corn mixture, stirring constantly. Cook 1 minute, stirring constantly. Remove from heat.

• **Stir** in olives and green onions. Gradually stir about one-fourth of hot mixture into egg substitute; add to remaining hot mixture, stirring constantly.

• **Spoon** into prepared pieplate; sprinkle with reserved cracker mixture and paprika.

• **Bake**, uncovered, at 400° for 20 minutes or until set. Serve with Fresh Tomato Salsa. **Yield:** 6 servings.

Fresh Tomato Salsa
2 cups peeled, chopped tomato
1 jalapeño pepper, seeded and finely chopped
½ cup thinly sliced green onions
2 tablespoons lemon juice
¼ teaspoon salt
½ teaspoon dried oregano
⅛ teaspoon pepper

• **Combine** all ingredients, stirring well. Cover and chill at least 3 hours. **Yield:** 2 cups.

Per serving: Calories 209 (39% from fat)
Fat 9.1g (2.0g saturated) Protein 7.1g Carbohydrate 28.6g
Fiber 2.3g Cholesterol 1mg Sodium 556mg

Buttercrust Corn Pie with
Fresh Tomato Salsa

Spinach Pie with Muenster Crust

LOW: • Calorie • Cholesterol • Sodium

We didn't believe it would work until we tried it—the crust for this spinach pie is made from overlapped slices of Muenster cheese. They melt together and then firm up to a sliceable consistency.

3 (10-ounce) packages frozen chopped spinach, thawed
12 ounces reduced-sodium Muenster cheese slices
Vegetable cooking spray
1 small onion, finely chopped
1 cup nonfat cottage cheese
¾ cup egg substitute
⅓ cup grated nonfat Parmesan cheese
¼ teaspoon pepper
2 small tomatoes, quartered

• **Drain** spinach well, pressing between layers of paper towels to remove excess moisture; set aside.
• **Cut** 2 cheese slices into small triangles, and reserve for garnish. Cover bottom and sides of a 9-inch pieplate coated with cooking spray with remaining cheese slices, overlapping cheese as needed.
• **Combine** spinach, onion, and next 4 ingredients; spoon into pieplate.
• **Bake,** uncovered, at 350° for 40 minutes or until set. Let stand 10 minutes before serving. Top with reserved cheese triangles and tomato wedges. **Yield:** 8 servings.

Per serving: Calories 238 (53% from fat)
Fat 14.1g (7.6g saturated)   Protein 20.6g   Carbohydrate 13.7g
Fiber 4.4g   Cholesterol 1mg   Sodium 341mg

Fresh Tomato Tart

LOW: • Calorie • Cholesterol

Strewn with a handful of sweet basil leaves, this fresh tomato tart is unbeatable summer fare.

½ (15-ounce) package refrigerated piecrusts
1½ cups (6 ounces) shredded part-skim mozzarella cheese
3 tablespoons chopped fresh basil, divided
3 medium-size ripe tomatoes, peeled and cut into ½-inch slices
Olive oil-flavored vegetable cooking spray
¼ teaspoon salt
¼ teaspoon pepper

• **Fit** piecrust into a 10-inch tart pan according to package directions; trim any excess pastry along edges. Generously prick bottom and sides of pastry with a fork.
• **Bake,** uncovered, at 400° for 5 minutes.
• **Sprinkle** cheese evenly into pastry shell, and top with 2 tablespoons basil. Arrange tomato slices on top; coat with cooking spray, and sprinkle with salt and pepper.
• **Bake,** uncovered, on lower rack of oven at 400° for 35 to 40 minutes. Remove from oven, and sprinkle with remaining 1 tablespoon basil. Let stand 5 minutes before serving. **Yield:** 5 servings.

Per serving: Calories 276 (55% from fat)
Fat 16.9g (8.3g saturated)   Protein 8.8g   Carbohydrate 23.0g
Fiber 0.8g   Cholesterol 28mg   Sodium 505mg

Winter Fruit Salad with Poppy Seed Dressing (page 86)

Salads

Winter Fruit Salad with Poppy Seed Dressing

LOW: • Cholesterol • Sodium

Winter citrus—orange and grapefruit—star in this tender lettuce salad. Drizzle it with poppy seed dressing, and sprinkle toasted almond slices on top for crunch.

4 oranges
4 pink grapefruit
2 cups purple or red seedless grapes
1 purple onion
2 heads Bibb lettuce
¼ cup sliced almonds, toasted
Poppy Seed Dressing

• **Peel** and section oranges and grapefruit; cut grapes in half. Cut onion into thin slices; separate into rings.
• **Line** individual serving plates with lettuce leaves. Arrange fruit, sliced onion, and toasted almonds over lettuce. Drizzle with Poppy Seed Dressing; serve immediately. **Yield:** 8 servings.

Poppy Seed Dressing

½ cup sugar
1 teaspoon dry mustard
⅓ cup cider vinegar
2 tablespoons chopped onion
½ cup reduced-fat mayonnaise
½ cup nonfat sour cream
1½ tablespoons poppy seeds

• **Combine** all ingredients, stirring with a wire whisk. Serve immediately or cover and store in refrigerator. Allow to come to room temperature before serving. **Yield:** 1⅔ cups.

Per serving: Calories 201 (31% from fat)
Fat 6.9g (0.9g saturated)   Protein 3.6g   Carbohydrate 34.9g
Fiber 3.5g   Cholesterol 5mg   Sodium 121mg

Holiday Cranberry Salad

LOW: • Fat • Calorie • Cholesterol • Sodium

Fresh cranberries ornament this crimson gelatin salad. We kept the celery, but replaced the walnuts with chopped Granny Smith apple for satisfying crunch without fat.

2 cups fresh or frozen cranberries, thawed
½ cup sugar
1 (0.3-ounce) package sugar-free lemon-flavored gelatin
1 cup boiling water
1 cup chopped celery
1 cup chopped Granny Smith apple
Vegetable cooking spray
Green leaf lettuce (optional)
Garnishes: celery leaves, cranberries

• **Position** knife blade in food processor bowl; add cranberries. Process 30 seconds or until chopped.
• **Combine** cranberries and sugar in a large bowl; let mixture stand 30 minutes or until sugar dissolves.
• **Combine** gelatin and boiling water in a large bowl; stir 2 minutes or until gelatin dissolves. Chill until the consistency of unbeaten egg white.
• **Stir** cranberry mixture, celery, and apple into gelatin mixture. Pour mixture into a 4-cup mold coated with cooking spray. Cover and chill until firm.
• **Unmold** salad onto a lettuce-lined serving plate, if desired. Garnish, if desired. **Yield:** 8 servings.

Per serving: Calories 80 (2% from fat)
Fat 0.2g (0.0g saturated)   Protein 0.8g   Carbohydrate 19.0g
Fiber 1.1g   Cholesterol 0mg   Sodium 43mg

Orange-Buttermilk Salad

LOW: • Calorie • Cholesterol • Sodium

*Crushed pineapple and whipped topping
add just the right amount of sweetness
to this salad.*

1 (20-ounce) can unsweetened crushed
   pineapple, undrained
1 (0.6-ounce) package sugar-free orange-
   flavored gelatin
2 cups nonfat buttermilk
1 (8-ounce) container frozen reduced-calorie
   whipped topping, thawed
1/3 cup finely chopped pecans
Vegetable cooking spray
16 lettuce leaves

• **Bring** pineapple and juice to a boil in a medium saucepan. Remove from heat; add gelatin. Stir 2 minutes or until gelatin dissolves; cool.
• **Add** buttermilk to pineapple mixture; chill until consistency of unbeaten egg white. Fold in whipped topping and pecans.
• **Spoon** mixture into a 9-cup mold coated with cooking spray; cover and chill until firm. Unmold onto a lettuce-lined serving plate. **Yield:** 16 servings.

Per serving: Calories 85 (39% from fat)
Fat 3.7g (0.7g saturated)   Protein 2.7g   Carbohydrate 11.1g
Fiber 0.5g   Cholesterol 1mg   Sodium 49mg

Cucumber Mousse with Dill Sauce

LOW: • Calorie • Sodium

*Cool, crisp cucumbers and the refreshing
flavor of dill make perfect partners.*

2 envelopes unflavored gelatin
3 tablespoons cold water
1 cup boiling water
2 large cucumbers, cut in half
1 cup 1% low-fat cottage cheese
1½ cups reduced-fat sour cream
3 tablespoons chopped fresh dill
2 tablespoons chopped green onions
1 tablespoon chopped fresh parsley
¼ teaspoon salt
¼ teaspoon ground white pepper
10 lettuce leaves
Dill Sauce

• **Sprinkle** gelatin over 3 tablespoons cold water; stir and let stand 1 minute. Add 1 cup boiling water; stir until gelatin dissolves. Set aside.
• **Peel** and seed 3 cucumber halves; thinly slice remaining cucumber half, and set aside.
• **Position** knife blade in food processor bowl; add peeled and seeded cucumber. Pulse 2 or 3 times or until cucumber is finely chopped.
• **Add** cottage cheese, and process 20 seconds, stopping once to scrape down sides. Pour gelatin gradually through food chute with processor running.
• **Combine** sour cream and next 5 ingredients in a large bowl; stir in cucumber mixture. Spoon into lightly oiled individual molds; cover and chill until firm.
• **Arrange** lettuce leaves on serving plates. Unmold salads onto prepared plates; top with Dill Sauce and cucumber slices. **Yield:** 10 servings.

Dill Sauce

1 (8-ounce) carton nonfat sour cream
2 tablespoons skim milk
2 tablespoons fresh lemon juice
2 teaspoons chopped fresh dill
½ teaspoon chopped fresh parsley

• **Combine** all ingredients in a small bowl, stirring well. **Yield:** 1 cup.

Per serving: Calories 102 (41% from fat)
Fat 4.7g (2.9g saturated)   Protein 7.6g   Carbohydrate 7.3g
Fiber 0.6g   Cholesterol 15mg   Sodium 191mg

Broccoli Salad

LOW: • Sodium

What's broccoli salad without crispy bits of bacon? This salad delivers the taste without as much fat, thanks to turkey bacon.

½ cup raisins
2 pounds broccoli, cut into flowerets
1 cup purple seedless grapes, halved
3 green onions, thinly sliced
⅔ cup reduced-fat mayonnaise
2 tablespoons tarragon vinegar
2 tablespoons slivered almonds, toasted
4 slices turkey bacon, cooked and crumbled

• **Soak** raisins in hot water 5 minutes; drain.
• **Combine** raisins and next 3 ingredients in a large bowl. Combine mayonnaise and vinegar; stir into broccoli mixture. Cover and chill.
• **Stir** in almonds and bacon just before serving. **Yield:** 8 servings.

Per serving: Calories 145 (52% from fat)
Fat 8.4g (1.2g saturated)   Protein 3.5g   Carbohydrate 16.5g
Fiber 2.4g   Cholesterol 11mg   Sodium 250mg

Corn Salad

LOW: • Fat • Calorie • Cholesterol • Sodium

Small, sweet kernels of white corn mingle with bright bits of purple onion and green bell pepper in this colorful sour cream-dressed salad.

2 (11-ounce) cans white shoepeg corn, drained
1 green bell pepper, chopped
½ cup chopped purple onion
½ cup nonfat sour cream
1 tablespoon white vinegar
¼ teaspoon celery salt
⅛ teaspoon pepper

• **Combine** all ingredients, stirring well. Cover and chill at least 3 hours. Serve with a slotted spoon. **Yield:** 8 servings.

Per serving: Calories 71 (5% from fat)
Fat 0.4g (0.1g saturated)   Protein 2.9g   Carbohydrate 15.8g
Fiber 1.0g   Cholesterol 0mg   Sodium 257mg

Summer Zucchini Salad

LOW: • Calorie • Cholesterol • Sodium

Zucchini's mild flavor comes alive with the addition of fresh basil and mint. Instead of a heavy olive oil dressing, we used a commercial lite olive oil vinaigrette.

8 medium zucchini, cut into thin strips (about 3 pounds)
¼ cup lite olive oil vinaigrette dressing
2 tablespoons finely chopped fresh basil
2 tablespoons finely chopped fresh mint
¼ teaspoon salt
3 tablespoons coarsely chopped pecans, toasted

• **Cook** zucchini in vinaigrette dressing in a large skillet over medium-high heat, stirring constantly, 3 minutes or until zucchini is tender. Remove zucchini mixture from skillet, and cool.
• **Combine** zucchini mixture, basil, mint, and salt in a large bowl, stirring gently. Serve salad at room temperature, or cover and chill. Sprinkle with pecans just before serving. **Yield:** 8 servings.

Per serving: Calories 50 (63% from fat)
Fat 3.5g (0.3g saturated)   Protein 1.5g   Carbohydrate 4.6g
Fiber 0.7g   Cholesterol 0mg   Sodium 137mg

Summer Zucchini Salad

Gazpacho-Stuffed Endive

LOW: • Calorie • Cholesterol • Sodium

Ingredients from gazpacho, the classic cold tomato soup, mingle in this endive salad. For another twist, serve the stuffed endive leaves on a platter as pick-up appetizers. You'll get a yield of about 6 dozen stuffed leaves.

6 green onions, sliced
2 cloves garlic, minced
1 tablespoon capers
2 tablespoons olive oil
2 tablespoons white wine vinegar
½ teaspoon freshly ground pepper
1⅓ pounds plum tomatoes
1 cucumber, peeled and seeded
½ red bell pepper
½ avocado, peeled and seeded
¼ cup loosely packed fresh basil leaves
2 ounces part-skim mozzarella cheese
4 heads Belgian endive

• **Combine** first 6 ingredients in a large bowl. Finely chop tomatoes and next 4 ingredients; add to green onion mixture. Cut cheese into small cubes; add to vegetable mixture. Cover and chill at least 2 hours.
• **Separate** endive into leaves; spoon vegetable mixture into leaves, using a slotted spoon. **Yield:** 10 servings.

Per serving: Calories 76 (59% from fat)
Fat 5.0g (1.2g saturated)   Protein 2.8g   Carbohydrate 6.4g
Fiber 1.6g   Cholesterol 3mg   Sodium 105mg

Roasted Onion Salad

LOW: • Calorie • Cholesterol • Sodium

The sweet essence of roasted onion provides a mellow base for the dominant flavors of blue cheese and garlic in this tender lettuce salad. We cut about a cup of oil from the recipe, which makes the flavors really sing.

5 medium onions, unpeeled and cut into
    ½-inch-thick slices
Olive oil-flavored vegetable cooking spray
8 cups loosely packed mixed baby lettuces
¼ cup chopped walnuts, toasted
½ cup crumbled blue cheese
Garlic Vinaigrette

• **Arrange** onion slices in a roasting pan coated with cooking spray. Coat slices lightly with cooking spray.
• **Bake,** uncovered, at 500° for 20 minutes or until onion slices are lightly charred; cool. Remove and discard outer skin of onion slices. Set slices aside.
• **Combine** lettuces, walnuts, and blue cheese; toss gently. Top with roasted onion slices; drizzle with Garlic Vinaigrette. **Yield:** 8 servings.

Garlic Vinaigrette

2 cloves garlic
1 tablespoon chopped shallot
¼ cup chopped fresh parsley
¼ teaspoon dried crushed red pepper
¼ teaspoon salt
½ teaspoon freshly ground black pepper
2 tablespoons white wine vinegar
½ cup plus 1 tablespoon canned vegetable
    broth
2½ tablespoons olive oil

• **Position** knife blade in food processor bowl; add garlic and shallot, and pulse 3 or 4 times. Add parsley and next 5 ingredients; process 20 seconds, stopping once to scrape down sides.
• **Pour** olive oil through food chute in a slow, steady stream with processor running; process until blended. **Yield:** 1 cup.

Per serving: Calories 121 (64% from fat)
Fat 8.6g (2.0g saturated)   Protein 4.2g   Carbohydrate 7.0g
Fiber 1.5g   Cholesterol 5mg   Sodium 259mg

Greens and Grapefruit Salad

LOW: • Fat • Calorie • Cholesterol • Sodium

This salad kept the crunch without the fat by substituting a sprinkling of sunflower kernels in place of the pine nuts in the original recipe.

8 cups loosely packed torn mixed salad greens
2 heads radicchio, separated into leaves
2 heads Belgian endive, separated into leaves
1 medium-size purple onion, thinly sliced
2 tablespoons chopped fresh basil
2 pink grapefruit, peeled and sectioned
Dijon Vinaigrette
3 tablespoons sunflower kernels

• **Combine** first 6 ingredients in a large bowl; drizzle with ¾ cup Dijon Vinaigrette. Sprinkle with sunflower kernels. Serve with remaining vinaigrette. **Yield:** 12 servings.

Dijon Vinaigrette

½ cup red wine vinegar
¼ cup Dijon mustard
2 tablespoons lime juice
¼ teaspoon freshly ground pepper
¼ cup water
½ cup canned no-salt-added chicken broth
2 tablespoons sugar

• **Combine** all ingredients in container of an electric blender; process until smooth, stopping once to scrape down sides. **Yield:** 1¾ cups.

Per serving: Calories 60 (23% from fat)
Fat 1.5g (0.1g saturated)   Protein 2.2g   Carbohydrate 9.7g
Fiber 1.0g   Cholesterol 0mg   Sodium 185mg

Mixed Greens with Parmesan Walnuts

LOW: • Calorie • Cholesterol • Sodium

Don't go nuts and give up all nuts. We cut the fat by halving the amount of walnuts in the original recipe and toasting them, using butter-flavored cooking spray instead of melted butter. They're just as crunchy that way.

¾ cup walnut pieces
Butter-flavored vegetable cooking spray
2 tablespoons grated nonfat Parmesan cheese
4 cups loosely packed torn iceberg lettuce
4 cups loosely packed torn leaf lettuce
3 cups loosely packed torn curly endive
3 cups loosely packed torn fresh spinach
2 cups loosely packed torn watercress
½ cup fat-free balsamic vinaigrette

• **Place** walnuts in an 8-inch square pan. Coat walnuts with cooking spray.
• **Bake** at 350° for 5 minutes. Sprinkle with cheese, tossing to coat; bake 4 to 5 additional minutes or until cheese is lightly browned. Cool completely.
• **Combine** iceberg lettuce and next 4 ingredients; toss. Drizzle with vinaigrette, and toss gently to coat. Top with walnuts, and serve immediately. **Yield:** 8 servings.

Per serving: Calories 101 (52% from fat)
Fat 5.8g (0.4g saturated)   Protein 3.5g   Carbohydrate 9.5g
Fiber 1.9g   Cholesterol 0mg   Sodium 270mg

Spinach Salad with the Blues

Spinach Salad with the Blues

True blue-cheese lovers can't get enough of this cheeky cheese, so we lightened up on the nuts and omitted the oil instead.

⅓ cup canned no-salt-added chicken broth
¼ cup white wine vinegar
1 tablespoon prepared mustard
1 teaspoon sugar
1 (10-ounce) package fresh spinach, washed, trimmed, and shredded
5 heads Belgian endive, washed and trimmed (about 10 ounces)
2 Red Delicious apples, cored and thinly sliced
¼ cup chopped walnuts, toasted
1 (4-ounce) package crumbled blue cheese

• **Combine** first 4 ingredients in a jar. Cover tightly, and shake vigorously. Set aside.
• **Combine** spinach and dressing in a large bowl, tossing gently. Divide spinach mixture evenly among six individual salad plates.
• **Arrange** endive leaves and apple slices beside shredded spinach.
• **Sprinkle** with walnuts and blue cheese. Yield: 6 servings.

Per serving: Calories 161 (48% from fat)
Fat 8.6g (3.8g saturated)   Protein 7.0g   Carbohydrate 15.9g
Fiber 4.1g   Cholesterol 14mg   Sodium 330mg

Winter Salad

LOW: • Fat • Calorie • Cholesterol • Sodium

Ruby-red radicchio leaves, with their thick, white veins, add a peppery accent to this mixed green salad. It's topped with creamy white slices of fresh fennel for celery-like crunch and then drizzled with a slightly sweet balsamic vinegar dressing.

2 heads fresh fennel
12 cups loosely packed torn mixed salad greens
2 heads radicchio, torn into bite-size pieces
Balsamic Dressing
12 lettuce leaves

• **Rinse** fennel thoroughly. Trim and discard fennel bulb bases. Trim stalks from bulbs, and discard hard outside stalks and leaves. Cut bulbs lengthwise into ⅛-inch slices; set aside.
• **Combine** salad greens and radicchio; drizzle with Balsamic Dressing, and toss gently. Spoon onto a lettuce-lined serving plate. Top with sliced fennel. Serve immediately. Yield: 12 servings.

Balsamic Dressing
⅔ cup canned reduced-sodium chicken broth
1 tablespoon olive oil
¼ cup balsamic vinegar
1 shallot, finely chopped
¼ teaspoon salt
¼ teaspoon freshly ground pepper

• **Combine** all ingredients in a jar. Cover tightly, and shake vigorously. Yield: 1 cup.

Per serving: Calories 53 (25% from fat)
Fat 1.5g (0.2g saturated)   Protein 3.8g   Carbohydrate 7.0g
Fiber 0.5g   Cholesterol 0mg   Sodium 119mg

Mixed Greens with Tarragon Vinaigrette

LOW: • Calorie • Cholesterol

The sharp, licorice-like flavor of tarragon accents the pineapple-inspired dressing for this green salad. Toasted sesame seeds add a nutty nuance.

½ teaspoon sugar
½ teaspoon dried tarragon
½ teaspoon minced onion
¼ teaspoon salt
¼ teaspoon dry mustard
⅛ teaspoon pepper
2 tablespoons unsweetened pineapple juice
1 tablespoon tarragon vinegar
1 tablespoon cider vinegar
2 teaspoons olive oil
2 cups loosely packed torn mixed salad greens
1 teaspoon sesame seeds, toasted

• **Combine** first 10 ingredients in a jar; cover tightly, and shake vigorously. Pour over salad greens; toss gently to coat. Sprinkle with sesame seeds. Yield: 2 servings.

Per serving: Calories 76 (65% from fat)
Fat 5.5g (0.7g saturated)   Protein 1.7g   Carbohydrate 5.3g
Fiber 0.2g   Cholesterol 0mg   Sodium 325mg

Blue Cheese Coleslaw

LOW: • Calorie • Cholesterol • Sodium

Blue cheese turns this slaw into one sassy salad. For extra crisp slaw, soak the shredded cabbage in ice water for an hour. Then drain the cabbage, pat dry, and chill in a plastic bag until ready to use.

3 tablespoons apple cider vinegar
2 tablespoons finely chopped onion
1 tablespoon sugar
¾ teaspoon celery seeds
⅛ teaspoon salt
⅛ teaspoon dry mustard
¼ teaspoon pepper
1 clove garlic, minced
¼ cup nonfat sour cream
1 pound cabbage, finely shredded
½ cup crumbled blue cheese

• **Combine** first 8 ingredients in a bowl; gradually add sour cream, stirring with a wire whisk until blended. Cover and chill at least 1 hour.
• **Combine** cabbage and cheese; chill 1 hour.
• **Pour** vinegar mixture over cabbage mixture; toss gently. Serve immediately. **Yield:** 6 servings.

Per serving: Calories 71 (37% from fat)
Fat 2.9g (1.8g saturated)   Protein 3.7g   Carbohydrate 8.1g
Fiber 1.9g   Cholesterol 7mg   Sodium 202mg

Mediterranean Salad

LOW: • Fat • Cholesterol

Add a twist to this recipe by using fusilli (spiral-shaped pasta) in place of spaghetti. We like both versions.

1 (8-ounce) package spaghetti
1 (14-ounce) can artichoke hearts, drained and coarsely chopped
1 (2¼-ounce) can sliced ripe olives, drained
1 cup frozen English peas, thawed
1 medium-size red bell pepper, chopped
1 small zucchini, chopped
½ small purple onion, thinly sliced
¼ cup grated nonfat Parmesan cheese
½ cup reduced-fat mayonnaise
½ cup fat-free Italian salad dressing
1 teaspoon dried parsley flakes
½ teaspoon dried dillweed
½ teaspoon coarsely ground pepper

• **Cook** spaghetti according to package directions, omitting salt and fat; drain. Rinse with cold water; drain.
• **Combine** artichokes and next 6 ingredients in a large bowl. Add spaghetti, tossing well.
• **Combine** mayonnaise and next 4 ingredients, stirring with a wire whisk until blended. Add to spaghetti mixture, and stir well. Cover and chill. **Yield:** 8 servings.

Per serving: Calories 209 (24% from fat)
Fat 5.5g (0.2g saturated)   Protein 6.1g   Carbohydrate 33.8g
Fiber 1.4g   Cholesterol 5mg   Sodium 416mg

Pasta-Vegetable Salad

LOW: • Fat • Calorie • Cholesterol

Feta cheese and oregano give this colorful pasta salad a distinct Greek flavor. Add the radishes just before serving. Otherwise, they'll bleed their red color onto the pasta and vegetables.

6 ounces tricolor rotini pasta, uncooked
1 pound broccoli, cut into flowerets
3 stalks celery, sliced
1 (8-ounce) can sliced water chestnuts, drained
1 (1.05-ounce) package fat-free Italian dressing mix
3 tablespoons chopped fresh oregano
¾ cup sliced radishes
⅓ cup crumbled reduced-fat feta cheese

• **Prepare** pasta according to package directions, omitting salt and fat; drain. Rinse with cold water; drain.
• **Combine** pasta, broccoli, celery, and water chestnuts in a bowl; set aside.
• **Prepare** dressing mix according to package directions; stir in oregano. Pour over pasta mixture, stirring to coat. Cover and chill at least 6 hours. Just before serving, stir in radishes, and sprinkle with cheese. **Yield:** 9 servings.

Per serving: Calories 124 (9% from fat)
Fat 1.2g (0.4g saturated)   Protein 4.3g   Carbohydrate 24.0g
Fiber 0.8g   Cholesterol 2mg   Sodium 343mg

Pasta-Vegetable Salad

Mexican Cornbread Salad

LOW: • Cholesterol

Crumbled cornbread spiced with sage and a Ranch-style sour cream dressing blankets pinto beans, Cheddar cheese, turkey bacon, and fresh vegetables in this layered Mexican salad.

1 (6-ounce) package Mexican cornbread mix
Dash of ground sage
1 (1.0-ounce) package Ranch-style salad dressing mix
1 (8-ounce) carton reduced-fat sour cream
1 cup reduced-fat mayonnaise
2 (16-ounce) cans pinto beans, drained
1 cup chopped green bell pepper
2 (15¼-ounce) cans no-salt-added whole kernel corn, drained
3 large tomatoes, chopped
4 slices turkey bacon, cooked and crumbled
1 cup (4 ounces) shredded reduced-fat Cheddar cheese
1 cup sliced green onions
8 lettuce leaves
2 small tomatoes, cut into wedges

• **Prepare** cornbread mix according to package directions, adding sage; cool.
• **Combine** salad dressing mix, sour cream, and mayonnaise; set aside.
• **Crumble** half of cornbread into a bowl. Top with half each of beans, sour cream mixture, bell pepper, and next 5 ingredients. Repeat layers.
• **Cover** and chill 2 hours. Serve in individual lettuce-lined salad bowls, and top evenly with tomato wedges. **Yield:** 8 servings.

Per serving: Calories 438 (40% from fat)
Fat 19.4g (6.0g saturated) Protein 19.0g Carbohydrate 46.4g
Fiber 5.7g Cholesterol 47mg Sodium 1,252mg

Mexican Chicken Tortilla Salads

LOW: • Fat • Cholesterol • Sodium

A creamy cilantro and jalapeño dressing drenches this chicken salad with feisty flavor. For a change of pace, we thought it would also be good topped with fat-free Ranch dressing or no-salt-added salsa.

¾ cup (3 ounces) shredded reduced-fat Monterey Jack cheese
¼ cup reduced-fat mayonnaise, divided
3 tablespoons nonfat sour cream
2 tablespoons chopped fresh cilantro
1 tablespoon finely chopped pickled jalapeño peppers
1 clove garlic, minced
4 (4-ounce) skinned and boned chicken breast halves
1 (7-ounce) package no-oil baked tortilla chips
9 cups shredded green leaf lettuce
3 Roma tomatoes, thinly sliced
¼ cup plus 2 tablespoons nonfat sour cream
Garnish: fresh cilantro sprigs

• **Combine** cheese, 3 tablespoons mayonnaise, 3 tablespoons sour cream, and next 3 ingredients. Set aside.
• **Place** chicken between two sheets of heavy-duty plastic wrap, and flatten to ¼-inch thickness, using a meat mallet or rolling pin.
• **Brush** both sides of chicken lightly with remaining 1 tablespoon mayonnaise; place on a rack in broiler pan.
• **Broil** chicken 5½ inches from heat (with electric oven door partially opened) 5 minutes on each side.
• **Spread** cheese mixture evenly on top of chicken.
• **Broil** 3 to 4 additional minutes or until mixture is browned. Coarsely shred chicken; set aside, and keep warm.
• **Layer** chips, lettuce, and tomato evenly on individual plates; top with chicken. Top each serving evenly with sour cream. Garnish, if desired. **Yield:** 6 servings.

Per serving: Calories 315 (22% from fat)
Fat 7.8g (1.9g saturated) Protein 26.6g Carbohydrate 33.1g
Fiber 2.4g Cholesterol 56mg Sodium 396mg

Moroccan Grilled Chicken Salad

LOW: • Calorie • Cholesterol

A Moroccan Spice Rub lends an exotic air to this main-dish salad. You may not be familiar with fenugreek in the rub; it's a seed with a pleasantly bitter flavor.

½ cup plain nonfat yogurt
3 tablespoons Moroccan Spice Rub
6 (4-ounce) boned chicken breast halves
Vegetable cooking spray
10 cups loosely packed torn mixed salad
    greens
Vinaigrette Dressing

• **Combine** yogurt and 3 tablespoons Moroccan Spice Rub, stirring well. Lift skin of chicken breast halves, and spread yogurt mixture under skin. Replace skin, and spread yogurt mixture over chicken. Cover and chill.
• **Coat** grill rack with cooking spray; place on grill over hot coals (400° to 500°).
• **Cook** chicken, skin side down, covered with grill lid, over hot coals about 4 minutes. Turn chicken; cook 2 additional minutes or until done.
• **Remove** and discard skin from chicken; cut chicken into thin strips.
• **Arrange** salad greens evenly on six individual serving plates; top evenly with chicken strips, and drizzle with Vinaigrette Dressing. **Yield:** 6 servings.

Moroccan Spice Rub
¼ cup paprika
1 tablespoon kosher salt
1 tablespoon sweet red pepper flakes
2 teaspoons instant minced onion
1 teaspoon cracked peppercorns
1 teaspoon ground ginger
1 teaspoon ground cardamom
1 teaspoon ground cumin
1 teaspoon fenugreek
Dash of ground cloves
Dash of ground cinnamon
Dash of ground allspice

• **Combine** all ingredients in a skillet; cook over medium-high heat, stirring constantly, 3 to 5 minutes or until spices are darker. Let cool.
• **Position** knife blade in food processor bowl; add spice mixture. Process 2 to 3 minutes. Store spice rub in an airtight container in a cool, dark place up to 3 months. Use on chicken or pork. **Yield:** ½ cup.

Vinaigrette Dressing
2 tablespoons olive oil
¼ cup canned reduced-sodium chicken broth
2 tablespoons red wine vinegar
1 tablespoon balsamic vinegar
1 teaspoon Dijon mustard
Dash of curry powder

• **Combine** all ingredients in a jar; cover tightly, and shake vigorously. **Yield:** ½ cup.

Per serving: Calories 221 (33% from fat)
Fat 8.0g (1.5g saturated)   Protein 29.7g   Carbohydrate 5.2g
Fiber 0.6g   Cholesterol 73mg   Sodium 614mg

Chicken Noodle Salad

LOW: • Fat • Calorie • Cholesterol

Be sure you buy the low-fat version of ramen noodles. Regular noodles can have as much as 17 grams of fat in a 3-ounce package.

1 (3-ounce) package low-fat Oriental-flavored
    ramen noodle soup mix
2 cups water
1 tablespoon reduced-calorie mayonnaise
2 teaspoons low-sodium soy sauce
1 teaspoon lemon juice
¼ teaspoon ground red pepper
1 stalk celery, chopped
1 large carrot, scraped and chopped
3 green onions, chopped
½ cup chopped green bell pepper
½ cup chopped cooked chicken breast (skinned
    before cooking and cooked without salt)

• **Remove** seasoning packet from soup mix.
• **Bring** water to a boil; stir in noodles, and cook 3 minutes. Drain and set aside.
• **Combine** mayonnaise and next 3 ingredients. Add to noodles; toss gently.
• **Combine** ½ seasoning packet from soup mix, celery, and remaining 4 ingredients in a medium bowl. Reserve remaining ½ seasoning packet for another use. Add noodles and seasoned vegetables, and toss. Cover and chill. **Yield:** 2 servings.

Per serving: Calories 176 (19% from fat)
Fat 3.8g (0.7g saturated)   Protein 12.0g   Carbohydrate 23.3g
Fiber 2.9g   Cholesterol 27mg   Sodium 442mg

Turkey Taco Salad

LOW: • Cholesterol

Part of the fun of eating a taco salad is in the trimmings. Turn to no-oil baked tortilla chips, reduced-fat cheese, nonfat sour cream, and salsa for lower calorie alternatives.

1 pound ground skinless turkey
1 (1¼-ounce) package taco seasoning mix
¾ cup water
6 cups no-oil baked tortilla chips
2 cups shredded lettuce
1 cup (4 ounces) shredded reduced-fat process American cheese
1 cup chopped tomato
¼ cup salsa
¼ cup nonfat sour cream

• **Brown** ground turkey in a large nonstick skillet over medium heat, stirring until it crumbles. Drain turkey, and pat dry with paper towels; wipe pan drippings from skillet. Return turkey to skillet. Stir in taco seasoning mix and water; cook, uncovered, 10 minutes, stirring often.
• **Layer** tortilla chips, lettuce, turkey mixture, cheese, and remaining 3 ingredients evenly on individual salad plates. **Yield:** 4 servings.

Per serving: Calories 381 (45% from fat)
Fat 19.1g (4.3g saturated)   Protein 25.3g   Carbohydrate 25g
Fiber 0.5g   Cholesterol 57mg   Sodium 1,034mg

Wild Tuna Salad

LOW: • Calorie • Cholesterol

Tuna takes a walk on the wild side when paired with long-grain and wild rice mix.

1 (6-ounce) package long-grain-and-wild rice mix
1 (12-ounce) can solid white tuna in spring water, drained and flaked
½ cup reduced-fat mayonnaise
½ cup finely chopped celery
¼ cup nonfat sour cream
¼ cup unsalted roasted cashews, chopped
2 tablespoons finely chopped onion
2 teaspoons Mrs. Dash table blend seasoning
½ teaspoon salt
6 lettuce leaves
¾ cup alfalfa sprouts

• **Cook** rice according to package directions, omitting seasoning packet; cover rice, and chill completely.
• **Add** tuna and next 7 ingredients, stirring well. Serve on lettuce leaves; top with alfalfa sprouts. **Yield:** 6 servings.

Per serving: Calories 254 (32% from fat)
Fat 9.1g (0.7g saturated)   Protein 17.4g   Carbohydrate 26.2g
Fiber 1.6g   Cholesterol 26mg   Sodium 542mg

Ham and Potato Salad

LOW: • Fat • Calorie • Cholesterol

Ham and frozen mixed vegetables perk up this chunky red potato salad. We diced the ham to give a smoky tidbit in every bite.

1 pound small round red potatoes, cut into ½-inch wedges (about 3 cups)
1 (16-ounce) package frozen mixed vegetables
⅓ cup reduced-fat mayonnaise
⅓ cup nonfat sour cream
½ cup sliced green onions
½ teaspoon pepper
½ teaspoon salt
1½ cups diced lean cooked ham

• **Cover** and cook potato in boiling water to cover 10 minutes or until tender (do not overcook); drain and set aside.
• **Cook** frozen mixed vegetables according to package directions, omitting salt and fat; drain and set aside.
• **Combine** mayonnaise and next 4 ingredients in a large bowl. Gently stir in potato, vegetables, and ham. Cover and chill at least 8 hours. **Yield:** 6 servings.

Per serving: Calories 207 (27% from fat)
Fat 6.1g (1.3g saturated)   Protein 13.1g   Carbohydrate 25.2g
Fiber 4.4g   Cholesterol 30mg   Sodium 924mg

Squash Dressing (page 118)

Side Dishes

Asparagus with Garlic Cream

LOW: • Calorie • Cholesterol • Sodium

Drizzle crisp-tender asparagus spears with a garlicky cream sauce; a sprinkling of fragrant snipped chives tops things off.

1 (8-ounce) carton reduced-fat sour cream
3 tablespoons skim milk
1 tablespoon white wine vinegar
2 cloves garlic, minced
⅛ teaspoon salt
⅛ teaspoon freshly ground pepper
2 pounds fresh asparagus
2 teaspoons chopped fresh chives

• **Stir** together first 6 ingredients. Cover and chill at least 2 hours.
• **Snap** off tough ends of asparagus; remove scales from stalks with a vegetable peeler, if desired.
• **Cover** and cook asparagus in a small amount of boiling water 4 minutes or until crisp-tender; drain. Plunge into ice water to stop the cooking process; drain. Cover and chill.
• **Serve** chilled asparagus on a serving platter. Top with sauce, and sprinkle with chives. **Yield:** 8 servings.

Per serving: Calories 58 (56% from fat)
Fat 3.6g (2.2g saturated) Protein 2.7g Carbohydrate 5.0g
Fiber 1.5g Cholesterol 11mg Sodium 51mg

Marinated Asparagus with Prosciutto

LOW: • Calorie • Cholesterol

Marinate this tender asparagus at least two hours to absorb the sweet-and-tangy honey-Dijon mixture. Use either lean ham or prosciutto to top this dish; ham is the lighter choice and is reflected in the nutritional analysis.

2 pounds fresh asparagus
½ cup vegetable broth
¼ cup white wine vinegar
2 tablespoons vegetable oil
2 tablespoons honey
2 tablespoons Dijon mustard
2 teaspoons dried tarragon
¼ pound thinly sliced lean cooked ham or prosciutto, cut into thin strips

• **Snap** off tough ends of asparagus; remove scales from stalks with a vegetable peeler, if desired.
• **Cover** and cook asparagus in a small amount of boiling water 4 minutes or until crisp-tender; drain. Plunge into ice water to stop the cooking process; drain. Place in a shallow baking dish; set aside.
• **Combine** broth and next 5 ingredients in a jar. Cover tightly, and shake vigorously. Pour over asparagus; cover and chill 2 to 4 hours.
• **Remove** asparagus, reserving marinade; arrange asparagus on a serving platter. Top with ham or prosciutto, and drizzle with reserved marinade. **Yield:** 8 servings.

Per serving: Calories 90 (47% from fat)
Fat 4.7g (0.9g saturated) Protein 4.9g Carbohydrate 8.3g
Fiber 0.8g Cholesterol 6mg Sodium 381mg

Broccoli with Stuffing

LOW: • Fat • Cholesterol

A mouth-watering mixture of sharp Cheddar, creamy mushroom soup, and crunchy seasoned stuffing mix enhances the fresh flavor of broccoli spears.

2 (10-ounce) packages frozen broccoli spears
Butter-flavored vegetable cooking spray
1 cup (4 ounces) shredded reduced-fat sharp
    Cheddar cheese
½ cup egg substitute
1 (10¾-ounce) can reduced-fat, reduced-
    sodium cream of mushroom soup,
    undiluted
½ cup nonfat mayonnaise
½ cup finely chopped onion
1 (6-ounce) box reduced-sodium stuffing mix
    for chicken

• **Cook** broccoli according to package directions; drain.
• **Arrange** broccoli in an 11- x 7- x 1½-inch baking dish coated with cooking spray. Sprinkle with cheese.
• **Combine** egg substitute and next 3 ingredients; spread over cheese.
• **Combine** ¾ cup stuffing mix and 2½ teaspoons of the mix's seasoning packet, tossing well. Reserve remaining stuffing mix and seasoning packet for another use. Sprinkle over casserole; coat with cooking spray.
• **Bake** at 350° for 30 minutes or until thoroughly heated. **Yield:** 8 servings.

Per serving: Calories 134 (28% from fat)
Fat 4.1g (1.9g saturated)   Protein 8.9g   Carbohydrate 16.1g
Fiber 1.7g   Cholesterol 13mg   Sodium 537mg

Braised Red Cabbage

LOW: • Fat • Calorie • Cholesterol • Sodium

Thin slices of red cabbage are simmered in tangy red wine vinegar until crisp-tender, and then mixed with aromatic bits of onion and garlic.

Olive oil-flavored vegetable cooking spray
1 teaspoon olive oil
1 small onion, chopped
1 clove garlic, minced
½ teaspoon dried thyme
½ teaspoon celery seeds
¼ teaspoon salt
¼ teaspoon ground white pepper
2 bay leaves
1½ quarts water
1 cup red wine vinegar
1 small red cabbage, thinly sliced (8 cups)
2 tablespoons red wine vinegar
¼ cup canned reduced-sodium chicken broth

• **Coat** a large nonstick skillet with cooking spray; add oil. Place over medium-high heat until hot. Add onion and garlic; cook, stirring constantly, until onion is tender. Stir in thyme and next 4 ingredients; cook 30 seconds. Remove from heat, and set aside.
• **Combine** water and 1 cup vinegar in a large Dutch oven; bring to a boil. Add cabbage, and cook 10 seconds, stirring constantly; drain. Add cabbage, 2 tablespoons vinegar, and chicken broth to onion mixture; bring to a boil.
• **Cover,** reduce heat, and simmer 15 minutes or until cabbage is crisp-tender. Remove and discard bay leaves. **Yield:** 8 servings.

Per serving: Calories 32 (25% from fat)
Fat 0.9g (0.1g saturated)   Protein 1.1g   Carbohydrate 5.9g
Fiber 1.5g   Cholesterol 0mg   Sodium 98mg

Corn Pudding

LOW: • Fat • Cholesterol

If you use plump milky kernels of fresh sweet corn, the whipping cream, butter, and eggs from the original recipe really aren't necessary. Evaporated skimmed milk, a bit of margarine, and egg substitute keep our pudding creamy and low in fat.

¼ cup sugar
¼ cup all-purpose flour
2 teaspoons baking powder
1 teaspoon salt
2 cups evaporated skimmed milk
1½ cups egg substitute
2 tablespoons margarine, melted
6 cups fresh corn kernels (about 12 ears)
Vegetable cooking spray

• **Combine** first 4 ingredients; set aside.
• **Combine** skimmed milk, egg substitute, and margarine in a large bowl. Gradually add sugar mixture, stirring until smooth. Stir in corn. Pour mixture into a 13- x 9- x 2-inch baking dish coated with cooking spray.
• **Bake**, uncovered, at 350° for 40 to 45 minutes or until deep golden and set. Let stand 5 minutes before serving. **Yield:** 8 servings.

Note: If fresh sweet corn is out of season, you can use frozen whole kernel corn that's been thawed and drained.

Per serving: Calories 243 (17% from fat)
Fat 4.5g (0.9g saturated)   Protein 13.7g   Carbohydrate 40.8g
Fiber 4.0g   Cholesterol 3mg   Sodium 486mg

Curried Corn and Sweet Red Peppers

LOW: • Fat • Calorie • Cholesterol • Sodium

This simple side dish exudes vibrant curry flavor. We like it alongside chicken or pork tenderloin.

1 tablespoon reduced-calorie margarine
¼ cup chopped red bell pepper
1 (15¼-ounce) can whole kernel corn, drained
1 teaspoon curry powder
⅛ teaspoon pepper
½ teaspoon cornstarch
¼ cup evaporated skimmed milk

• **Melt** margarine in a medium nonstick skillet over medium heat; add red pepper, and cook, stirring constantly, until tender. Stir in corn, curry powder, and pepper; cook 3 minutes, stirring often.
• **Combine** cornstarch and skimmed milk, stirring until smooth. Add to corn mixture, and cook, stirring constantly, until mixture thickens. **Yield:** 3 servings.

Per serving: Calories 114 (24% from fat)
Fat 3.0g (0.6g saturated)   Protein 3.8g   Carbohydrate 20.2g
Fiber 1.1g   Cholesterol 1mg   Sodium 293mg

Curried Corn and Sweet Red Peppers

Balsamic-Flavored Eggplant

A splash of balsamic vinegar brightens the subtle flavors of these grilled vegetables.

2 medium tomatoes, sliced
1 medium-size purple onion, sliced and separated into rings
12 pitted ripe olives, drained
¾ cup balsamic vinegar
1 medium eggplant
½ teaspoon salt
Olive oil-flavored vegetable cooking spray
6 ounces part-skim firm farmer cheese, cut into ½-inch cubes

• **Combine** first 3 ingredients in a shallow dish; drizzle with vinegar. Cover and chill 2 hours.
• **Cut** eggplant into 1-inch slices. Sprinkle both sides of slices with salt; drain on paper towels 30 minutes. Rinse and pat dry. Coat both sides of slices with cooking spray.
• **Cook,** covered with grill lid, over medium-hot coals (350° to 400°) about 4 minutes on each side or until tender. Remove from heat, and cool.
• **Remove** vegetables from marinade, reserving marinade.
• **Arrange** vegetables and eggplant slices on a serving plate. Sprinkle with cheese, and drizzle with ¼ cup marinade. **Yield:** 6 servings.

Per serving: Calories 162 (53% from fat)
Fat 9.6g (5.2g saturated)   Protein 9.1g   Carbohydrate 12.3g
Fiber 3.0g   Cholesterol 20mg   Sodium 578mg

Eggplant Parmigiana

LOW: • Fat

Tender eggplant slices have a spongelike capacity for soaking up oil when fried, so don't fry them. Coat the breaded eggplant slices with cooking spray instead, and bake them until crisp and golden.

12 ounces spaghetti, uncooked
½ cup egg substitute
¼ cup skim milk
1 tablespoon chopped fresh parsley
½ teaspoon garlic powder
¼ teaspoon salt
¼ teaspoon pepper
1 cup fine, dry breadcrumbs
½ cup grated Parmesan and Romano cheese blend, divided
¼ cup all-purpose flour
1 (1½-pound) eggplant, peeled and cut into ½-inch-thick slices
Vegetable cooking spray
1 (15½-ounce) jar no-salt-added spaghetti sauce
1½ cups (6 ounces) shredded part-skim mozzarella cheese

• **Cook** spaghetti according to package directions, omitting salt and fat; drain, set aside, and keep warm.
• **Combine** egg substitute and next 5 ingredients in a shallow bowl, stirring well; set aside.
• **Combine** breadcrumbs and 2 tablespoons cheese blend in a shallow bowl; set aside.
• **Place** flour in a large heavy-duty, zip-top plastic bag; add eggplant. Shake gently to coat.
• **Dip** eggplant in egg substitute mixture, and dredge in breadcrumb mixture. Place eggplant on a large baking sheet coated with cooking spray. Coat slices with cooking spray. Bake at 400° for 20 minutes or until lightly browned.
• **Arrange** half of eggplant slices in an 11- x 7- x 1½-inch baking dish coated with cooking spray. Spread half of spaghetti sauce over eggplant, and sprinkle with 3 tablespoons cheese blend. Repeat procedure.
• **Bake,** uncovered, at 350° for 25 minutes. Sprinkle with mozzarella cheese; bake 10 additional minutes or until cheese melts. Serve over spaghetti. **Yield:** 6 servings.

Per serving: Calories 509 (19% from fat)
Fat 10.9g (5.4g saturated)   Protein 25.7g   Carbohydrate 73.5g
Fiber 3.8g   Cholesterol 27mg   Sodium 649mg

Collard Greens

LOW: • Calorie • Cholesterol • Sodium

Collard greens seasoned with bacon drippings are a Southern classic, but we found that liquid smoke accents the greens in similar fashion without adding fat.

2 (2-pound) packages washed fresh collard
    greens
Vegetable cooking spray
2 teaspoons vegetable oil
½ cup chopped onion
1 (16-ounce) can reduced-sodium chicken broth
¼ cup water
½ teaspoon seasoned salt
½ teaspoon sugar
½ teaspoon freshly ground pepper
¼ teaspoon liquid smoke

• **Remove** coarse stems and discolored spots from greens; coarsely chop greens, and set aside.
• **Coat** a large Dutch oven with cooking spray. Add oil; place over medium-high heat until hot. Add onion; cook, stirring constantly, until tender. Add greens, broth, and remaining ingredients.
• **Bring** to a boil over medium-high heat. Cover, reduce heat, and simmer 1 hour or until tender. **Yield:** 6 servings.

Per serving: Calories 35 (44% from fat)
Fat 1.7g (0.3g saturated) Protein 1.6g Carbohydrate 3.4g
Fiber 0.7g Cholesterol 0mg Sodium 206mg

Turnip Greens

LOW: • Fat • Calorie • Cholesterol

Serve this popular soul food with our Oven-Fried Chicken (page 65) or Oven-Fried Catfish (page 74). If you can't find fresh greens, use three 10-ounce packages of frozen chopped turnip greens.

2 quarts water
1 teaspoon salt
3 pounds fresh turnip greens, trimmed and
    rinsed
2 tablespoons sugar
1 tablespoon hot sauce
1 tablespoon dry white wine
¼ pound lean cooked ham, chopped

• **Combine** water and salt in a stockpot, and bring to a boil.

• **Add** greens, a few at a time, to stockpot; add sugar, hot sauce, and wine. Cover and cook over medium heat 40 minutes.
• **Stir** in chopped ham, and cook 20 additional minutes or until greens are tender; drain. **Yield:** 9 servings.

Per serving: Calories 47 (15% from fat)
Fat 0.8g (0.3g saturated) Protein 3.5g Carbohydrate 6.8g
Fiber 1.6g Cholesterol 6mg Sodium 477mg

Mushroom Casserole

This strata-like dish is a must-try for mushroom lovers. We used the common button variety, but you can also use shiitake, crimini, or portobello. If you choose portobellos chop them instead of slicing them because they're so large.

1 tablespoon reduced-calorie stick margarine
3 (8-ounce) packages sliced fresh mushrooms
1¼ cups chopped onion
½ cup chopped celery
½ cup chopped green bell pepper
½ cup reduced-fat mayonnaise
8 (1-ounce) slices white bread, cut into 1-inch
    pieces
Vegetable cooking spray
½ cup egg substitute
1½ cups skim milk
1 (10¾-ounce) can reduced-fat cream of mush-
    room soup, undiluted
1 cup freshly grated Romano cheese

• **Melt** margarine in a large Dutch oven. Add mushrooms and next 3 ingredients, and cook over medium-high heat, stirring constantly, until tender; drain well. Stir in mayonnaise.
• **Place** half of bread evenly into a 13- x 9- x 2-inch baking dish coated with cooking spray. Spoon mushroom mixture evenly over bread. Top with remaining bread.
• **Combine** egg substitute and milk; pour over bread. Cover and chill at least 8 hours.
• **Pour** soup over casserole; top with cheese.
• **Bake**, uncovered, at 350° for 1 hour or until hot and bubbly. **Yield:** 8 servings.

Per serving: Calories 273 (42% from fat)
Fat 12.8g (4.7g saturated) Protein 13.4g Carbohydrate 24.4g
Fiber 2.5g Cholesterol 23mg Sodium 895mg

Grilled Shiitakes

Grilled Shiitakes

LOW: • Calorie • Cholesterol • Sodium

The simple ingredients in this recipe belie its complex, intriguing flavor. Shiitake mushrooms impart their bold, meaty taste, while generous amounts of garlic and freshly ground pepper add savory sparks. Large shiitakes are a must— they won't fall through the grill rack.

1 pound large fresh shiitake mushrooms
¼ cup chopped fresh parsley
¼ cup canned reduced-sodium chicken broth
3 tablespoons reduced-calorie margarine, melted
4 cloves garlic, minced
½ teaspoon freshly ground pepper
¼ teaspoon salt

• **Remove** stems from mushrooms; discard. Combine parsley and remaining 5 ingredients; brush evenly on both sides of mushroom caps.
• **Cook** mushrooms, without grill lid, over medium-hot coals (350° to 400°) 8 minutes, turning once. **Yield:** 4 servings.

Per serving: Calories 95 (54% from fat)
Fat 5.7g (0.1g saturated)   Protein 1.7g   Carbohydrate 12.4g
Fiber 1.7g   Cholesterol 0mg   Sodium 268mg

Grilled Stuffed Onions

LOW: • Fat • Cholesterol

We loaded sweet and juicy onions with sharp Cheddar and seasoned stuffing mix to create one of the best sides ever.

1 (6-ounce) box reduced-sodium stuffing mix for chicken
1 cup (4 ounces) shredded sharp reduced-fat Cheddar cheese
½ cup canned reduced-sodium chicken broth
2 tablespoons reduced-calorie margarine, melted
1 teaspoon poultry seasoning
6 medium-size sweet onions
Vegetable cooking spray
Garnish: fresh oregano sprigs

• **Combine** 1½ cups stuffing mix and 1½ tablespoons of the mix's seasoning packet in a medium bowl, tossing well. Reserve remaining stuffing mix and seasoning packet for another use. Add cheese and next 3 ingredients, stirring well; set aside.
• **Cut** each onion horizontally into 3 slices. Spread 2 tablespoons stuffing mixture between slices, and reassemble onions. Place each onion on a 12-inch-square piece of heavy-duty aluminum foil coated with cooking spray; bring opposite corners together, and twist foil to seal.
• **Cook,** covered with grill lid, over medium-hot coals (350° to 400°) 25 minutes or until tender. Garnish, if desired. **Yield:** 6 servings.

Per serving: Calories 222 (28% from fat)
Fat 7.0g (2.2g saturated)   Protein 10.5g   Carbohydrate 31.4g
Fiber 4.3g   Cholesterol 13mg   Sodium 362mg

Onion Pudding

LOW: • Fat • Cholesterol

*Sweet caramelized onions take center stage
in this exquisite pudding.*

¼ cup sugar
¼ cup all-purpose flour
2 teaspoons baking powder
1 teaspoon salt
2 cups evaporated skimmed milk
1½ cups egg substitute
2 tablespoons margarine, melted
Vegetable cooking spray
2 tablespoons margarine
6 cups thinly sliced sweet onion

• **Combine** first 4 ingredients; set aside.
• **Combine** skimmed milk, egg substitute, and 2 tablespoons melted margarine, stirring well. Gradually add flour mixture to milk mixture, stirring until smooth. Set aside.
• **Coat** a large Dutch oven with cooking spray, and add 2 tablespoons margarine. Place over medium-high heat until margarine melts. Add onion, and cook 20 minutes or until onion is caramel colored, stirring often. Stir onion mixture into milk mixture. Pour into a 13- x 9- x 2-inch baking dish coated with cooking spray.
• **Bake**, uncovered, at 350° for 30 minutes or until set. Let stand 5 minutes before serving. **Yield:** 8 servings.

Per serving: Calories 211 (26% from fat)
Fat 6.2g (1.2g saturated)   Protein 11.2g   Carbohydrate 28.3g
Fiber 2.4g   Cholesterol 3mg   Sodium 505mg

Buttermilk-Basil Mashed Potatoes

LOW: • Fat • Cholesterol

*A smattering of fresh basil for flavor and a
splash of buttermilk for fluff make a good thing
even better in these spunky spuds.*

3½ pounds baking potatoes, peeled and cut
    into 1-inch pieces
1 onion, chopped
3 stalks celery, cut in half
12 cloves garlic, peeled
½ teaspoon salt
¾ cup nonfat cottage cheese
½ cup nonfat buttermilk
2 to 4 tablespoons chopped fresh basil
1 teaspoon salt
¼ teaspoon freshly ground pepper

• **Combine** first 5 ingredients in a Dutch oven; add water to cover. Bring to a boil over high heat; reduce heat, and simmer 20 minutes or until potato is tender. Drain; remove and discard celery. Mash potato mixture.
• **Position** knife blade in food processor bowl; add cottage cheese and buttermilk. Process until smooth, stopping once to scrape down sides.
• **Add** cottage cheese mixture to potato mixture; stirring until smooth. Stir in basil, 1 teaspoon salt, and pepper.
• **Cook** over low heat until thoroughly heated. Serve immediately. **Yield:** 8 servings.

Per serving: Calories 205 (1% from fat)
Fat 0.3g (0.1g saturated)   Protein 10.9g   Carbohydrate 41.2g
Fiber 3.8g   Cholesterol 2mg   Sodium 639mg

Roasted Garlic Mashed Potatoes

LOW: • Fat • Cholesterol • Sodium

The mellow sweetness of roasted garlic permeates this crowd-pleaser. If you prefer a smoother version, puree the garlic pulp.

4 heads garlic
1 tablespoon olive oil
4 pounds baking potatoes, peeled and cut into
   1-inch pieces
3 tablespoons reduced-calorie margarine
1 cup skim milk
1 teaspoon salt
½ teaspoon pepper

- **Place** garlic on a square of aluminum foil; drizzle with oil, and wrap in foil.
- **Bake** at 425° for 30 minutes; set aside.
- **Cook** potato in boiling water to cover 15 to 20 minutes or until tender; drain. Transfer to a large mixing bowl of a heavy-duty electric mixer. Add margarine and remaining 3 ingredients; beat at medium speed 2 minutes or until fluffy.
- **Cut** off ends of garlic; squeeze pulp from cloves. Stir into potato mixture. **Yield:** 11 servings.

Per serving: Calories 192 (16% from fat)
Fat 3.4g (0.7g saturated) Protein 4.6g Carbohydrate 36.7g
Fiber 2.5g Cholesterol 0mg Sodium 268mg

Peppery Potato Casserole

LOW: • Fat • Cholesterol

There's pepper aplenty in this cheese-sauced potato casserole—green bell, jalapeño, and black.

8 large baking potatoes, unpeeled (about
   5 pounds)
Vegetable cooking spray
1 tablespoon reduced-calorie margarine
1 cup chopped green bell pepper
1 small jalapeño pepper, seeded and minced
2 cloves garlic, minced
1½ tablespoons all-purpose flour
1½ cups skim milk
12 ounces reduced-fat loaf process cheese
   spread
¼ teaspoon salt
¼ teaspoon pepper

- **Cook** potatoes in boiling water to cover 25 minutes or until tender; drain and cool.
- **Coat** a Dutch oven with cooking spray; add margarine. Place over medium-high heat until margarine melts. Add green pepper, jalapeño, and garlic, and cook, stirring constantly, until tender. Remove vegetables from pan; set aside.
- **Combine** flour and milk, stirring until smooth. Gradually add milk mixture to pan. Cook over medium heat, stirring constantly, until mixture is thickened and bubbly.
- **Stir** in cheese, and cook, stirring constantly, until cheese melts. Remove from heat.
- **Peel** potatoes, and cut into thin slices. Layer potato in a 13- x 9- x 2-inch baking dish coated with cooking spray. Sprinkle each layer evenly with vegetable mixture, salt, and pepper.
- **Spoon** cheese mixture over potato. Bake, uncovered, at 375° for 30 minutes or until thoroughly heated. **Yield:** 12 servings.

Per serving: Calories 232 (16% from fat)
Fat 4.0g (2.1g saturated) Protein 11.7g Carbohydrate 36.3g
Fiber 3.4g Cholesterol 11mg Sodium 509mg

Rutabaga Whip

LOW: • Fat • Cholesterol • Sodium

Whip mellow rutabagas and humble potatoes into this rich, distinctive side dish.

2 pounds rutabagas, peeled and chopped
6 cups water
2 pounds baking potatoes, peeled and chopped
¼ cup plus 2 tablespoons evaporated skimmed
   milk
2 tablespoons reduced-calorie margarine,
   softened
2 tablespoons reduced-fat sour cream
½ teaspoon salt
½ teaspoon pepper

- **Combine** rutabagas and water in a Dutch oven; bring to a boil, and cook 15 minutes. Add potato, and cook 15 minutes or until tender; drain.
- **Combine** vegetables, skimmed milk, and remaining ingredients in a large mixing bowl. Beat at medium speed with an electric mixer until fluffy. **Yield:** 7 servings.

Per serving: Calories 175 (15% from fat)
Fat 3.0g (0.7g saturated) Protein 4.6g Carbohydrate 33.5g
Fiber 2.8g Cholesterol 2mg Sodium 244mg

Sweet Potato-Eggnog Casserole

Sweet Potato-Eggnog Casserole

LOW: • Fat • Cholesterol • Sodium

Turn this sweet side into holiday fare with brandy-soaked golden raisins and a touch of eggnog. Crumbled fat-free oatmeal cookies adorn it.

5 pounds large sweet potatoes
½ cup golden raisins
2 tablespoons brandy
2 tablespoons hot water
⅔ cup refrigerated eggnog
2 tablespoons sugar
1 tablespoon reduced-calorie margarine, melted
⅛ teaspoon salt
Oatmeal Cookie Topping

• **Cook** sweet potatoes in water to cover in a large Dutch oven 40 minutes or until tender; drain sweet potatoes, and cool to touch. Peel sweet potatoes, and mash.
• **Combine** raisins, brandy, and water; let stand 30 minutes. Drain.
• **Combine** mashed sweet potato, eggnog, and next 3 ingredients; reserve 2 cups sweet potato mixture. Stir raisin mixture into remaining sweet potato mixture. Spoon into a 2-quart baking dish. Sprinkle top with Oatmeal Cookie Topping.
• **Pipe** or dollop reserved 2 cups sweet potato mixture around edge of casserole.
• **Bake**, uncovered, at 350° for 20 minutes. **Yield:** 8 servings.

Oatmeal Cookie Topping

2 (3-inch) fat-free oatmeal cookies, crumbled
2 tablespoons dark brown sugar
2 tablespoons chopped pecans, toasted

• **Combine** all ingredients in a small bowl. **Yield:** ½ cup.

Per serving: Calories 356 (10% from fat)
Fat 4.1g (1.2g saturated)   Protein 5.9g   Carbohydrate 73.7g
Fiber 4.9g   Cholesterol 12mg   Sodium 276mg

Sweet Potato Peaks

LOW: • Fat • Cholesterol • Sodium

Peaks of mashed sweet potato seem an unlikely topping for pineapple slices, but with a sweet and crunchy cereal-pecan coating, they're sure to win raves.

2 cups mashed cooked sweet potato, cooled
½ cup sugar
⅓ cup crushed corn flakes cereal
1 tablespoon margarine, softened
½ teaspoon ground cinnamon
½ cup finely chopped pecans
½ cup crushed corn flakes cereal
1 (15¼-ounce) can unsweetened sliced pineapple, undrained
Vegetable cooking spray
2 tablespoons honey

• **Combine** first 5 ingredients, stirring until blended; shape into 8 cones. Coat cones with pecans and ½ cup crushed cereal; cover and chill at least 4 hours.
• **Drain** pineapple, reserving juice. Arrange pineapple slices in a single layer in an 11- x 7- x 1½-inch baking dish coated with cooking spray; place cones upright on pineapple rings, and set aside.
• **Combine** 2 tablespoons reserved pineapple juice and honey; set aside. Reserve remaining juice for another use.
• **Bake** sweet potato cones, uncovered, at 350° for 30 minutes, spooning honey mixture over cones during last 10 minutes of baking. **Yield:** 8 servings.

Per serving: Calories 232 (25% from fat)
Fat 6.4g (0.7g saturated)   Protein 2.0g   Carbohydrate 43.7g
Fiber 1.9g   Cholesterol 0mg   Sodium 99mg

Spinach-Artichoke Bake

This casserole may not win a beauty contest, but it more than makes up for its simple look in rich taste. It's best served with roasted chicken or beef.

2 (10-ounce) packages frozen chopped spinach
Vegetable cooking spray
1 tablespoon reduced-calorie margarine
½ cup finely chopped onion
1 (14-ounce) can quartered artichoke hearts, drained
1 (16-ounce) carton reduced-fat sour cream
¼ teaspoon salt
¼ teaspoon pepper
½ cup freshly grated Parmesan cheese, divided

• **Cook** spinach according to package directions; drain well, pressing between layers of paper towels to remove excess moisture. Set spinach aside.

• **Coat** a large nonstick skillet with cooking spray; add margarine. Place over medium heat until margarine melts. Add onion; cook until tender. Gently stir in spinach, artichoke hearts, and next 3 ingredients; stir in ¼ cup Parmesan cheese.

• **Spoon** mixture into a 1½-quart casserole coated with cooking spray; sprinkle with remaining ¼ cup Parmesan cheese.

• **Bake,** uncovered, at 350° for 25 to 30 minutes or until hot and bubbly. **Yield:** 6 servings.

Per serving: Calories 199 (60% from fat)
Fat 13.3g (7.5g saturated)   Protein 9.9g   Carbohydrate 12.9g
Fiber 3.3g   Cholesterol 35mg   Sodium 406mg

Spinach Squares

These quiche-like squares of spinach, rice, and Swiss cheese are moistened with a creamy mushroom soup mixture.

2 (10-ounce) packages frozen chopped spinach, thawed
1 cup cooked rice (cooked without salt or fat)
1 cup (4 ounces) shredded reduced-fat Swiss cheese
¼ cup sliced green onions
1 (10¾-ounce) can reduced-fat cream of mushroom soup, undiluted
¾ cup egg substitute
⅛ teaspoon salt
⅛ teaspoon pepper
⅛ teaspoon dried basil
⅛ teaspoon dried oregano
Vegetable cooking spray
¼ cup soft breadcrumbs
2 tablespoons grated Parmesan cheese
1 tablespoon reduced-calorie margarine, melted

• **Drain** spinach well, pressing between layers of paper towels to remove excess moisture.

• **Combine** spinach and next 3 ingredients in a large bowl; set aside. Combine mushroom soup and next 5 ingredients; add to spinach mixture, stirring well. Spoon into an 8-inch square baking dish coated with cooking spray.

• **Combine** breadcrumbs, Parmesan cheese, and margarine; sprinkle over spinach mixture.

• **Bake,** uncovered, at 325° for 40 minutes or until thoroughly heated. Let stand 10 minutes before cutting into squares; serve immediately. **Yield:** 6 servings.

Per serving: Calories 189 (36% from fat)
Fat 7.6g (3.5g saturated)   Protein 13.1g   Carbohydrate 18.4g
Fiber 3.7g   Cholesterol 17mg   Sodium 640mg

Squash Soufflé

Buttery cracker crumbs and extra sharp Cheddar fill this yellow squash dish with rich, golden goodness.

1 pound yellow squash, chopped
1 medium onion, chopped
1 tablespoon reduced-calorie margarine
1½ cups (6 ounces) shredded reduced-fat extra sharp Cheddar cheese, divided
1½ cups reduced-fat round buttery cracker crumbs, divided
¼ cup skim milk
¼ teaspoon salt
¼ teaspoon pepper
¾ cup egg substitute
Vegetable cooking spray

• **Cook** squash and onion in boiling water to cover 5 minutes or until tender; drain and mash.
• **Add** margarine, 1¼ cups cheese, 1¼ cups cracker crumbs, milk, salt, and pepper. Stir in egg substitute.
• **Spoon** mixture into a 2-quart casserole coated with cooking spray. Sprinkle with remaining ¼ cup cheese and ¼ cup cracker crumbs.
• **Bake**, uncovered, at 350° for 45 minutes or until puffed and golden. **Yield:** 6 servings.

Per serving: Calories 228 (41% from fat)
Fat 10.5g (4.7g saturated)   Protein 11.7g   Carbohydrate 19.6g
Fiber 1.7g   Cholesterol 20mg   Sodium 571mg

Microwave Ratatouille

LOW: • Calorie • Cholesterol • Sodium

This eggplant medley typically calls for cooking the vegetables in olive oil. Use your microwave oven instead to eliminate the oil and to get the ratatouille to the table in record time.

3 cups chopped unpeeled eggplant
2 cups chopped yellow squash
2 cups chopped zucchini
1 red bell pepper, chopped
1 yellow bell pepper, chopped
Vegetable cooking spray
1 medium onion, chopped
4 cloves garlic, minced
1½ cups spaghetti sauce
¼ cup coarsely chopped fresh flat-leaf parsley
1 teaspoon dried oregano
1 teaspoon dried thyme
1 tablespoon finely chopped fresh basil

• **Place** eggplant in a 9-inch pieplate; cover with a paper towel, and microwave at HIGH 4 minutes. Transfer to a large bowl. Repeat procedure with squash, zucchini, and peppers. Set vegetable mixture aside.
• **Coat** a very large skillet or Dutch oven with cooking spray; place over medium heat until hot. Add onion and garlic, and cook, stirring constantly, until tender.
• **Stir** in vegetable mixture, spaghetti sauce, and next 3 ingredients. Cook 4 minutes, stirring occasionally. Stir in basil. **Yield:** 6 servings.

Per serving: Calories 97 (36% from fat)
Fat 3.9g (0.1g saturated)   Protein 2.9g   Carbohydrate 15.4g
Fiber 2.0g   Cholesterol 0mg   Sodium 272mg

Vegetarian Sauté

Vegetarian Sauté

LOW: • Cholesterol

A satisfying measure of extra sharp Cheddar cheese melts invitingly atop this one-skillet stew of beans and vegetables.

Vegetable cooking spray
1 tablespoon olive oil
1 medium onion, chopped
1 medium-size green bell pepper, chopped
1 medium zucchini, chopped
2 cloves garlic, minced
1 stalk celery, chopped
1 (14.5-ounce) can no-salt-added stewed
   tomatoes
1 (15-ounce) can dark red kidney beans,
   drained
1 tablespoon sugar
½ teaspoon dried oregano
¼ teaspoon salt
¼ teaspoon pepper
½ cup (2 ounces) shredded reduced-fat extra
   sharp Cheddar cheese

• **Coat** a large nonstick skillet with cooking spray; add oil. Place over medium-high heat until hot. Add onion and next 4 ingredients; cook, stirring constantly, until tender.
• **Stir** in tomatoes and next 5 ingredients. Bring to a boil; reduce heat to medium, and cook, uncovered, 5 minutes or until liquid is almost absorbed, stirring often. Sprinkle with cheese. Serve immediately. **Yield:** 4 servings.

Per serving: Calories 198 (32% from fat)
Fat 7.1g (2.5g saturated)   Protein 9.2g   Carbohydrate 25.9g
Fiber 6.1g   Cholesterol 10mg   Sodium 505mg

Hot Tomato Grits

LOW: • Fat • Cholesterol

Sometimes less is more, as in the case of these cheese grits. Switching to sharp reduced-fat Cheddar let us halve the original amount of regular Cheddar and keep the pleasant pungency. Smoky bits of turkey bacon heighten the cheese flavor even more.

1 slice turkey bacon, chopped
2 (14½-ounce) cans ready-to-serve chicken
   broth
1 cup quick-cooking grits
2 large ripe tomatoes, peeled and chopped
2 tablespoons canned chopped green chiles
½ cup (2 ounces) shredded reduced-fat sharp
   Cheddar cheese

• **Cook** chopped bacon in a large heavy saucepan over medium heat until browned, stirring often. Gradually add broth; bring to a boil.
• **Stir** in grits, tomatoes, and chiles; return to a boil, stirring often. Reduce heat, and simmer 15 to 20 minutes, stirring often.
• **Stir** in cheese; cover and let stand 5 minutes or until cheese melts. **Yield:** 6 servings.

Per serving: Calories 161 (23% from fat)
Fat 4.1g (1.6g saturated)   Protein 7.5g   Carbohydrate 24.1g
Fiber 2.1g   Cholesterol 9mg   Sodium 819mg

Tomato-Basil Risotto

LOW: • Fat • Cholesterol

*The key to making risotto creamy is to add
the warm broth to the rice mixture a small amount
at a time and then stir constantly until the liquid is
absorbed before adding more. The rice will remain
creamy, and the grains separate and firm.*

8 cups canned reduced-sodium chicken broth
2 tablespoons reduced-calorie margarine,
　　divided
¼ cup chopped onion
3 cups chopped plum tomatoes (about
　　6 tomatoes)
2 cups Arborio rice
¼ cup chopped fresh basil
¼ cup grated Parmesan cheese
¼ teaspoon salt
¼ teaspoon pepper

• **Cook** broth in a saucepan over medium heat
until hot.
• **Melt** 1 tablespoon margarine in a large
Dutch oven over medium-high heat; add onion,
and cook 2 minutes, stirring constantly.
• **Add** tomato; cook 2 minutes, stirring constantly. Add rice, and cook 5 minutes, stirring
constantly. Reduce heat to medium.
• **Add** broth, ½ cup at a time, stirring constantly; allow rice to absorb liquid before adding
more broth.
• **Stir** in remaining 1 tablespoon margarine,
chopped basil, and remaining ingredients. **Yield:**
7 servings.

Per serving:　Calories 264 (12% from fat)
Fat 3.5g (1.0g saturated)　Protein 7.3g　Carbohydrate 49.8g
Fiber 1.9g　Cholesterol 2mg　Sodium 724mg

Lemon-Garlic Pasta

LOW: • Fat • Cholesterol • Sodium

*Simplicity makes this dish special.
With so few ingredients, fresh garlic and
lemon juice are a must.*

8 ounces thin spaghetti, uncooked
4 cloves garlic, minced
1 tablespoon reduced-calorie margarine,
　　melted
1 tablespoon olive oil
3 tablespoons fresh lemon juice
3 tablespoons canned reduced-sodium chicken
　　broth
¼ teaspoon salt
½ teaspoon pepper
⅓ cup chopped fresh parsley

• **Cook** spaghetti according to package directions, omitting salt and fat; drain and set aside.
• **Cook** garlic in margarine and olive oil in a
large skillet over medium-high heat, stirring constantly, until lightly browned. Add lemon juice
and next 3 ingredients.
• **Bring** to a boil; pour mixture over pasta. Add
parsley; toss gently. Serve immediately. **Yield:** 4
servings.

Per serving:　Calories 272 (20% from fat)
Fat 6.1g (1.0g saturated)　Protein 7.9g　Carbohydrate 45.6g
Fiber 1.6g　Cholesterol 0mg　Sodium 206mg

French Onion Casserole

*Echoing the flavors of French onion soup,
this creamy casserole soaks the bread mixture
in a mushroom sauce.*

3 medium-size sweet onions
Vegetable cooking spray
1 tablespoon reduced-calorie margarine
1 (8-ounce) package fresh mushrooms, sliced
2 cups (8 ounces) shredded reduced-fat Swiss
    cheese, divided
1 (10¾-ounce) can reduced-fat, reduced-
    sodium cream of mushroom soup,
    undiluted
⅔ cup evaporated skimmed milk
2 teaspoons reduced-sodium soy sauce
6 (½-inch-thick) slices French bread
¼ cup finely chopped fresh parsley

• **Cut** onions crosswise into ¼-inch slices; cut each slice in half.
• **Coat** a large nonstick skillet with cooking spray; add margarine, and place over medium-high heat until hot. Add onions and mushrooms, and cook, stirring constantly, until tender.
• **Spoon** mixture into a 2-quart baking dish coated with cooking spray. Sprinkle with 1 cup cheese.
• **Combine** soup, evaporated milk, and soy sauce, stirring well; pour over cheese. Top with bread slices, and sprinkle with remaining 1 cup cheese and parsley.
• **Cover** and chill 4 to 8 hours. Remove baking dish from refrigerator, and let stand at room temperature 30 minutes.
• **Cover** and bake at 375° for 30 minutes. Uncover and bake 15 additional minutes or until thoroughly heated. Let stand 5 minutes before serving. **Yield:** 6 servings.

Per serving: Calories 275 (37% from fat)
Fat 11.3g (5.9g saturated) Protein 17.0g Carbohydrate 27.1g
Fiber 3.0g Cholesterol 33mg Sodium 439mg

Nannie's Cornbread Dressing

LOW: • Fat

*Bits of fresh jalapeño pepper distinguish this
go-with-everything dressing. Some people might
mistake it for a potato casserole because it's so light
in color—until they take the first scrumptious bite.*

2 cups self-rising flour
1 cup self-rising white cornmeal
2 cups nonfat buttermilk
⅓ cup margarine, melted
1 large egg, lightly beaten
2 egg whites, lightly beaten
Vegetable cooking spray
1 cup chopped celery
1 medium onion, chopped
1 jalapeño pepper, seeded and chopped
¼ teaspoon pepper
3 cups canned reduced-sodium chicken broth
⅛ teaspoon paprika
Garnish: celery leaves

• **Combine** flour and cornmeal in a large bowl; make a well in center of mixture.
• **Combine** buttermilk and next 3 ingredients, stirring well; add to dry ingredients, stirring just until moistened. Spoon batter into a 9-inch square pan coated with cooking spray.
• **Bake,** uncovered, at 400° for 25 minutes or until golden. Cool in pan on a wire rack, and crumble cornbread into a large bowl.
• **Add** celery and next 3 ingredients, stirring well. Stir in chicken broth. (Mixture will be thick and moist.) Lightly spoon into a 13- x 9-x 2-inch baking dish coated with cooking spray (do not pack down).
• **Bake,** uncovered, at 350° for 35 minutes or until lightly browned. Sprinkle with paprika. Garnish, if desired. **Yield:** 8 servings.

Per serving: Calories 286 (30% from fat)
Fat 9.4g (2.0g saturated) Protein 9.9g Carbohydrate 40.4g
Fiber 0.7g Cholesterol 30mg Sodium 960mg

Sausage-Cornbread Dressing

We liked this hearty dressing so much that we gave it our highest rating. One of the secrets in keeping its full flavor is using turkey breakfast sausage in place of pork sausage.

2 (7½-ounce) packages complete yellow corn muffin mix
Vegetable cooking spray
1 pound freshly ground turkey breakfast sausage
2 cups chopped onion
1¾ cups chopped celery
3 cups white bread cubes, toasted
2 teaspoons rubbed sage
1 teaspoon pepper
4 cups canned reduced-sodium chicken broth
½ cup egg substitute

• **Prepare** muffin mix according to package directions for cornbread, using skim milk. Let cool, and crumble; set aside.
• **Coat** a large nonstick skillet with cooking spray. Place over medium heat until hot. Add sausage, onion, and celery; cook, stirring constantly, until sausage crumbles and vegetables are tender. Drain and pat dry with paper towels.
• **Combine** cornbread, bread cubes, sage, and pepper in a large bowl; stir in sausage mixture. Add chicken broth and egg substitute, stirring well. Spoon mixture into a 13- x 9- x 2-inch baking dish coated with cooking spray.
• **Bake**, uncovered, at 350° for 1 hour or until browned. **Yield:** 12 servings.

Note: For the corn muffin mix, we used Martha White brand that has egg in the mix.

Per serving: Calories 143 (33% from fat)
Fat 5.3g (3.0g saturated)   Protein 9.6g   Carbohydrate 13.8g
Fiber 1.2g   Cholesterol 24mg   Sodium 501mg

Squash Dressing

LOW: • Fat • Cholesterol • Sodium

Slices of yellow squash give this spicy Mexican cornbread dressing its unusual texture and taste.

2 (6-ounce) packages Mexican cornbread mix
2 pounds yellow squash, sliced
2 cups water
Vegetable cooking spray
2 tablespoons margarine, melted
1 cup chopped onion
1 cup chopped celery
½ cup chopped green bell pepper
½ cup sliced green onions
1 (10¾-ounce) can reduced-fat cream of chicken soup, undiluted
2 cups skim milk
¼ teaspoon pepper

• **Prepare** cornbread mix according to package directions, using skim milk. Let cool, and crumble; set aside.
• **Combine** squash and water in a large saucepan; bring to a boil. Cover, reduce heat, and simmer 8 minutes or until tender; drain well, and set aside.
• **Coat** a large nonstick skillet with cooking spray; add margarine. Place over medium-high heat until margarine melts. Add onion and next 3 ingredients, and cook, stirring constantly, until tender.
• **Combine** cornbread, squash, onion mixture, soup, and remaining ingredients, stirring gently. Spoon into a 13- x 9- x 2-inch baking dish coated with cooking spray.
• **Bake**, uncovered, at 350° for 40 minutes or until thoroughly heated. **Yield:** 10 servings.

Per serving: Calories 255 (14% from fat)
Fat 4.1g (1.1g saturated)   Protein 3.9g   Carbohydrate 11.0g
Fiber 2.5g   Cholesterol 9mg   Sodium 348mg

Chile Verde (page 124)

Soups, Sandwiches & Sauces

Chilled Cucumber-Buttermilk Soup

Snippets of fresh green onions, parsley, and dill briskly season and brightly color this cool cucumber soup.

5 cucumbers (about 2¾ pounds)
½ teaspoon salt
6 green onions, chopped
½ cup chopped fresh parsley
1 tablespoon chopped fresh dill
1 quart nonfat buttermilk
1 (16-ounce) carton reduced-fat sour cream
¼ cup lemon juice
¼ teaspoon salt
¼ teaspoon ground white pepper
Garnishes: thinly sliced cucumber, fresh
    parsley sprigs

• **Peel** cucumbers; cut in half lengthwise, and scoop out seeds. Place cucumber shells on a paper towel; sprinkle ½ teaspoon salt evenly over both sides of cucumber. Let stand 30 minutes. Drain; coarsely chop.
• **Combine** cucumber, green onions, and next 7 ingredients. Place one-third of mixture in container of an electric blender; process 1 minute or until smooth. Pour into a 3-quart container. Repeat procedure twice with remaining mixture. Cover and chill at least 3 hours. Garnish, if desired. **Yield: 11 cups.**

Per 1-cup serving: Calories 109 (45% from fat)
Fat 5.4g (3.4g saturated)   Protein 5.6g   Carbohydrate 10.8g
Fiber 1.5g   Cholesterol 19mg   Sodium 279mg

Macaroni and Cheese Soup

Tender morsels of macaroni and vegetables mingle in this velvety cheese soup. We first tried skim milk, but the soup was thin and watery. Using 1% low-fat milk made it rich tasting and creamy.

1 cup elbow macaroni, uncooked
Butter-flavored vegetable cooking spray
2 tablespoons margarine
½ cup finely chopped carrot
½ cup finely chopped celery
1 small onion, finely chopped
4 cups 1% low-fat milk
1 tablespoon chicken-flavored bouillon
    granules
½ teaspoon ground white pepper
2 tablespoons cornstarch
2 tablespoons water
6 ounces reduced-fat loaf process cheese
    spread, cubed
1 cup frozen whole kernel corn, thawed
½ cup frozen English peas, thawed

• **Cook** macaroni according to package directions, omitting salt and fat; drain. Rinse with cold water; drain and set aside.
• **Coat** a large skillet with cooking spray; add margarine. Place over medium-high heat until margarine melts. Add carrot, celery, and onion, and cook, stirring constantly, until tender. Remove vegetable mixture from heat; set aside.
• **Combine** milk, bouillon granules, and white pepper in a large saucepan. Combine cornstarch and water, stirring until smooth; stir into milk mixture. Stir in vegetable mixture, and cook over medium heat, stirring constantly, until mixture thickens and comes to a boil. Boil 1 minute, stirring constantly.
• **Add** cheese, and cook over medium heat, until cheese melts, stirring often.
• **Add** macaroni, corn, and peas; cook over low heat, stirring constantly, just until thoroughly heated. **Yield: 7 cups.**

Per 1-cup serving: Calories 181 (40% from fat)
Fat 8.1g (3.4g saturated)   Protein 12.3g   Carbohydrate 25.0g
Fiber 1.7g   Cholesterol 6mg   Sodium 839mg

Cream of Roasted Sweet Red Pepper Soup

LOW: • Fat • Calorie • Cholesterol

Roasting red bell peppers until their skins are charred and blistered brings out the sweetness of their crimson flesh. We found that the roasting method in this recipe is the quickest and easiest.

3 pounds red bell peppers (about 6 large)
Vegetable cooking spray
6 cloves garlic, minced
1 small onion, chopped
2 (10½-ounce) cans low-sodium chicken broth
1 cup dry white wine
1 bay leaf
½ teaspoon salt
¼ teaspoon pepper
2 tablespoons all-purpose flour
2 tablespoons water
1 (12-ounce) can evaporated skimmed milk
1 (8-ounce) carton nonfat sour cream
Garnish: fresh basil leaves, cut into thin strips

• **Cut** red bell peppers in half lengthwise; remove and discard seeds and membranes. Place peppers, skin side up, on a baking sheet; flatten with palm of hand. Broil peppers 5½ inches from heat (with electric oven door partially opened) 15 to 20 minutes or until charred. Place peppers in ice water until cool. Remove peppers from water; peel and discard skins. Coarsely chop peppers. Set aside.

• **Coat** a large Dutch oven with cooking spray, and place over medium-high heat until hot. Add garlic and onion; cook, stirring constantly, until tender. Add chicken broth and next 4 ingredients; bring to a boil. Reduce heat, and simmer, uncovered, 30 minutes. Pour broth mixture through a large wire-mesh strainer into a large container, reserving solids. Remove and discard bay leaf. Set broth mixture aside.

• **Position** knife blade in food processor bowl; add reserved solids and roasted peppers. Process 2 minutes or until pepper mixture is smooth, stopping twice to scrape down sides; set pepper puree aside.

• **Combine** flour and water in a Dutch oven, stirring until smooth. Add chicken broth mixture, stirring well. Cook over medium heat, stirring constantly, until mixture is thickened and bubbly. Stir in pepper puree. Gradually stir in evaporated milk and sour cream. Cook over low heat until thoroughly heated. Garnish, if desired. **Yield:** 8 cups.

Per 1-cup serving: Calories 139 (11% from fat)
Fat 1.7g (0.4g saturated) Protein 8.2g Carbohydrate 19.8g
Fiber 3.0g Cholesterol 3mg Sodium 258mg

Cream of Shiitake Soup

LOW: • Fat • Calorie • Cholesterol

Use shiitake mushrooms, with their full-bodied, steaklike flavor, to elevate cream of mushroom soup to new culinary heights. A creamy combo of evaporated skimmed milk and nonfat sour cream duplicates the texture of the whipping cream of the original recipe.

½ pound fresh shiitake mushrooms
3 tablespoons reduced-calorie margarine
2 cups chopped onion
3 tablespoons all-purpose flour
¼ teaspoon ground nutmeg
¼ teaspoon pepper
2 (14½-ounce) cans reduced-sodium chicken broth
1 (12-ounce) can evaporated skimmed milk
1 (8-ounce) carton nonfat sour cream

• **Remove** stems from mushrooms; discard. Finely chop mushroom caps.

• **Melt** margarine in a large saucepan over medium-high heat; add chopped mushroom caps and onion, and cook, stirring constantly, until tender.

• **Add** flour, nutmeg, and pepper; cook 1 minute, stirring constantly. Gradually add broth; cook, stirring constantly, until thickened. Remove from heat.

• **Gradually** stir skimmed milk into sour cream; stir sour cream mixture into broth mixture. Cook over low heat just until thoroughly heated. **Yield:** 7½ cups.

Per 1½-cup serving: Calories 194 (22% from fat)
Fat 4.8g (0.8g saturated) Protein 12.5g Carbohydrate 24.9g
Fiber 1.9g Cholesterol 3mg Sodium 628mg

Creamy Asparagus-and-Chicken Soup

*Spring green asparagus highlights this
splendid chicken soup, and nonfat sour cream gives
the broth richness and body. Be sure you cook
the soup over low heat after adding the sour cream.
If the soup boils, the sour cream might curdle.*

4 (4-ounce) skinned and boned chicken breast
　　halves
4 cups water
1 medium onion, quartered
2 large celery stalks, cut into 1-inch pieces
1 teaspoon salt
½ teaspoon pepper
1½ pounds fresh asparagus
1 cup nonfat sour cream
1 cup skim milk
Garnish: chopped fresh parsley

• **Combine** first 6 ingredients in a saucepan.
Bring to a boil; cover, reduce heat, and simmer
35 minutes or until chicken is tender.

• **Remove** chicken, reserving broth and vegetables in pan. Let chicken cool slightly; shred
into bite-size pieces. Set aside.

• **Snap** off tough ends of asparagus; remove
scales from stalks with a vegetable peeler, if
desired. Cut asparagus into 2-inch pieces; add to
reserved chicken broth and vegetables.

• **Bring** to a boil; cover, reduce heat, and simmer 10 minutes or until asparagus is tender.
Drain vegetable mixture, reserving broth in pan.

• **Position** knife blade in food processor bowl;
add vegetables and 1 cup reserved broth. Process
until smooth, stopping once to scrape down
sides. Add sour cream; process until smooth.

• **Gradually** add puree to broth remaining in
pan; stir in milk and chicken. Cook over low heat
until thoroughly heated (do not boil). Garnish, if
desired. **Yield:** 8 cups.

Per 1-cup serving:　Calories 119 (8% from fat)
Fat 1.0g (0.3g saturated)　Protein 18.2g　Carbohydrate 8.6g
Fiber 1.3g　Cholesterol 33mg　Sodium 386mg

Sweet Potato-and-Sausage Soup

*Smoky slices of sausage, shreds of fresh cabbage,
and soulful crowder peas impart a healthy dose of
heartiness to this chunky sweet potato soup.*

½ pound reduced-fat smoked sausage, cut into
　　½-inch slices
1 medium-size sweet potato, peeled and cut
　　into ½-inch cubes
1 cup coarsely shredded cabbage
½ cup chopped green bell pepper
½ cup chopped celery
½ cup chopped onion
1 (16-ounce) can no-salt-added tomatoes,
　　undrained and chopped
1 (15.8-ounce) can crowder peas, undrained
1 (14¼-ounce) can no-salt-added beef broth
¼ teaspoon hot sauce

• **Combine** all ingredients in a large Dutch
oven; bring to a boil over medium-high heat.
Cover, reduce heat, and simmer 30 minutes or
until potato is tender, stirring occasionally. **Yield:**
7 cups.

Per 1-cup serving:　Calories 310 (35% from fat)
Fat 11.9g (5.2g saturated)　Protein 15.9g　Carbohydrate 36.5g
Fiber 2.4g　Cholesterol 30mg　Sodium 886mg

Tamale Soup

You don't have to travel any farther than your pantry to cook up this snappy southwestern soup. Cans of creamed corn, pinto beans, stewed tomatoes, and tamales lead the way.

1 pound ground round
1 medium onion, chopped
1 green bell pepper, chopped
1 (14¼-ounce) can stewed tomatoes, undrained
2 (16-ounce) cans pinto beans, undrained
1 (15-ounce) can no-salt-added creamed corn
1 (14¼-ounce) can no-salt-added beef broth
2 (14.5-ounce) cans tamales, drained and cut into 1-inch pieces

• **Cook** first 3 ingredients in a large Dutch oven until meat is browned, stirring until meat crumbles. Drain and pat dry with paper towels. Wipe drippings from Dutch oven with paper towels. Add stewed tomatoes and next 3 ingredients; simmer, uncovered, 1 hour, stirring occasionally.
• **Stir** in tamale pieces, and serve immediately. **Yield:** 10 cups.

Per 1-cup serving: Calories 332 (31% from fat)
Fat 11.4g (3.8g saturated) Protein 17.9g Carbohydrate 38.8g
Fiber 8.2g Cholesterol 40mg Sodium 664mg

Five-Ingredient Chili

LOW: • Fat • Calorie

This brazen chili dares to be low fat, low calorie, and low effort—it has only five ingredients, and you can make it in mere minutes.

1½ pounds ground round
1 medium onion, chopped
4 (16-ounce) cans chili-hot beans, undrained
1 (1¾-ounce) package chili seasoning mix
1 (46-ounce) can no-salt-added tomato juice

• **Cook** ground round and onion in a Dutch oven, stirring until meat crumbles; drain. Stir in beans and remaining ingredients.
• **Bring** to a boil; reduce heat, and simmer, uncovered, 30 minutes or to desired consistency, stirring occasionally. **Yield:** 14 cups.

Per 1-cup serving: Calories 220 (16% from fat)
Fat 3.9g (1.6g saturated) Protein 17.8g Carbohydrate 26.1g
Fiber 6.2g Cholesterol 30mg Sodium 803mg

Black Bean Chili Marsala

LOW: • Fat • Calorie

Chunks of sirloin steak stud this hearty chili—it's thick with black beans and meaty mushrooms. Marsala wine adds a smoky touch. If you don't have a cup of this fortified wine on hand, substitute 1 cup of dry white wine plus 1½ tablespoons of brandy.

Vegetable cooking spray
1 large onion, chopped
2 cloves garlic, minced
1 (1½-pound) lean boneless top sirloin steak, trimmed and chopped
4 (8-ounce) cans tomato sauce
2 (6-ounce) cans tomato paste
3 (4-ounce) cans sliced mushrooms, drained
1 (14¼-ounce) can no-salt-added beef broth
1 cup Marsala wine
1 cup water
¼ cup chili powder
1 teaspoon seasoned salt
1 teaspoon salt-free herb-and-spice blend
1 teaspoon freshly ground pepper
2 (15-ounce) cans black beans, drained
4½ cups cooked long-grain rice (cooked without salt or fat)
Garnish: strips of lime rind or fresh cilantro sprigs

• **Coat** a large Dutch oven with cooking spray; place over medium-high heat until hot. Add onion and garlic, and cook, stirring constantly, until tender. Add meat and next 10 ingredients.
• **Bring** to a boil; cover, reduce heat, and simmer 1 hour, stirring occasionally.
• **Add** beans, and cook until thoroughly heated. Serve over rice. Garnish, if desired. **Yield:** 13½ cups.

Per 1-cup serving: Calories 272 (11% from fat)
Fat 3.4g (1.0g saturated) Protein 17.0g Carbohydrate 40.5g
Fiber 5.4g Cholesterol 26mg Sodium 1,001mg

Chili Verde

LOW: • Fat • Calorie

*Appease hearty appetites with this robust
two-meat chili. Red wine, salsa, green chiles,
and fresh cilantro flame the flavor.*

¾ pound lean boneless round steak, cut into
    1-inch cubes
¾ pound pork tenderloin, cut into 1-inch
    cubes
1 large onion, chopped
1 large green bell pepper, chopped
1 clove garlic, minced
Vegetable cooking spray
2 (14½-ounce) cans no-salt-added whole
    tomatoes, undrained and chopped
2 (4½-ounce) cans chopped green chiles,
    undrained
1 cup dry red wine
1 cup no-salt-added salsa
¼ cup chopped fresh cilantro
2 beef bouillon cubes
1 tablespoon brown sugar
3 tablespoons lemon juice
4 cups cooked long-grain rice (cooked without
    salt and fat)
Garnish: fresh cilantro sprigs

• **Combine** first 5 ingredients in a Dutch oven
coated with cooking spray. Cook over medium-
high heat, stirring constantly, until meat is
browned.
• **Add** tomatoes and next 7 ingredients. Bring
to a boil; cover, reduce heat, and simmer 1 hour
or until meat is tender, stirring occasionally.
Serve over rice; garnish, if desired. **Yield:** 8 cups.

Per 1-cup serving: Calories 295 (10% from fat)
Fat 3.2g (1.0g saturated)   Protein 22.9g   Carbohydrate 38.3g
Fiber 2.5g   Cholesterol 52mg   Sodium 345mg

Bell Pepper-Cheese Chowder

LOW: • Calorie • Cholesterol

*This is beer-cheese soup with an attitude. Bold
rosemary flaunts an herbal fragrance, while red
and yellow peppers add subtle sweetness.*

2 tablespoons margarine
1 cup chopped red bell pepper
1 cup chopped yellow bell pepper
½ cup chopped carrots
½ cup sliced celery
½ cup chopped onion
2 cloves garlic, minced
¾ cup all-purpose flour
3 cups 1% low-fat milk
2½ cups canned reduced-sodium chicken
    broth
½ teaspoon dry mustard
¼ teaspoon dried rosemary, crushed
¼ teaspoon salt
¼ teaspoon ground red pepper
½ teaspoon freshly ground black pepper
1½ cups (6 ounces) shredded reduced-fat
    sharp Cheddar cheese
1½ cups flat light beer
Garnish: fresh rosemary sprigs

• **Melt** margarine in a large Dutch oven over
medium-high heat. Add red bell pepper and next
5 ingredients; cook, stirring constantly, 5 minutes or until tender.
• **Combine** flour, milk, and chicken broth,
stirring until smooth. Gradually stir into vegetable mixture; cook, stirring constantly, until
thick and bubbly.
• **Stir** in mustard and next 4 ingredients; gradually add cheese and beer, stirring until cheese
melts. Garnish, if desired, and serve immediately. **Yield:** 10 cups.

Per 1-cup serving: Calories 167 (36% from fat)
Fat 6.6g (2.9g saturated)   Protein 9.7g   Carbohydrate 16.4g
Fiber 1.2g   Cholesterol 14mg   Sodium 395mg

Bell Pepper-Cheese Chowder

Open-Face Eggplant Sandwiches

LOW: • Fat • Cholesterol

Even the staunchest meat lover will enjoy this sandwich. It tricks the palate with thick slices of eggplant and savory seasonings—fennel seeds, hickory-flavored barbecue sauce, and tahini. Tahini is a thick paste made from ground sesame seeds. Look for it next to the peanut butter at most grocery stores.

¼ cup plain low-fat yogurt
1½ tablespoons tahini
1½ tablespoons water
1 tablespoon lemon juice
1 clove garlic, minced
Vegetable cooking spray
½ teaspoon fennel seeds
½ teaspoon ground cumin
½ teaspoon ground red pepper
1 small eggplant, cut into ½-inch-thick slices
    (about ¾ pound)
¼ cup hickory-flavored barbecue sauce
1 small onion, sliced and separated into
    rings
1 small green bell pepper, cut into rings
1 clove garlic, pressed
¼ cup dry red wine
1 medium tomato, sliced
4 (1-inch-thick) slices French bread,
    toasted

• **Combine** first 5 ingredients; set aside.
• **Coat** a 12-inch cast-iron or large electric skillet with cooking spray; heat over high heat until hot. Add fennel seeds, cumin, and red pepper; cook, stirring constantly, until toasted.
• **Brush** 1 side of each eggplant slice with barbecue sauce. Place slices, brushed side down, in skillet, and brush top sides with remaining sauce.
• **Cook** eggplant 1 to 2 minutes or until browned. Turn slices, and push to one side of skillet.
• **Add** onion, green pepper, and garlic to skillet; cook 1 to 2 minutes or until vegetables are slightly tender and eggplant is blackened, stirring frequently.
• **Add** wine; cover, reduce heat, and simmer 2 minutes. Remove vegetables from skillet, and keep warm.
• **Add** tomato slices to skillet; cook 1 minute on each side. Remove from skillet.

• **Place** 2 bread slices on each serving plate; top evenly with vegetables. Drizzle with yogurt mixture. Serve immediately. **Yield:** 2 servings.

Per serving: Calories 377 (26% from fat)
Fat 10.9g (1.7g saturated) Protein 12.6g Carbohydrate 61g
Fiber 7.6g Cholesterol 3mg Sodium 598mg

Italian Chicken-Mozzarella Melt

LOW: • Fat

A crusty bun and layers of mozzarella and Parmesan cheeses invite you to sample this shredded zucchini and pizzeria-style chicken sandwich.

4 (4-ounce) skinned and boned chicken breast
    halves
1 tablespoon olive oil
¼ teaspoon salt
½ teaspoon dried oregano, divided
1 cup pizza pasta sauce
½ teaspoon dried basil
4 (2.8-ounce) hoagie rolls, halved and toasted
1 small zucchini, shredded
¼ cup (2 ounces) shredded part-skim
    mozzarella cheese
¼ cup grated Parmesan cheese
Garnish: fresh basil sprigs

• **Brush** each piece of chicken with olive oil; sprinkle with salt and ¼ teaspoon oregano.
• **Cook** chicken in a large nonstick skillet over medium-high heat about 4 minutes on each side or until done. Set chicken aside.
• **Combine** pizza pasta sauce, basil, and remaining ¼ teaspoon oregano in skillet; cook over medium-high heat until thoroughly heated.
• **Remove** sauce from heat; add chicken, and keep warm.
• **Place** rolls on a baking sheet; spread sauce mixture evenly on bottom half of each roll. Top evenly with chicken, zucchini, and cheeses.
• **Broil** 3 inches from heat (with electric oven door partially opened) 2 to 3 minutes or until cheeses melt. Cover each bottom half with tops of rolls. Garnish, if desired. **Yield:** 4 servings.

Per serving: Calories 509 (26% from fat)
Fat 14.6g (3.2g saturated) Protein 41.7g Carbohydrate 50.9g
Fiber 2.1g Cholesterol 78mg Sodium 1,062mg

Italian Chicken-Mozzarella Melt

Tuna Burgers

LOW: • Fat

These hearty burgers burst with the bold flavors of garlic, onion, cracked pepper, and thyme.

3 (6-ounce) cans solid white tuna in spring
    water, drained and flaked
2 cups soft breadcrumbs
½ cup egg substitute
1 teaspoon low-sodium Worcestershire sauce
1 small onion, finely chopped
2 tablespoons dried parsley flakes
2 drops of hot sauce
1 teaspoon lemon juice
1 teaspoon salt-free lemon and pepper
    seasoning
½ teaspoon onion powder
½ teaspoon garlic powder
1 teaspoon cracked black pepper
½ teaspoon dried thyme
Vegetable cooking spray
6 kaiser rolls, split
6 lettuce leaves
6 slices tomato
¼ cup plus 2 tablespoons reduced-calorie
    mayonnaise
2 tablespoons sweet pickle relish

• **Combine** first 9 ingredients; shape tuna mixture into 6 patties.
• **Combine** onion powder and next 3 ingredients; sprinkle evenly on both sides of patties.
• **Cook** patties in a large nonstick skillet coated with cooking spray 4 minutes on each side or until done.
• **Place** each patty on a roll with lettuce and tomato slices; serve with mayonnaise and pickle relish. **Yield:** 6 servings.

Per serving: Calories 453 (22% from fat)
Fat 11.1g (1.2g saturated)   Protein 30.9g   Carbohydrate 56.4g
Fiber 1.7g   Cholesterol 35mg   Sodium 1,042mg

Green Tomato Sandwich Spread

LOW: • Fat • Calorie • Cholesterol

Green tomatoes don't have to be fried to be fabulous. Here's a versatile spread that's a must-try for an end-of-the-season stash. We liked it as a sandwich spread, especially on hot dogs and hamburgers.

3 medium-size green tomatoes, quartered
    (about 1¼ pounds)
1 medium onion, coarsely chopped
1 large green bell pepper, coarsely chopped
¾ teaspoon salt
½ cup sugar
⅓ cup white vinegar
2 tablespoons all-purpose flour
½ cup nonfat mayonnaise
2 tablespoons prepared mustard
2 tablespoons chopped pimiento-stuffed olives

• **Position** knife blade in food processor bowl; add half of first 3 ingredients. Process until finely chopped (do not puree), stopping once to scrape down sides. Repeat procedure with remaining half of first 3 ingredients.
• **Combine** tomato mixture and salt in a large nonaluminum saucepan; cover and let stand 2 to 3 hours.
• **Drain** tomato mixture, discarding liquid. Return tomato mixture to saucepan, and stir in sugar and vinegar; bring to a boil. Reduce heat, and simmer, uncovered, 10 minutes, stirring occasionally.
• **Combine** ½ cup tomato mixture and flour, stirring well. Return to remaining tomato mixture in pan; cook, stirring constantly, 5 minutes or until thickened. Remove from heat.
• **Stir** in mayonnaise, mustard, and olives; cool. Cover and store in refrigerator up to 1 week. **Yield:** 3½ cups.

Per 1-tablespoon serving: Calories 15 (6% from fat)
Fat 0.1g (0.0g saturated)   Protein 0.2g   Carbohydrate 3.5g
Fiber 0.3g   Cholesterol 0mg   Sodium 70mg

Roasted Red Bell Pepper Butter

LOW: • Cholesterol

Soft and satiny nonfat cream cheese melds with margarine to create the base for this spread. A roasted sweet red bell pepper illuminates the buttery blend with color and character.

1 large red bell pepper
½ cup margarine, softened
½ cup nonfat cream cheese, softened
½ teaspoon grated lemon rind
¼ teaspoon ground red pepper

• **Cut** pepper in half lengthwise; discard seeds and membrane. Place pepper, skin side up, on a baking sheet, and flatten with palm of hand.
• **Broil** 5½ inches from heat (with electric oven door partially opened) 15 to 20 minutes or until charred. Place in ice water until cool; peel and discard skins. Coarsely chop pepper.
• **Position** knife blade in food processor bowl; add margarine and next 3 ingredients. Process until smooth, stopping once to scrape sides.
• **Add** roasted pepper; pulse 3 or 4 times.
• **Serve** as a spread on French bread slices. **Yield:** 1½ cups.

Per 1-tablespoon serving: Calories 39 (87% from fat)
Fat 3.8g (0.8g saturated)   Protein 0.8g   Carbohydrate 0.6g
Fiber 0.1g   Cholesterol 1mg   Sodium 73mg

Blueberry Chutney

LOW: • Fat• Calorie • Cholesterol

Plump, smooth-skinned blueberries plus bits of fresh ginger, garlic, and mint are gilded with curry to make this pleasantly pungent accompaniment with chicken, turkey, lamb, or pork.

4 cups fresh or frozen blueberries
1 large onion, finely chopped
2 tablespoons minced fresh ginger
2 tablespoons minced garlic
¼ cup sugar
¼ cup raisins
¼ cup white wine vinegar
2 tablespoons curry powder
½ teaspoon salt
¼ cup chopped fresh mint

• **Combine** first 9 ingredients in a non-aluminum saucepan; bring to a boil over medium heat, stirring occasionally. Reduce heat, and cook 25 to 30 minutes or until mixture is thickened, stirring often. Remove from heat, and cool.
• **Stir** in mint. Cover and store in refrigerator up to 5 days. **Yield:** 3 cups.

Per 2-tablespoon serving: Calories 32 (5% from fat)
Fat 0.2g (0.0g saturated)   Protein 0.4g   Carbohydrate 8.0g
Fiber 1.5g   Cholesterol 0mg   Sodium 51mg

Brandied Cranberries

LOW: • Fat • Calorie • Cholesterol • Sodium

The sour juices of fresh cranberries are sugared and spiced during baking and then splashed with spirits before serving. This sweet-sour spread gives new meaning to sandwiches made with leftover turkey.

3 (12-ounce) packages fresh or frozen cranberries, thawed
Vegetable cooking spray
2 cups sugar
1 teaspoon ground cinnamon
½ teaspoon ground cloves
⅓ cup brandy
Garnish: fresh thyme sprigs

• **Place** cranberries in a single layer in two 15- x 10- x 1-inch jellyroll pans coated with cooking spray.
• **Combine** sugar, cinnamon, and cloves in a bowl; pour over cranberries. Cover tightly with aluminum foil.
• **Bake** at 350° for 1 hour.
• **Spoon** cranberries into a large serving bowl; gently stir in brandy. Cool.
• **Serve** chilled or at room temperature. Garnish, if desired. Cover and store cranberries in refrigerator up to 1 week. **Yield:** 4 cups.

Per 1-tablespoon serving: Calories 35 (3% from fat)
Fat 0.1g (0.0g saturated)   Protein 0.1g   Carbohydrate 8.3g
Fiber 0.2g   Cholesterol 0mg   Sodium 0mg

Zesty Black-Eyed Pea Relish

Zesty Black-Eyed Pea Relish

LOW: • Fat • Cholesterol

In this colorful relish, black-eyed peas and a bevy of vegetables bask in the gusto of Italian salad dressing. Sprinkle with crumbled turkey bacon just before serving to preserve its crispness.

2 (15.8-ounce) cans black-eyed peas, rinsed
   and drained
1 cup chopped celery
1 green bell pepper, chopped
1 large tomato, peeled and chopped
2 cloves garlic, minced
4 green onions, sliced
1 (4-ounce) jar sliced mushrooms, drained
1 (4-ounce) jar diced pimiento, drained
1 (8-ounce) bottle fat-free Italian salad
   dressing
½ teaspoon pepper
3 slices turkey bacon, cooked and crumbled

• **Combine** all ingredients except bacon in a large bowl, tossing gently. Cover and chill at least 3 hours, stirring occasionally. (Relish will be ready after 1 hour, but will have more flavor with longer chilling.)
• **Sprinkle** with bacon just before serving. **Yield:** 7½ cups.

Per ½-cup serving: Calories 63 (13% from fat)
Fat 0.9g (0.2g saturated)   Protein 3.9g   Carbohydrate 10.2g
Fiber 1.2g   Cholesterol 2mg   Sodium 221mg

Eggplant Relish

LOW: • Fat • Cholesterol

Oyster sauce anoints this relish with the saltiness of soy without overpowering the eggplant flavor. Serve the relish over pasta or as a condiment for meats and side dishes.

4 pounds eggplant (about 4 medium)
Olive oil-flavored vegetable cooking spray
1 tablespoon olive oil
3 cups chopped onion (about 3 medium)
1 (14½-ounce) can no-salt-added whole
   tomatoes, undrained and chopped
1 (8-ounce) can no-salt-added tomato sauce
¼ cup chopped fresh parsley
¼ cup oyster sauce
1½ tablespoons minced fresh oregano or
   1½ teaspoons dried oregano
½ teaspoon pepper
2 tablespoons minced garlic
⅛ teaspoon ground red pepper
⅛ teaspoon hot sauce

• **Peel** eggplant, if desired, and cut into ½-inch cubes.
• **Combine** eggplant and water to cover in a large Dutch oven; bring to a boil. Reduce heat, and simmer, uncovered, 10 minutes or until tender. Drain and set aside.
• **Coat** Dutch oven with cooking spray. Add olive oil; cook onion in Dutch oven over medium-high heat, stirring constantly, until tender. Add eggplant and tomatoes; cook 10 minutes or until liquid is almost absorbed, stirring often.
• **Add** tomato sauce and remaining ingredients; cook 5 minutes, stirring occasionally. Serve immediately, or cover and store in refrigerator up to 5 days. **Yield:** 7 cups.

Per ½-cup serving: Calories 57 (19% from fat)
Fat 1.2g (0.2g saturated)   Protein 1.7g   Carbohydrate 11.0g
Fiber 1.7g   Cholesterol 0mg   Sodium 98mg

Lemon Basting Sauce

LOW: • Calorie • Cholesterol • Sodium

Minty thyme tames the tart flavors of fresh lemon and wine vinegar in this basting sauce. Use fat-free Italian salad dressing in place of olive oil vinaigrette if you'd like to cut the fat further.

1½ lemons, peeled, sectioned, and finely chopped
2 tablespoons white wine vinegar
2 tablespoons water
⅓ cup reduced-fat olive oil vinaigrette
1½ teaspoons dried thyme
¼ teaspoon cracked peppercorns

• **Combine** all ingredients in a bowl. Cover and store in refrigerator up to 1 week. Use as a basting sauce for fish or chicken. **Yield:** ¾ cup.

Per 1-tablespoon serving: Calories 15 (78% from fat)
Fat 1.3g (0.1g saturated)   Protein 0.1g   Carbohydrate 1.4g
Fiber 0.1g   Cholesterol 0mg   Sodium 50mg

Lemony Tartar Sauce

LOW: • Calorie • Cholesterol

Make this quick-and-easy sauce to serve with your catch-of-the-day or as a sandwich spread. You can use nonfat mayonnaise to eliminate the fat from this recipe, but we prefer the flavor using the reduced-fat version.

½ cup reduced-fat mayonnaise
2 tablespoons finely chopped green onions
1 teaspoon grated lemon rind
2 tablespoons sweet pickle relish
2 teaspoons lemon juice

• **Combine** all ingredients. Serve with seafood or as a sandwich spread. **Yield:** ⅔ cup.

Per 1-tablespoon serving: Calories 33 (82% from fat)
Fat 3.0g (0.1g saturated)   Protein 0.0g   Carbohydrate 1.8g
Fiber 0.0g   Cholesterol 3mg   Sodium 108mg

Papaya Vinaigrette Dressing

LOW: • Fat • Calorie • Cholesterol • Sodium

The golden flesh of a fragrant papaya gives this dressing a sweet melon perspective. Garlic, onion, pepper, and sherry wine vinegar balance the sweetness.

1 ripe papaya, peeled and seeded
5 cloves garlic
2 tablespoons sugar
2 tablespoons chopped onion
½ teaspoon pepper
½ cup sherry wine vinegar
⅓ cup club soda
½ cup chicken broth
1 tablespoon olive oil

• **Position** knife blade in food processor bowl; add first 7 ingredients. Process until smooth, stopping occasionally to scrape down sides.
• **Pour** broth and oil gradually through food chute with processor running; process until smooth. Serve over fresh spinach. **Yield:** 2 cups.

Per 1-tablespoon serving: Calories 15 (30% from fat)
Fat 0.5g (0.1g saturated)   Protein 0.2g   Carbohydrate 1.8g
Fiber 0.1g   Cholesterol 0mg   Sodium 35mg

Orange-Strawberry Shortcake (page 144)

Desserts

Pears with Orange-Caramel Sauce

LOW: • Fat • Calorie • Cholesterol • Sodium

Fragrant orange juice and rind punctuate this syrupy pear dessert. Serve it warm over silky scoops of vanilla ice cream.

6 medium-size ripe pears
¾ cup orange juice, divided
⅓ cup unsalted margarine
¼ cup sugar
1 tablespoon grated orange rind
1 tablespoon pear liqueur
6 cups vanilla nonfat ice cream

• **Peel** and core pears; cut each into 6 wedges. Place in a large bowl; drizzle with ¼ cup orange juice, and toss gently to coat. Set aside.

• **Melt** margarine in a large heavy skillet over medium heat. Add sugar, and cook 2 minutes, stirring constantly. Add pear wedges, and cook 10 to 15 minutes or until the syrup thickens and pear wedges are tender, stirring often. (Do not overcook.)

• **Remove** pear wedges with a slotted spoon; set aside. Continue cooking 10 minutes or until mixture is a light caramel color, stirring often. (Mixture will look curdled.)

• **Add** remaining ½ cup orange juice, orange rind, and liqueur, stirring with a wire whisk until smooth.

• **Return** pear wedges to skillet, and cook 1 minute or until thoroughly heated. Serve immediately with ice cream. **Yield:** 12 servings.

Per serving: Calories 210 (23% from fat)
Fat 5.3g (1.0g saturated)   Protein 3.4g   Carbohydrate 39.8g
Fiber 1.8g   Cholesterol 0mg   Sodium 51mg

Baked Pears á la Mode

LOW: • Fat • Calorie • Cholesterol • Sodium

Spoonfuls of vanilla-scented ice cream will puddle invitingly when set atop these warm honeyed pear halves. A dusting of almond cookie crumbs adds crisp detail.

2 (16-ounce) cans pear halves in lite juice, drained
2 tablespoons honey
1 tablespoon reduced-calorie margarine, melted
¾ cup crumbled amaretti cookies
2 cups vanilla nonfat ice cream

• **Arrange** pears in an 11- x 7- x 1½-inch baking dish. Set aside.

• **Combine** honey and margarine; drizzle over pears.

• **Bake**, uncovered, at 350° for 10 minutes. Sprinkle cookie crumbs over pears; bake 10 additional minutes. Serve warm with ice cream. **Yield:** 6 servings.

Per serving: Calories 248 (8% from fat)
Fat 2.2g (0.2g saturated)   Protein 4.0g   Carbohydrate 51.7g
Fiber 1.2g   Cholesterol 0mg   Sodium 117mg

Eggnog Dessert

LOW: • Calorie • Sodium

Freshly grated nutmeg showers this velvety eggnog enticer with spicy sweetness.

1 quart canned eggnog, divided
2 tablespoons sugar
2 envelopes unflavored gelatin
1 teaspoon rum extract
2⅔ cups frozen reduced-calorie whipped topping, thawed and divided
¼ teaspoon freshly grated nutmeg

• **Combine** 1 cup eggnog and sugar in a heavy saucepan. Sprinkle gelatin over mixture; let stand 1 minute. Cook over low heat, stirring until sugar and gelatin dissolve (about 4 minutes). Stir in rum extract and remaining 3 cups eggnog.
• **Cover** and chill until consistency of unbeaten egg white.
• **Fold** in 2 cups whipped topping. Spoon into individual dishes. Dollop or pipe with remaining ⅔ cup whipped topping; sprinkle with nutmeg. **Yield:** 10 servings.

Per serving: Calories 182 (46% from fat)
Fat 9.4g (6.2g saturated)   Protein 4.9g   Carbohydrate 20.1g
Fiber 0.0g   Cholesterol 60mg   Sodium 78mg

Boiled Christmas Custard

LOW: • Fat • Calorie • Cholesterol • Sodium

One taste of this smooth, old-fashioned custard will evoke memories of simpler times.

1 quart skim milk
1 cup egg substitute
½ cup sugar
2 tablespoons all-purpose flour
2 teaspoons vanilla extract

• **Cook** skim milk in a medium-size heavy nonaluminum saucepan (to avoid discoloring) over medium heat 10 minutes or until hot.
• **Combine** egg substitute and remaining 3 ingredients in a small bowl, beating with a wire whisk until blended. Gradually stir 1 cup hot milk into egg mixture, and add to remaining hot milk, stirring constantly.
• **Cook** over medium heat, stirring constantly, 6 to 8 minutes or until mixture begins to thicken and thermometer registers 180° (do not boil).
• **Remove** from heat, and pour mixture through a nonaluminum strainer into a bowl, if desired. Place heavy-duty plastic wrap directly on surface of custard (to keep "skin" from forming), and chill. **Yield:** 5 cups.

Per ½-cup serving: Calories 93 (2% from fat)
Fat 0.2g (0.1g saturated)   Protein 5.9g   Carbohydrate 16.4g
Fiber 0.0g   Cholesterol 2mg   Sodium 87mg

Sweet Potato Flan

Sweet Potato Flan

LOW: • Fat • Calorie • Cholesterol • Sodium

Spiced with cinnamon, allspice, and cloves, this sweet potato sensation is splendid. You can substitute 1 cup of canned mashed sweet potato for the fresh sweet potato.

1 large sweet potato (about 1 pound)
½ cup sugar
2 (14-ounce) cans fat-free sweetened condensed milk
2 cups skim milk
2½ cups egg substitute
1 teaspoon ground cinnamon
½ teaspoon ground allspice
¼ teaspoon ground cloves
1 teaspoon vanilla extract
1 tablespoon flaked coconut, toasted

• **Pierce** sweet potato several times with a fork; place on a baking sheet.
• **Bake** at 375° for 1 hour or until done; cool to touch. Peel sweet potato, and mash. Set aside 1 cup mashed sweet potato. Reserve any remaining sweet potato for another use.
• **Sprinkle** sugar in a 10-inch round cakepan; place over medium heat, and cook, shaking pan constantly, until sugar melts and turns light golden brown. Remove from heat; set aside. (Caramelized sugar may crack slightly as it cools.)
• **Combine** ½ cup sweet potato, 1 can sweetened condensed milk, and half of next 6 ingredients in container of an electric blender; process until smooth, stopping once to scrape down sides. Pour mixture into a large bowl. Repeat procedure; add mixture to bowl, stirring well with a wire whisk.
• **Pour** mixture over caramelized sugar in cakepan; cover with aluminum foil, and place in a larger shallow pan. Add hot water to larger pan to depth of ½ inch.
• **Bake** at 325° for 1 hour and 15 minutes or until a knife inserted in center comes out clean. Remove pan from water, and uncover; cool in pan on a wire rack 30 minutes.
• **Cover** and chill at least 8 hours.
• **Run** a knife around edge of flan to loosen; invert onto a serving plate. Sprinkle with toasted coconut. **Yield:** 16 servings.

Per serving: Calories 101 (3% from fat)
Fat 0.3g (0.2g saturated)   Protein 9.0g   Carbohydrate 45.7g
Fiber 0.9g   Cholesterol 1mg   Sodium 127mg

Flan de Queso

LOW: • Fat

A golden layer of caramelized sugar mirrors the sweetness of this lush flan.

⅓ cup sugar
1 (14-ounce) can fat-free sweetened condensed milk
1 (8-ounce) package Neufchâtel cheese, cubed and softened
1 cup egg substitute
3 slices reduced-calorie white bread, torn
1 cup water
⅔ cup evaporated skimmed milk
3 tablespoons reduced-calorie margarine, melted
1 teaspoon vanilla extract

• **Sprinkle** sugar in a 9-inch round cakepan; place over medium heat. Shake pan occasionally until sugar melts and turns light golden brown; cool. (Caramelized sugar may crack slightly as it cools.)
• **Combine** condensed milk and remaining 7 ingredients in container of an electric blender; process until smooth, stopping once to scrape down sides. Pour over caramelized sugar.
• **Place** cakepan in a larger shallow pan. Add hot water to larger pan to depth of 1 inch.
• **Bake**, uncovered, at 350° for 55 minutes or until a knife inserted in center of flan comes out clean.
• **Remove** cakepan from water; cool flan on a wire rack 30 minutes.
• **Run** a knife around edge of flan to loosen; invert flan onto a serving plate. Cool. **Yield:** 8 servings.

Per serving: Calories 313 (27% from fat)
Fat 9.4g (4.6g saturated)   Protein 11.9g   Carbohydrate 44.6g
Fiber 0.7g   Cholesterol 22mg   Sodium 312mg

Chocolate Pots de Crème with
Orange Meringues

Chocolate Pots de Crème with Orange Meringues

LOW: • Fat • Calorie • Cholesterol • Sodium

Slip your spoon into a little pot of this satiny chocolate custard, and slowly savor each bite. The orange meringues provide crunchy companions.

½ cup sugar
⅓ cup unsweetened cocoa
3 tablespoons cornstarch
¾ cup 1% low-fat milk
1 tablespoon bourbon
1 teaspoon vanilla extract
Orange Meringues

• **Combine** first 3 ingredients in a heavy saucepan; gradually stir in milk. Cook over medium heat, stirring constantly, until mixture comes to a boil; cook 1 additional minute. Remove from heat; stir in bourbon and vanilla.
• **Pour** into six 4-ounce pots de crème cups or custard cups; cool. Cover and chill. Serve each with 2 Orange Meringues. **Yield:** 6 servings.

Orange Meringues
3 egg whites
¼ teaspoon cream of tartar
⅛ teaspoon salt
½ cup superfine sugar
¼ teaspoon vanilla extract
1 teaspoon grated orange rind

• **Beat** egg whites in a large bowl at high speed with an electric mixer until foamy. Add cream of tartar and salt; beat until soft peaks form.
• **Add** sugar, 1 tablespoon at a time, beating until stiff peaks form. Stir in vanilla and rind.
• **Drop** ¼ cup mixture onto a parchment paper-lined baking sheet; spread into a 3-inch circle. Repeat procedure with remaining mixture.
• **Bake** at 200° for 2 hours or until almost dry. Turn oven off; cool in oven at least 8 hours. Remove from paper; store in an airtight container at room temperature up to 2 days. **Yield:** 1 dozen.

Note: If meringues become soft or sticky, bake at 200° for 5 minutes. Turn oven off; let meringues cool in oven until dry.

Per serving: Calories 194 (5% from fat)
Fat 1.0g (0.6g saturated) Protein 4.1g Carbohydrate 41.2g
Fiber 0.0g Cholesterol 1mg Sodium 93mg

Chocolate Truffle Mousse with Raspberry Sauce

LOW: • Sodium

A drizzle of scarlet raspberry sauce magnifies the chocolateyness of this sinfully rich mousse.

1⅓ cups (8 ounces) reduced-fat semisweet
    chocolate baking chips
3 tablespoons light corn syrup
3 tablespoons margarine
¼ cup evaporated skimmed milk
1 egg yolk, lightly beaten
½ teaspoon vanilla extract
1½ cups frozen reduced-calorie whipped
    topping, thawed
Raspberry Sauce

• **Combine** first 3 ingredients in a heavy saucepan; cook over low heat, stirring constantly, until chocolate melts and mixture is smooth.
• **Add** milk and egg yolk; cook over medium-low heat, stirring constantly, until a thermometer registers 160° and mixture is thickened. Let cool slightly. Cover and chill 30 minutes.
• **Stir** vanilla into chocolate mixture. Gently fold whipped topping into chocolate mixture.
• **Spoon** into individual serving dishes; cover and chill at least 2 hours. Serve with Raspberry Sauce. **Yield:** 5 servings.

Raspberry Sauce
1 (10-ounce) package unsweetened
    raspberries, thawed
1 teaspoon cornstarch
2 tablespoons light corn syrup

• **Place** raspberries in container of an electric blender; process 1 minute or until smooth, stopping once to scrape down sides. Pour mixture in a wire-mesh strainer into a small saucepan; press with back of a spoon against the sides of the strainer to squeeze out juice. Discard pulp and seeds remaining in strainer.
• **Add** cornstarch to juice in pan, stirring well. Stir in corn syrup. Cook over medium heat, stirring constantly, until mixture boils. Boil 1 minute, stirring constantly. Remove from heat; let cool. **Yield:** ½ cup.

Per serving: Calories 392 (35% from fat)
Fat 15.3g (9.0g saturated) Protein 2.6g Carbohydrate 60.6g
Fiber 4.0g Cholesterol 44mg Sodium 136mg

Butter Pecan Mousse

LOW: • Calorie

*Buttery-rich pecan pieces partner with crunchy
nutlike cereal nuggets to saturate this creamy
mousse with taste and texture.*

⅓ cup chopped pecans
Butter-flavored vegetable cooking spray
⅓ cup crunchy nutlike cereal nuggets
1 (8-ounce) package Neufchâtel cheese,
    softened
2 tablespoons sugar
2 tablespoons brown sugar
½ teaspoon vanilla extract
2 tablespoons evaporated skimmed milk
3 cups frozen reduced-calorie whipped
    topping, thawed

• **Place** pecans on a baking sheet; coat with
cooking spray. Bake at 350° for 5 minutes or until
toasted; cool. Combine pecans and cereal; set
aside.

• **Beat** cheese at medium speed with an electric mixer until smooth. Add sugars, vanilla, and
milk; beat well. Stir in ½ cup pecan mixture.

• **Fold** whipped topping into pecan mixture;
spoon or pipe into serving dishes. Top evenly
with remaining pecan mixture. **Yield:** 8 servings.

Per serving: Calories 203 (59% from fat)
Fat 13.3g (7.7g saturated)   Protein 4.8g   Carbohydrate 17.2g
Fiber 0.8g   Cholesterol 22mg   Sodium 169mg

Buttermilk Bread Pudding with Butter-Rum Sauce

LOW: • Fat • Cholesterol

*A spirited sauce soaks into this dense,
currant-studded pudding, bathing it in richness.*

1 (16-ounce) loaf unsliced French bread
Butter-flavored vegetable cooking spray
2 tablespoons reduced-calorie margarine
1 quart nonfat buttermilk
½ cup currants
¾ cup firmly packed light brown sugar
½ cup egg substitute
1 tablespoon vanilla extract
Butter-Rum Sauce

• **Tear** enough bread into 1-inch pieces to
measure 7½ cups. Reserve remaining bread for
another use.

• **Coat** a 13- x 9- x 2-inch pan with cooking
spray; add margarine. Place in a 350° oven for 3
minutes or until margarine melts.

• **Combine** reserved bread pieces, buttermilk,
and currants in a large bowl; set aside.

• **Combine** brown sugar, egg substitute, and
vanilla, stirring well with a wire whisk.

• **Add** egg mixture to bread mixture, stirring
gently. Pour into pan of melted margarine.

• **Bake**, uncovered, at 350° for 1 hour and 5
minutes or until lightly browned. Serve warm or
cold with Butter-Rum Sauce. **Yield:** 10 servings.

Butter-Rum Sauce
1 tablespoon cornstarch
⅓ cup water
⅓ cup sugar
¼ cup reduced-calorie margarine
¼ cup rum

• **Combine** cornstarch and water in a small
saucepan, stirring well. Add sugar and margarine.

• **Cook** over medium heat until sugar dissolves
and sauce begins to boil. Boil 1 minute, stirring
constantly. Remove from heat, and stir in rum.
Yield: 1 cup.

Per serving: Calories 332 (15% from fat)
Fat 5.7g (1.2g saturated)   Protein 9.1g   Carbohydrate 56.5g
Fiber 1.1g   Cholesterol 5mg   Sodium 462mg

All Seasons Lemon Trifle

LOW: • Fat • Calorie • Cholesterol

*A trio of fresh berries cuddles up with fluffy
pillows of angel food cake and lemon cream sauce
in this heavenly trifle.*

1 (14½-ounce) package angel food cake mix
1 (14-ounce) can low-fat sweetened condensed
   milk
2 teaspoons grated lemon rind
⅓ cup fresh lemon juice
1 (8-ounce) carton lemon low-fat yogurt
1 (8-ounce) container frozen reduced-calorie
   whipped topping, thawed and divided
1 cup sliced fresh strawberries
1 cup fresh blueberries or blackberries
1 cup fresh raspberries
½ cup flaked coconut, lightly toasted

• **Prepare** cake mix according to package
directions; bake in a 10-inch tube pan. Invert
pan; cool completely.
• **Cut** cake into bite-size pieces, and set aside.
• **Combine** condensed milk, lemon rind,
lemon juice, and yogurt. Fold in 2 cups thawed
whipped topping, and set aside.
• **Place** one-third of cake pieces in bottom of
4-quart trifle bowl; top with one-third of lemon
mixture. Top with strawberries. Repeat layers
twice, using remaining cake pieces, lemon mixture, and first blueberries, and then raspberries.
• **Spread** remaining whipped topping over
raspberries; sprinkle with toasted coconut.
• **Cover** and chill 8 hours. **Yield:** 16 servings.

Per serving: Calories 244 (15% from fat)
Fat 4.2g (3.5g saturated)   Protein 5.4g   Carbohydrate 46.9g
Fiber 1.4g   Cholesterol 4mg   Sodium 240mg

Tropical Trifle

LOW: • Fat • Cholesterol

*Orange juice-kissed cubes of pound cake
and creamy pudding entertain layers of strawberries,
pineapple, and banana. Cap the creation
with a crown of toasted coconut.*

1 (3-ounce) package vanilla-flavored pudding
   mix
2 cups skim milk
1 (16-ounce) package fat-free pound cake
½ cup orange juice
1 (10-ounce) package frozen sliced
   strawberries, thawed and undrained
1 (20-ounce) can crushed unsweetened
   pineapple, undrained
2 bananas, peeled and sliced
1 (8-ounce) container frozen reduced-calorie
   whipped topping, thawed
¼ cup flaked coconut, toasted

• **Combine** pudding mix and skim milk in a
large saucepan; bring to a boil over medium heat,
stirring constantly. Remove from heat, and cool.
• **Cut** pound cake into 10 slices; cut each slice
into 6 cubes.
• **Place** half of cake cubes in bottom of a 2½-
quart trifle bowl. Sprinkle with half of orange juice.
• **Spoon** half of strawberries with juice over
cake cubes; spread with half of pudding.
• **Combine** undrained pineapple and banana
slices, stirring to coat fruit. Drain fruit, discarding liquid.
• **Spoon** half of fruit mixture over pudding;
spread half of whipped topping over top. Repeat
layers, ending with whipped topping. Sprinkle
with toasted coconut.
• **Cover** with plastic wrap, and chill at least 6
hours. **Yield:** 12 servings.

Per serving: Calories 258 (11% from fat)
Fat 3.2g (0.5g saturated)   Protein 4.0g   Carbohydrate 53.3g
Fiber 1.2g   Cholesterol 13mg   Sodium 280mg

Caramel Ice Cream Dessert

LOW: • Fat • Cholesterol • Sodium

A gooey caramel topping and a hearty mix of oats, brown sugar, and pecans cloak a frosty layer of ice cream in this easy make-ahead dessert.

1 cup all-purpose flour
½ cup quick-cooking oats, uncooked
⅓ cup firmly packed brown sugar
¼ cup finely chopped pecans
¼ cup reduced-calorie margarine, melted
Vegetable cooking spray
1 (12.25-ounce) jar fat-free caramel ice cream topping
4 cups vanilla nonfat ice cream, softened

• **Combine** first 4 ingredients, and stir in margarine; press mixture firmly in a 15- x 10- x 1-inch jellyroll pan coated with cooking spray.
• **Bake** at 350° for 12 minutes or until lightly browned; cool and crumble.
• **Sprinkle** two-thirds of crumbs in bottom of a 9-inch springform pan coated with cooking spray. Drizzle with half of caramel topping. Spread ice cream over topping. Drizzle with remaining caramel topping; sprinkle with remaining cookie crumbs. Cover and freeze until firm. **Yield:** 12 servings.

Per serving: Calories 252 (14% from fat)
Fat 4.0g (0.2g saturated)   Protein 3.8g   Carbohydrate 49.1g
Fiber 0.7g   Cholesterol 0mg   Sodium 145mg

Strawberry-Champagne Sorbet

LOW: • Fat • Calorie • Cholesterol • Sodium

This lightly sweetened sorbet boasts fresh strawberries and champagne—a divine dessert duo.

½ cup sugar
½ cup water
1 (10-ounce) package frozen strawberries, thawed and undrained
2 tablespoons lemon juice
1½ cups champagne
½ cup sliced fresh strawberries

• **Combine** sugar and water in a heavy saucepan; cook over medium heat, stirring constantly, until sugar dissolves. Remove sugar syrup from heat; cool.
• **Place** thawed strawberries in container of an electric blender or food processor; process until smooth, stopping once to scrape down sides. Pour through a wire-mesh strainer into an 8-inch square pan, pressing with back of a spoon against the sides of the strainer to squeeze out juice. Discard pulp and seeds. Stir lemon juice, sugar syrup, and champagne into strawberry puree. Cover and freeze at least 4 hours.
• **Position** knife blade in food processor bowl; add frozen mixture, and process until smooth, stopping once to scrape down sides. Return to pan, freeze until firm. Repeat processing procedure, and return mixture to pan; freeze until firm.
• **Spoon** into glasses, and top evenly with sliced strawberries. **Yield:** 3 cups.

Per ½-cup serving: Calories 129 (1% from fat)
Fat 0.2g (0.0g saturated)   Protein 0.6g   Carbohydrate 22.1g
Fiber 1.6g   Cholesterol 0mg   Sodium 3mg

Strawberry-Champagne Sorbet

Orange Butter Cakes

LOW: • Fat • Calorie • Cholesterol • Sodium

Once you taste this tender graham cracker cake, you'll be happy the recipe makes two loaves. Eat the cake by itself, team it with fresh berries, or serve it alongside ice cream.

¼ cup vegetable oil
¾ cup firmly packed light brown sugar
¼ cup sugar
2 cups all-purpose flour
1 cup reduced-fat graham cracker crumbs
1 teaspoon baking powder
1 teaspoon baking soda
¼ teaspoon salt
1 teaspoon ground cinnamon
1 tablespoon grated orange rind
1 cup orange juice
5 egg whites
Vegetable cooking spray

• **Beat** oil and sugars at medium speed with an electric mixer 2 minutes.
• **Combine** flour and next 6 ingredients; add to sugar mixture alternately with orange juice, beginning and ending with flour mixture. Mix at low speed just until blended after each addition.
• **Beat** egg whites at high speed with an electric mixer until stiff peaks form. Fold beaten egg white into batter. Pour batter into two 8½- x 4½- x 3-inch loafpans coated with cooking spray.
• **Bake** at 350° for 40 minutes or until a wooden pick inserted in center comes out clean. Cool in pans on wire racks 10 minutes; remove from pans, and let cool completely on wire racks. **Yield:** 32 servings.

Per serving: Calories 85 (20% from fat)
Fat 1.9g (0.4g saturated)   Protein 1.5g   Carbohydrate 15.4g
Fiber 0.3g   Cholesterol 0mg   Sodium 84mg

Orange-Strawberry Shortcake

LOW: • Fat • Cholesterol

Expect the unexpected from this low-fat strawberry shortcake recipe—it adds mandarin oranges and a splash of orange-flavored liqueur to the strawberries, and spices the shortcake with cinnamon.

2 pints fresh strawberries, sliced
2 (11-ounce) cans mandarin oranges, undrained
1½ tablespoons Triple Sec or other orange-flavored liqueur
2¼ cups reduced-fat biscuit and baking mix
⅔ cup skim milk
3 tablespoons reduced-calorie margarine, melted
1 tablespoon sugar
1½ teaspoons ground cinnamon
Vegetable cooking spray
¼ cup nonfat sour cream
2 cups frozen reduced-calorie whipped topping, thawed
Garnishes: strawberry leaves, strawberry blossoms

• **Combine** first 3 ingredients; cover and chill 2 hours.
• **Combine** biscuit mix and next 4 ingredients; stir with a fork until dry ingredients are moistened. Turn out onto a lightly floured surface; knead 4 or 5 times. Place dough on a baking sheet coated with cooking spray; press into a 7-inch round.
• **Bake** at 425° for 15 minutes. Carefully remove from pan; cool on a wire rack.
• **Gently** fold sour cream into whipped topping; set aside.
• **Split** biscuit round in half horizontally. Place bottom half on a serving platter. Drain fruit, reserving 2 tablespoons liquid. Spoon two-thirds of fruit on bottom round; drizzle with reserved liquid. Spoon half of whipped topping mixture over fruit. Add top biscuit round. Top with remaining fruit and whipped topping mixture. Garnish, if desired. **Yield:** 8 servings.

Per serving: Calories 285 (22% from fat)
Fat 7.1g (3.0g saturated)   Protein 4.7g   Carbohydrate 49.0g
Fiber 1.9g   Cholesterol 1mg   Sodium 465mg

Cute-as-a-Button Cherry Pound Cake

LOW: • Cholesterol • Sodium

Sweet bits of red maraschino cherries speckle this cake with a blush of color, while melt-away mints nestled in the frosting create a button effect.

Vegetable cooking spray
2 teaspoons sifted cake flour
3½ cups sifted cake flour
1¾ cups sugar
1 tablespoon baking powder
¼ teaspoon salt
1 cup vegetable oil
1 cup skim milk
½ teaspoon almond extract
½ teaspoon vanilla extract
6 egg whites
1 (6-ounce) jar red maraschino cherries, drained and chopped
Cream Cheese Drizzle
⅓ cup melt-away mints

• Coat a 10-inch tube pan with cooking spray; dust pan with 2 teaspoons flour, and set aside.
• Combine 3½ cups cake flour and next 3 ingredients in a large mixing bowl. Add oil and milk; beat at medium speed with an electric mixer until smooth. Stir in flavorings.
• Beat egg whites at high speed until stiff peaks form. Fold about one-third of beaten egg white into batter. Gently fold in remaining egg white. Gently fold in cherries.
• Pour batter into prepared pan. Bake at 300° for 1½ hours or until a wooden pick inserted in center comes out clean. Cool in pan on a wire rack 10 minutes; remove from pan, and cool completely on wire rack.
• Spoon Cream Cheese Drizzle over top of cake, and top evenly with melt-away mints. Yield: 16 servings.

Cream Cheese Drizzle
¼ cup plus 1 tablespoon Neufchâtel cheese, softened
¼ cup light butter, softened
½ (16-ounce) package powdered sugar, sifted
1 teaspoon vanilla extract

• Combine Neufchâtel cheese and butter. Beat at medium speed with an electric mixer until smooth. Gradually add sugar and vanilla; beat until smooth. Yield: 1¼ cups.

Note: For melt-away mints, we used Smooth 'n Melty Petite Mints by Guittard Chocolate Company.

Per serving: Calories 425 (37% from fat)
Fat 17.6g (5.2g saturated) Protein 4.2g Carbohydrate 62.9g
Fiber 0.0g Cholesterol 9mg Sodium 108mg

Marble Pound Cake

A sumptuous swirl of chocolate permeates this cake with goodness.

Vegetable cooking spray
2 teaspoons all-purpose flour
3 cups sifted cake flour
1½ cups sugar
1 tablespoon baking powder
1 teaspoon salt
¾ cup vegetable oil
¾ cup skim milk
2 teaspoons vanilla extract
2 eggs
4 egg whites
½ cup reduced-calorie chocolate syrup

• Coat a 12-cup Bundt or 10-inch tube pan with cooking spray; dust pan with 2 teaspoons flour, and set aside.
• Combine cake flour and next 7 ingredients in a large mixing bowl; beat at low speed with an electric mixer until blended.
• Beat egg whites at high speed with an electric mixer until stiff peaks form; gently fold into batter.
• Combine 1 cup batter and chocolate syrup; set aside.
• Divide remaining batter in half; pour 1 portion into prepared pan. Spoon half of reserved chocolate batter on top; repeat layers. Gently swirl batter with a knife to create a marbled effect.
• Bake at 350° for 50 minutes. Cover loosely with aluminum foil after 40 minutes to prevent excessive browning. Cool in pan on a wire rack 10 to 15 minutes; remove from pan, and cool completely on wire rack. Yield: 16 servings.

Per serving: Calories 262 (38% from fat)
Fat 11.1g (2.1g saturated) Protein 3.5g Carbohydrate 36.9g
Fiber 0.0g Cholesterol 27mg Sodium 183mg

Quick Chocolate Cola Cake

LOW: • Fat • Cholesterol

*You can have your cake, and eat it, too.
Our chocolate cake is a low-fat fooler made with light
cake and pudding mixes plus a bottle of diet cola.*

1 (18.25-ounce) package light devil's food
    cake mix
1 (3.8-ounce) package fat-free chocolate-
    flavored instant pudding mix
1 cup egg substitute
1/3 cup vegetable oil
1 (10-ounce) bottle diet cola-flavored
    carbonated beverage (1 1/4 cups)
Vegetable cooking spray
Chocolate-Cola Frosting
1/2 cup finely chopped pecans, toasted

• **Combine** first 4 ingredients in a mixing bowl; beat at medium speed with an electric mixer until blended.
• **Pour** cola gradually into cake batter, beating at low speed. Increase speed to medium; beat 2 minutes.
• **Pour** batter into a 13- x 9- x 2-inch pan coated with cooking spray.
• **Bake** at 350° for 30 minutes. Cool in pan on a wire rack 10 minutes.
• **Spread** Chocolate-Cola Frosting over top of warm cake; sprinkle with pecans. Cool cake completely on wire rack. **Yield: 15 servings.**

Chocolate-Cola Frosting
1/3 cup reduced-calorie margarine
3 tablespoons diet cola-flavored carbonated
    beverage
3 tablespoons unsweetened cocoa
1 (16-ounce) package powdered sugar, sifted
1 teaspoon vanilla extract

• **Combine** first 3 ingredients in a large saucepan; cook over medium heat, stirring constantly, until margarine melts. (Do not boil.) Remove from heat; add powdered sugar and vanilla, stirring until smooth. **Yield: 1 3/4 cups.**

Note: For light devil's food cake mix, we used Betty Crocker Reduced Fat Sweet Rewards Devil's Food Cake Mix.

Per serving: Calories 376 (26% from fat)
Fat 11.0g (2.4g saturated) Protein 3.4g Carbohydrate 66.0g
Fiber 1.5g Cholesterol 0mg Sodium 416mg

Chocolate Chiffon Cake with Coffee Buttercream

*Morsels of chocolate-covered coffee beans top
these three layers of lusciousness and hint at the
flavors to come. A crafty combination of vegetable oil
and margarine in place of butter keeps the cake moist
and the frosting rich and creamy.*

Butter-flavored vegetable cooking spray
6 egg whites
3/4 teaspoon cream of tartar
1 1/3 cups sugar
1 cup unsweetened cocoa
1/2 cup water
1/3 cup vegetable oil
1/4 cup margarine, melted
3 egg yolks
2 cups sifted cake flour
2 teaspoons baking soda
1/8 teaspoon salt
1 cup reduced-fat sour cream
2 teaspoons vanilla extract
Coffee Buttercream
1/3 cup chocolate-covered coffee beans,
    coarsely chopped

• **Coat** three 9-inch round cakepans with cooking spray; line with wax paper. Spray wax paper; set aside.
• **Beat** egg whites and cream of tartar at high speed with an electric mixer until stiff peaks form; set aside.
• **Combine** sugar and next 4 ingredients in a large mixing bowl. Beat at low speed with an electric mixer until smooth. Add egg yolks, one at a time, beating just until blended after each addition.
• **Combine** flour, baking soda, and salt; add to cocoa mixture alternately with sour cream, beginning and ending with flour mixture. Mix at low speed after each addition until blended. Stir in vanilla. Fold one-third of egg white into batter; fold in remaining egg white. Pour batter into prepared pans.
• **Bake** at 350° for 18 minutes or until a wooden pick inserted in center comes out clean. Cool in pans on wire racks 10 minutes; remove cake layers from pans. Cool cake layers completely on wire racks.
• **Spread** Coffee Buttercream between cake layers and on top and sides of cake. Sprinkle chocolate-covered coffee beans on top of cake. **Yield: 12 servings.**

Coffee Buttercream

2 teaspoons boiling water
¼ cup instant coffee granules
1 cup light butter, softened
7 cups sifted powdered sugar

• **Combine** water and coffee granules, stirring until coffee dissolves.
• **Beat** butter at medium speed with an electric mixer until creamy; gradually add powdered sugar, beating until blended. Gradually add coffee mixture; beat until spreading consistency. **Yield:** 3⅓ cups.

Per serving: Calories 679 (31% from fat)
Fat 23.6g (10.1g saturated)   Protein 7.0g   Carbohydrate 113.1g
Fiber 0.2g   Cholesterol 79mg   Sodium 413mg

Coconut-Lemon Cake

LOW: • Fat • Cholesterol • Sodium

A fresh lemon filling joins tender layers of cake crowned with fluffy frosting and coconut. Our version is temptingly trim—each lush serving gets only 24% of its calories from fat.

Vegetable cooking spray
¾ cup skim milk
½ cup vegetable oil
1 teaspoon vanilla extract
2⅔ cups sifted cake flour
1½ cups superfine sugar
1 tablespoon baking powder
⅛ teaspoon salt
8 egg whites
½ teaspoon cream of tartar
Lemon Filling
Fluffy White Frosting
½ cup flaked coconut

• **Coat** three 9-inch round cakepans with cooking spray; line with wax paper. Spray wax paper; set aside.
• **Combine** milk, oil, and vanilla in a large mixing bowl, stirring well. Combine flour, sugar, baking powder, and salt. Gradually add flour mixture to milk mixture, beating at medium speed with an electric mixer just until blended.
• **Beat** egg whites and cream of tartar at high speed with an electric mixer until stiff peaks form. Fold about one-third of beaten egg white into batter; fold in remaining egg white. Pour batter into prepared pans.

• **Bake** at 350° for 15 minutes or until a wooden pick inserted in center comes out clean. Cool in pans on wire racks 10 minutes; remove from pans, and cool completely on wire racks.
• **Spread** Lemon Filling between layers. Immediately spread Fluffy White Frosting on top and sides of cake. Sprinkle top of cake with coconut. **Yield:** 12 servings.

Lemon Filling

½ cup sugar
2½ tablespoons cornstarch
1 cup boiling water
2 tablespoons egg substitute
⅓ cup fresh lemon juice
1 tablespoon reduced-calorie margarine

• **Combine** sugar and cornstarch in a medium saucepan; stir in water. Cook over medium heat, stirring constantly, until mixture boils; boil 1 minute.
• **Gradually** stir about one-fourth of hot mixture into egg substitute; add to remaining hot mixture, stirring constantly with a wire whisk. Add lemon juice and margarine, stirring until margarine melts. Remove from heat. Let cool. **Yield:** 1½ cups.

Fluffy White Frosting

1½ cups water
1 cup sugar
2 tablespoons light corn syrup
4 egg whites
¼ teaspoon cream of tartar
1 teaspoon coconut extract

• **Combine** first 3 ingredients in a small heavy saucepan; cook over medium heat, stirring constantly, until clear. Cook, without stirring, until mixture reaches soft ball stage or candy thermometer registers 240° (15 to 20 minutes).
• **Beat** egg whites and cream of tartar at high speed with an electric mixer until soft peaks form; slowly add syrup mixture, beating constantly. Add coconut extract; continue beating just until stiff peaks form and frosting is desired consistency. **Yield:** 7½ cups.

Per serving: Calories 421 (24% from fat)
Fat 11.4g (3.0g saturated)   Protein 6.1g   Carbohydrate 74.6g
Fiber 0.2g   Cholesterol 0mg   Sodium 115mg

Basic Cookie Dough

Triple your baking pleasure with this versatile dough. One recipe makes three types of cookies, each requiring one-fourth of the dough. Try all three varieties, and then bake an extra batch of your favorite.

1 cup stick margarine, softened
⅔ cup reduced-calorie stick margarine, softened
¾ cup firmly packed brown sugar
¾ cup sugar
½ cup egg substitute
6½ cups all-purpose flour
1 tablespoon plus 1 teaspoon baking powder
1 teaspoon salt
¼ cup skim milk
1 tablespoon vanilla extract

• **Beat** softened margarines in a mixing bowl at medium speed with an electric mixer until fluffy; gradually add sugars, beating well. Add egg substitute, beating well.

• **Combine** flour, baking powder, and salt; add to margarine mixture alternately with milk, beginning and ending with flour mixture. Beat at low speed after each addition until blended. Stir in vanilla.

• **Divide** dough into 4 equal portions; wrap each portion in plastic wrap to prevent drying out. Chill. Proceed with cookie instructions of choice. **Yield:** 4 pounds.

Per pound: Calories 1579 (38% from fat)
Fat 66.7g (11.7g saturated)   Protein 23.3g   Carbohydrate 223.2g
Fiber 5.1g   Cholesterol 0mg   Sodium 1,485mg

Apricot Cookies

LOW: • Fat • Calorie • Cholesterol • Sodium

Apricot preserves flavor these cookies inside and out.

½ cup low-sugar apricot preserves, divided
¼ Basic Cookie Dough recipe (at left)
Vegetable cooking spray
¼ cup sugar
1¼ cups sifted powdered sugar
2 teaspoons reduced-calorie margarine, softened
¼ cup sliced almonds, toasted

• **Knead** 2 tablespoons low-sugar apricot preserves into Basic Cookie Dough. (Dough will be sticky.)

• **Shape** dough into 1-inch balls, and place on cookie sheets coated with cooking spray. Dip a flat-bottomed glass in ¼ cup sugar, and flatten each ball to ¼-inch thickness.

• **Bake** at 350° for 10 to 12 minutes or until cookies are lightly browned. Remove to wire racks to cool completely.

• **Combine** remaining ¼ cup plus 2 tablespoons low-sugar apricot preserves, powdered sugar, and margarine in a small mixing bowl. Beat at medium speed with an electric mixer until well blended. Spread frosting evenly over cookies. Place 3 almond slices on each cookie. **Yield:** 2½ dozen.

Per cookie: Calories 96 (26% from fat)
Fat 2.8g (0.4g saturated)   Protein 0.9g   Carbohydrate 16.9g
Fiber 0.3g   Cholesterol 0mg   Sodium 52mg

Christmas Jammies

LOW: • Calorie • Cholesterol • Sodium

Raspberry jam glistens through star cutouts in these festive little cookies. Use a heart-shaped cutter to create cutouts for Valentine's Day.

¼ **Basic Cookie Dough recipe (opposite page)**
Vegetable cooking spray
¼ **cup seedless raspberry jam**

• **Roll** Basic Cookie Dough to ⅛-inch thickness on a lightly floured surface.
• **Cut** with a 2-inch round cutter, and place on cookie sheets coated with cooking spray. Cut and remove center from half of cookies with a 1-inch star-shaped cutter.
• **Bake** at 350° for 8 to 10 minutes or until cookies are lightly browned. Remove to wire racks to cool completely.
• **Spread** ½ teaspoon raspberry jam on solid cookies, and top with cutout cookies. **Yield: 2 dozen.**

Per cookie: Calories 75 (34% from fat)
Fat 2.8g (0.5g saturated)   Protein 1.0g   Carbohydrate 11.5g
Fiber 0.2g   Cholesterol 0mg   Sodium 62mg

Sugarplum Sticks

LOW: • Calorie • Cholesterol • Sodium

Sweet and chewy bits of apricots and dates make these log-shaped cookies tempting to the palate as well as the eye.

½ **cup finely chopped pecans**
⅓ **cup chopped dried apricot halves**
⅓ **cup chopped pitted whole dates**
¼ **Basic Cookie Dough recipe (opposite page)**
Vegetable cooking spray
2 **tablespoons sifted powdered sugar**

• **Knead** pecans and dried fruit into Basic Cookie Dough until well blended.
• **Shape** dough into 2- x ½-inch logs, and place on cookie sheets coated with cooking spray.
• **Bake** at 350° for 12 minutes or until cookies are lightly browned. Remove to wire racks to cool completely. Sprinkle with powdered sugar. **Yield: 3 dozen.**

Per cookie: Calories 64 (42% from fat)
Fat 3.0g (0.4g saturated)   Protein 0.9g   Carbohydrate 8.9g
Fiber 0.5g   Cholesterol 0mg   Sodium 42mg

Toasted Oatmeal Cookies

LOW: • Calorie • Cholesterol • Sodium

Toasting the oats gives these chewy cookies their wholesome taste. Instead of toasting them in a skillet with melted butter, we roasted them in a pan coated with butter-flavored vegetable cooking spray.

Butter-flavored vegetable cooking spray
2 cups quick-cooking oats, uncooked
¼ cup margarine, softened
¾ cup firmly packed brown sugar
½ cup egg substitute
1 teaspoon vanilla extract
¾ cup all-purpose flour
1 teaspoon ground cinnamon
½ teaspoon baking soda
½ teaspoon salt
½ cup coarsely chopped pecans

• **Coat** a 15- x 10- x 1-inch jellyroll pan with cooking spray; add oats. Bake at 350° for 10 minutes or until oats are golden, stirring once. Cool.
• **Beat** margarine at medium speed with an electric mixer. Gradually add sugar, beating well.
• **Add** egg substitute and vanilla, beating well.
• **Combine** flour and remaining 4 ingredients; stir in toasted oats. Add oat mixture to sugar mixture, stirring well.
• **Drop** dough by rounded teaspoonfuls 3 inches apart, onto cookie sheets coated with cooking spray.
• **Bake** at 350° for 12 minutes or until golden. Cool on cookie sheets 5 minutes; remove to wire racks to cool completely. **Yield:** 3½ dozen.

Per cookie: Calories 57 (36% from fat)
Fat 2.3g (0.3g saturated)   Protein 1.1g   Carbohydrate 8.3g
Fiber 0.5g   Cholesterol 0mg   Sodium 56mg

Midnight Delights

LOW: • Calorie • Cholesterol • Sodium

Top these tart-like cookies with a pearly dollop of whipped topping just before serving.

1¾ cups all-purpose flour
⅓ cup unsweetened cocoa
¼ cup sugar
Dash of salt
½ cup reduced-calorie stick margarine
¼ cup plus 2 tablespoons strongly brewed coffee
Vegetable cooking spray
3 tablespoons skim milk
1 tablespoon reduced-calorie stick margarine
2 cups (12 ounces) reduced-fat semisweet chocolate baking chips, melted
¼ cup sugar
½ cup egg substitute
¼ cup finely chopped pecans
½ cup frozen reduced-calorie whipped topping, thawed
2 teaspoons strongly brewed coffee

• **Combine** first 4 ingredients; cut in ½ cup margarine with pastry blender until mixture is crumbly. Sprinkle ¼ cup plus 2 tablespoons coffee, 1 tablespoon at a time, over flour mixture. Stir with a fork until dry ingredients are moistened.
• **Turn** dough out, and knead 2 or 3 times. Wrap in wax paper, and chill at least 2 hours.
• **Shape** dough into ¾-inch balls; press into miniature (1¾-inch) muffin pans coated with cooking spray, using a tart tamper or back of a spoon. Cover and chill slightly.
• **Combine** milk and 1 tablespoon margarine in a small saucepan. Cook over low heat until margarine melts, stirring often. Combine margarine mixture, melted baking chips, and ¼ cup sugar in a medium mixing bowl. Beat at medium speed with an electric mixer until smooth. Add egg substitute and pecans; beat well. Spoon 1 rounded teaspoonful mixture into each shell.
• **Bake** at 350° for 20 minutes. Cool in pans on wire racks 15 minutes; remove from pans, and cool completely on wire racks.
• **Combine** whipped topping and 2 teaspoons coffee. Dollop onto each cookie just before serving. **Yield:** 4 dozen.

Per cookie: Calories 73 (46% from fat)
Fat 3.7g (1.9g saturated)   Protein 1.0g   Carbohydrate 10.7g
Fiber 0.2g   Cholesterol 0mg   Sodium 29mg

Midnight Delights

Coffee Nuggets

LOW: • Calorie • Cholesterol • Sodium

Coffee aficionados will appreciate these not-so-sweet cookies.

2 tablespoons instant coffee granules
1 cup sifted powdered sugar, divided
2 cups all-purpose flour
½ cup finely chopped pecans
½ cup margarine, melted
2 teaspoons vanilla extract
Vegetable cooking spray

• **Crush** coffee granules into a fine powder, using a mortar and pestle or back of a spoon. Combine coffee powder, ⅓ cup powdered sugar, flour, and pecans; add margarine and vanilla. Beat at medium speed with an electric mixer until blended. Cover and chill at least 1 hour.
• **Shape** dough into 1-inch balls; place on cookie sheets coated with cooking spray.
• **Bake** at 350° for 12 minutes or until lightly browned. Remove to wire racks to cool completely. Roll cookies in remaining ⅔ cup powdered sugar. **Yield:** 3½ dozen.

Per cookie: Calories 61 (47% from fat)
Fat 3.2g (0.5g saturated)   Protein 0.7g   Carbohydrate 7.4g
Fiber 0.2g   Cholesterol 0mg   Sodium 26mg

Chocolate-Hazelnut Biscotti

LOW: • Calorie • Cholesterol • Sodium

Toasted hazelnuts and a splash of hazelnut-flavored liqueur double the nutty flavor of these crispy dunking cookies.

2 large eggs
⅔ cup sugar
1 tablespoon Frangelico or other hazelnut-flavored liqueur
2 cups sifted cake flour
1½ teaspoons baking powder
¼ teaspoon salt
1½ tablespoons unsweetened cocoa
⅔ cup hazelnuts, chopped and toasted
Vegetable cooking spray

• **Beat** eggs at medium speed with an electric mixer until foamy. Gradually add sugar, beating at high speed until thick and pale. Add liqueur, beating until blended. Combine flour and next 3 ingredients; fold into egg mixture. Fold in nuts. Cover and chill 30 minutes.
• **Coat** a large cookie sheet with cooking spray. Divide dough into 3 portions, and spoon portions onto cookie sheet 2 inches apart. Shape each portion into an 8- x 1½-inch strip. Cover and chill 30 minutes; reshape dough, if necessary.
• **Bake** at 375° for 20 minutes or until lightly browned. Remove to wire racks to cool. Cut diagonally into ½-inch-thick slices. Lay slices flat on a cookie sheet. Bake at 375° for 5 minutes; turn slices over, and bake 5 additional minutes. Remove to wire racks to cool. **Yield:** 3½ dozen.

Per cookie: Calories 50 (31% from fat)
Fat 1.7g (0.2g saturated)   Protein 1.0g   Carbohydrate 7.9g
Fiber 0.1g   Cholesterol 11mg   Sodium 17mg

Miniature Orange Éclairs

LOW: • Fat • Calorie • Cholesterol • Sodium

*A splash of orange-flavored liqueur
and a drizzle of fudge sauce make these
diminutive éclairs delightful.*

1¼ cups frozen reduced-calorie whipped
    topping, thawed
2 drops of yellow liquid food coloring
2 drops of red liquid food coloring
24 ladyfingers
¼ cup Grand Marnier or other orange-flavored
    liqueur
½ cup fat-free fudge sauce
Garnishes: orange rind strips, fresh mint sprigs

• **Combine** first 3 ingredients with a wire whisk; set aside.
• **Separate** ladyfinger halves. Brush inside of ladyfingers with Grand Marnier.
• **Spread** whipped topping mixture evenly over bottom halves. Cover with top halves of ladyfingers.
• **Spoon** fudge sauce into a small zip-top plastic bag; seal bag. Snip a tiny hole in one corner of bag, using scissors. Pipe about 2 teaspoons fudge sauce on top of each éclair. Garnish, if desired. **Yield:** 2 dozen.

Per éclair: Calories 53 (15% from fat)
Fat 0.9g (0.5g saturated) Protein 1.0g Carbohydrate 9.4g
Fiber 0.3g Cholesterol 13mg Sodium 72mg

Coffee Napoleons

LOW: • Fat • Calorie

*Sugar-coated wonton wrappers crisped in
the oven provide crunchy layers for light Napoleons.*

2 teaspoons instant coffee granules
1 tablespoon hot water
1 (8-ounce) package Neufchâtel cheese,
    softened
1¼ cups skim milk
1 (3.8-ounce) package fat-free chocolate-
    flavored instant pudding mix
1 cup frozen reduced-calorie whipped topping,
    thawed
36 wonton wrappers
Butter-flavored vegetable cooking spray
½ cup sugar
1½ tablespoons skim milk
1 teaspoon instant coffee granules
½ cup (3 ounces) reduced-fat semisweet
    chocolate baking chips
1 tablespoon powdered sugar

• **Dissolve** 2 teaspoons coffee granules in 1 tablespoon hot water. Beat Neufchâtel cheese at medium speed with an electric mixer until creamy; add coffee mixture, 1¼ cups skim milk, and pudding mix. Beat at low speed until thickened. Fold in whipped topping; cover and chill.
• **Coat** both sides of each wonton wrapper with cooking spray; dredge in ½ cup sugar. Place on two 15- x 10- x 1-inch jellyroll pans lined with parchment paper. Bake at 375° for 3½ minutes; turn wrappers, and bake an additional 1½ minutes or until edges are golden. Transfer to wire racks to cool.
• **Combine** 1½ tablespoons skim milk, 1 teaspoon coffee granules, and baking chips in a heavy saucepan; cook over low heat, stirring constantly, until chips melt. Cool slightly, and spoon into a small zip-top plastic bag; seal bag. Snip a tiny hole in one corner of bag, using scissors. Drizzle mixture evenly over 12 wonton wrappers; set aside.
• **Pipe** or spoon half of filling evenly on 12 plain wonton wrappers. Top each with a plain wrapper. Spoon remaining half of filling on top of plain wrappers; top with drizzled wrappers. Sprinkle evenly with powdered sugar, and serve immediately. **Yield:** 12 servings.

Per serving: Calories 217 (26% from fat)
Fat 6.3g (3.1g saturated) Protein 5.4g Carbohydrate 34.7g
Fiber 0.0g Cholesterol 17mg Sodium 348mg

Apple-Bourbon Pie

Apple-Bourbon Pie

LOW: • Fat • Cholesterol

Bourbon-soaked currants spike this all-American apple pie, and toasted pecans deliver the crunch.

⅓ cup currants
⅓ cup bourbon
3 pounds cooking apples
½ cup sugar
2 tablespoons all-purpose flour
1 teaspoon ground cinnamon
¼ teaspoon salt
⅛ teaspoon ground nutmeg
¼ cup finely chopped pecans or walnuts, toasted
1 (15-ounce) package refrigerated piecrusts
2 teaspoons low-sugar apricot spread
1 teaspoon nonfat buttermilk
1 teaspoon sugar

• **Combine** currants and bourbon, and let soak 2 hours.
• **Peel** apples, and cut into ½-inch slices; arrange apple slices in a steamer basket over boiling water. Cover and steam 10 minutes or until apple slices are tender.
• **Combine** ½ cup sugar and next 4 ingredients in a large bowl; add apple slices, currant mixture, and pecans, stirring to combine.
• **Fit** 1 piecrust into a 9-inch pieplate according to package directions; brush apricot spread over piecrust. Spoon apple mixture into piecrust.
• **Unfold** remaining piecrust, and press out fold lines; cut piecrust in half. Reserve remaining half of piecrust for another use. Cut remaining half into 2 leaves and an apple with a 3-inch leaf-shaped cutter and apple-shaped cutter. Mark veins on leaves with pastry wheel or sharp knife. Arrange leaves and apple cutouts over apple mixture; brush with buttermilk, and sprinkle with 1 teaspoon sugar.
• **Bake** at 450° on lower rack of oven 15 minutes. Cover edges of pastry with strips of aluminum foil to prevent excessive browning. Bake at 350° for 30 minutes. Let cool 1 hour before serving. **Yield:** 8 servings.

Per serving: Calories 337 (28% from fat)
Fat 10.3g (3.6g saturated)   Protein 0.9g   Carbohydrate 58.3g
Fiber 4.8g   Cholesterol 6mg   Sodium 234mg

White Chocolate Chess Tart

LOW: • Cholesterol

This rich-tasting, ivory-colored tart uses a lighter piecrust recipe instead of a ready-made crust. The key to working with the lighter piecrust is to place it between two sheets of plastic wrap and chill as directed before rolling.

1¼ cups all-purpose flour
⅓ cup margarine
2 to 3 tablespoons cold water
1 (4-ounce) white chocolate bar, chopped
½ cup nonfat buttermilk
¾ cup egg substitute
1 tablespoon vanilla extract
¾ cup sugar
3 tablespoons all-purpose flour
1 tablespoon cornmeal
⅛ teaspoon salt

• **Place** flour in a medium bowl; cut in margarine with pastry blender until mixture is crumbly. Sprinkle cold water, 1 tablespoon at a time, evenly over surface; stir with a fork until dry ingredients are moistened. Shape into a ball.
• **Place** dough between two sheets of heavy-duty plastic wrap, and gently press into a 4-inch circle. Chill 20 minutes. Roll dough into a 12-inch circle. Place in freezer 5 minutes or until plastic wrap can be removed easily.
• **Remove** top sheet of plastic wrap. Invert pastry into a 9-inch tart pan with removable bottom; trim edges. Line pastry with aluminum foil, and fill with pie weights or dried beans.
• **Bake** at 450° for 8 minutes. Remove weights and foil; bake 3 to 4 additional minutes. Cool piecrust on a wire rack.
• **Combine** chocolate and buttermilk in a saucepan; cook over low heat, stirring constantly, until smooth. Cool 15 minutes.
• **Combine** egg substitute and vanilla in a large bowl; gradually add to white chocolate mixture, stirring until blended.
• **Combine** sugar and remaining 3 ingredients; gradually add to chocolate mixture, stirring until blended. Pour into piecrust.
• **Bake** at 325° for 50 minutes or until a knife inserted in center comes out clean. Cool on wire rack. **Yield:** 8 servings.

Per serving: Calories 317 (35% from fat)
Fat 12.5g (4.4g saturated)   Protein 5.8g   Carbohydrate 44.6g
Fiber 0.6g   Cholesterol 2mg   Sodium 171mg

Index

Credits

Oxmoor House wishes to thank the following merchants:

Annieglass, Santa Cruz, CA
Augusta Glass Studio, Augusta, MO
Biot, New York, NY
Boda Nova, Höganäs, Sweden
Charlotte & Co., Inc., Birmingham, AL
Cyclamen Studio, Berkeley, CA
Daisy Arts, Venice, CA
Barbara Eigen, Jersey City, NJ
Fioriware, New York, NY
Le Creuset of America, Inc., Yemassee, SC
The Loom Company, Aletha Soulé, New York, NY
Potluck, Modena, NY
Sabre Flatware, Dallas, TX
Scof, Dallas, TX
Southern Settings, Birmingham, AL
Stonefish Pottery, Hartford, CT
Swid Powell, New York, NY

Additional Photography:

Jim Bathie: page 57
Mark Gooch: pages 41, 55, 67, 80, 99, 138

Additional Photo Styling:

Katie Baker: page 64

Metric Equivalents

The recipes that appear in this cookbook use the standard United States method for measuring liquid and dry or solid ingredients (teaspoons, tablespoons, and cups). The information in the following charts is provided to help cooks outside the U.S. successfully use these recipes. All equivalents are approximate.

METRIC EQUIVALENTS FOR DIFFERENT TYPES OF INGREDIENTS

A standard cup measure of a dry or solid ingredient will vary in weight depending on the type of ingredient. A standard cup of liquid is the same volume for any type of liquid. Use the following chart when converting standard cup measures to grams (weight) or milliliters (volume).

Standard Cup	Fine Powder (ex. flour)	Grain (ex. rice)	Granular (ex. sugar)	Liquid Solids (ex. butter)	Liquid (ex. milk)
1	140 g	150 g	190 g	200 g	240 ml
¾	105 g	113 g	143 g	150 g	180 ml
⅔	93 g	100 g	125 g	133 g	160 ml
½	70 g	75 g	95 g	100 g	120 ml
⅓	47 g	50 g	63 g	67 g	80 ml
¼	35 g	38 g	48 g	50 g	60 ml
⅛	18 g	19 g	24 g	25 g	30 ml

USEFUL EQUIVALENTS FOR LIQUID INGREDIENTS BY VOLUME

¼ tsp				=	1 ml	
½ tsp				=	2 ml	
1 tsp				=	5 ml	
3 tsp	=	1 tbls		= ½ fl oz	=	15 ml
		2 tbls	= ⅛ cup	= 1 fl oz	=	30 ml
		4 tbls	= ¼ cup	= 2 fl oz	=	60 ml
		5⅓ tbls	= ⅓ cup	= 3 fl oz	=	80 ml
		8 tbls	= ½ cup	= 4 fl oz	=	120 ml
		10⅔ tbls	= ⅔ cup	= 5 fl oz	=	160 ml
		12 tbls	= ¾ cup	= 6 fl oz	=	180 ml
		16 tbls	= 1 cup	= 8 fl oz	=	240 ml
	1 pt	= 2 cups	= 16 fl oz	=	480 ml	
	1 qt	= 4 cups	= 32 fl oz	=	960 ml	
			33 fl oz	= 1000 ml	= 1 l	

USEFUL EQUIVALENTS FOR DRY INGREDIENTS BY WEIGHT

(To convert ounces to grams, multiply the number of ounces by 30)

1 oz	=	1/16 lb	=	30 g
4 oz	=	¼ lb	=	120 g
8 oz	=	½ lb	=	240 g
12 oz	=	¾ lb	=	360 g
16 oz	=	1 lb	=	480 g

USEFUL EQUIVALENTS FOR LENGTH

(To convert inches to centimeters, multiply the number of inches by 2.5)

1 in			=	2.5 cm		
6 in	= ½ ft		=	15 cm		
12 in	= 1 ft		=	30 cm		
36 in	= 3 ft	= 1 yd	=	90 cm		
40 in			=	100 cm	=	1 m

USEFUL EQUIVALENTS FOR COOKING/OVEN TEMPERATURES

	Fahrenheit	Celcius	Gas Mark
Freeze Water	32° F	0° C	
Room Temperature	68° F	20° C	
Boil Water	212° F	100° C	
Bake	325° F	160° C	3
	350° F	180° C	4
	375° F	190° C	5
	400° F	200° C	6
	425° F	220° C	7
	450° F	230° C	8
Broil			Grill